The Church in My Rearview Mirror

Also by Tim Sledge

Making Peace with Your Past (1992)

Moving Beyond Your Past (1994)

Making Peace with Your Past – South Korea (1996)

Making Peace with Your Past – Peru (2001)

Goodbye Jesus (2018)

A Meta-Spiritual Handbook (2018)

* * *

You can contact Tim Sledge on his website, MovingTruths.com, where he shares insights for personal growth.

The Church in My Rearview Mirror

A Case Study in Forced Termination

Tim Sledge

INSIGHTING GROWTH
Publications Inc.

Tim Sledge
www.MovingTruths.com.

Printed in the United States of America

First Edition: December 2018

Insighting Growth Publications
One Riverway Suite 1700
Houston, TX 77056

www.IGrowPub.com

ISBN–13: 978-0-9998435-5-0 (Paperback)
ISBN–13: 978-0-9998435-6-7 (E-Book)

Contents

1 – Brother Bill 1
2 – Evangelism Conference 4
3 – Permian High 6
4 – Falling Back 8
5 – Promised Land 12
6 – Seminary Training 16
7 – New York 20
8 – Farming Town 25
9 – Main Event 30
10 – Priority Driven 34
11 – Prayer Force 38
12 – Wholehearted Growth 42
13 – Panic Attacks 45
14 – Treatment Center 48
15 – Vulnerable Preaching 52
16 – Older Brothers 55
17 – Breaking Ground 58
18 – Quiet Courage 60
19 – Encouragement Center 64
20 – Too Close 65
21 – Two Congregations 71
22 – Growth Pattern 73
23 – Ocean View 76
24 – Bethlehem Boulevard 80
25 – Bedroom Wall 83
26 – Theological War 90
27 – Megachurch Steamroller 93
28 – Protester Buses 99
29 – Book Tour 102
30 – Dream Year 108
31 – Wind Factor 112
32 – Mixed Messages 115
33 – Intention Tension 119
34 – Balancing Act 124
35 – Triple Threat 129
36 – Acute Deaconitis 137
37 – Under Scrutiny 142
38 – Turning Point 148
39 – Fast Lane 150
40 – Problem Solving 154
41 – Galveston Gang 156

42 – Too Vulnerable 159
43 – Law Office 161
44 – Downward Spiral 166
45 – Shocked Members... 180
46 – Shocked Me.. 184
47 – Debriefing Myself.. 191
48 – Predictable Pattern 202
49 – Left Behind 207
50 – Freelance Minister.. 214
51 – South Korea.. 220
52 – Still Struggling 226
53 – Prison Sentences 230
54 – High Tech... 235
55 – Longest Hour.. 241
56 – New Purpose 243
57 – Self-Care 245

Preface

This is a book for ministers and lay leaders. It is my story of a lost ministry in a church that was in every way I could imagine the best place in the world for me to be a pastor.

To help you better understand the main event, I have briefly shared some information about my early steps in ministry: my call to be a minister, my first preaching experiences, my educational path, and some material about the churches I served before landing at the Kingsland Baptist Church in Katy, Texas.

I have attempted to tell the story in a way that allows you to live it with me and to feel the joy and the pain I experienced. And I have attempted to analyze what happened, to make sense of it, and to take responsibility for my part in it.

I am one of the estimated one in ten ministers who eventually left the ministry after a forced termination. But I still feel a deep affinity for individuals who dedicate themselves to lead congregations, to be present and available, to help, to guide, and to inspire.

It is my hope that this book will in some way help churches and ministers avoid the trauma I experienced. And if you are a minister who has already experienced a similar loss, it is my aim that this book will provide some comfort and support as you work through what happened.

And just so you know, the following names are pseudonyms for real individuals who are part of the story: Adam, Blake, Cheryl, Ellen, Elliot, Gilbert, Jason, Merrill, Nelson, Pat, Rodney, Stan, Stuart, Vic, and Wendell. CNI refers to an actual company that goes by another name.

Tim Sledge

1 – Brother Bill

I sometimes wonder what my life might have looked like if Bill Hogue had not become pastor of the Crescent Park Baptist Church in Odessa, Texas, in the spring of 1964. I was a 16-year-old high school sophomore when I first met Brother Bill—he asked that everyone call him that—and I remember the exact spot in the church office where I was standing at that moment.

I remember how Brother Bill was smiling as he looked me in the eye and firmly clasped my right hand. I was caught off guard by how outgoing and friendly he was, and by how much attention he was paying to a teenager like me. He talked to me like an equal and seemed just as interested in knowing me as he would have been if I were an adult.

Only as an adult would I realize how far-reaching was Brother Bill's influence on me. While he may have come across initially like any other 35-year-old man going about his business in Odessa, Texas—of average height and average build, with short brown hair and glasses that resembled LBJ's—there was nothing average about the man himself. He was intuitive about people, a discerning listener, and his one-to-one communication skills were off the charts. Quite simply, he had a genius for relationships.

His devotion to God, to his congregation, and over the course of many years—to me—became an example I would emulate. Just as our previous pastor taught me the impact of an interesting, challenging, and inspiring sermon, Brother Bill showed me how effective a pastor could be based on his genuine love for the members of his church.

My father had experienced a dramatic spiritual turnaround after nearly dying when his appendix burst a few years earlier, but still struggled with occasional alcoholic relapses. As much as I loved my father, I was looking for another model of how to be an admirable man, and Bill Hogue was it. Looking back, I think the way Brother Bill related to people reminded me of Jesus. It wasn't long before I began to think of him not only as my pastor, but as my friend, and even as a second father.

Brother Bill's involvement in the future direction of my life was almost immediate. Not long after his arrival, one Sunday morning as the worship service ended, I felt something inexplicable—a sort of emotional stirring.

I had been taught to be sensitive to hearing God speak in my life and that God speaks in mysterious ways. After the Sunday morning episode, I talked to Brother Bill and asked for his thoughts.

Since we didn't know what this stirring meant, he said, I should simply tell God that I was listening and available. With great intensity and complete sincerity, that's exactly what I did. In Brother Bill's office, I prayed aloud: "God, whatever you want me to do, I will do. Whatever you want me to be, I will be. Wherever you want me to go, I will go."

I meant every word. I didn't take the commitment I was making lightly. And I believed God would eventually let me know what else I was supposed to do.

The theological underpinnings for my prayer that day had been drilled in countless times with concepts that applied not just to me, but to every believer. God knew you even before you were born. God loves you and has a wonderful plan for your life. You can expect God to lead you through Bible passages you read, through preaching and teaching, through the opening and closing of doors in your life, and through an inner still small voice. You need to listen for God's voice and be ready to claim what he has for you when he gives you direction. I had no doubts about the truth of these concepts.

A few months later, in October of my junior year, our church held a revival. For Baptist revival services, an outside speaker would come to address the normal Sunday morning and evening worship services. This was followed by evening services each weekday for the remainder of the revival week. At the end of each service, an altar call was offered as the visiting minister invited worshippers to walk to the front of the sanctuary to make a public decision.

As far as we were concerned, the most important decision anyone could make was becoming a follower of Jesus by turning one's life over to him. By anyone, we meant *anyone*—irreligious people, people of other faiths, even people from Christian churches, including Baptists, who had just gone through the motions and never wholeheartedly committed to Jesus. This was the decision to be born again. This was how one became a Christian. And when you made this decision, you were expected to let other people know by walking the aisle to make your decision public. This public decision was usually accompanied by a request to be baptized as a symbol of the rebirth that resulted from praying the prayer of commitment to Jesus. These were all steps I had taken at age nine.

The second type of public decision was a recommitment to Jesus. These decisions were often the result of sorrow for some recent sinful behavior or lack of consistency in the practice of faith. Sometimes, people recommitted their lives to Christ when they decided to re-embrace life in the church after a long absence. In our view, once you made a sincere commitment, you couldn't lose your relationship with God, but you could fall out of fellowship with him, and a recommitment decision was a way of regaining that fellowship.

The third type of public decision: Individuals and families often came forward during the invitation to publicly move their church membership from a Baptist congregation in another city or even from across town.

Seeing someone walk the aisle to make one of these three kinds of decisions was a regular occurrence. But one other kind of response to the invitation at the end of a Baptist worship service was rare—so rare that I had only seen this type of decision once. This was the decision I made during the Wednesday night service of the revival: I walked the aisle and shared with the visiting minister, my pastor, and the congregation that I felt called to be a minister.

Shortly after this decision, I wrote a pamphlet titled, "When God Called Me," in which I described my call to ministry.

> As the music leader sang a solo, I heard only one line, "If I had a thousand lives, they should be thine." When the sermon began, a desire to preach the word of God began to burn within me, and that line of the song kept running through my mind. "If I had a thousand lives, they should be thine. If I had a thousand lives, they should be thine." It was then that I realized that God had a place for me in the ministry.

> When the first strains of the organ began, I was halfway down the aisle. I knew without a doubt that God was calling me to be a preacher.

Brother Bill believed in getting things started quickly. Within a few weeks, I preached my first sermon at our Wednesday evening service, and it was titled, "The Happy Christian." As I shared my words, I was overcome with emotion and on the verge of tears multiple times. I'm not sure I sounded very happy, but I did sound extremely sincere.

After my sermon that evening, a woman who worked with a nearby Spanish-speaking church that our congregation sponsored asked me to speak there on a Sunday evening, and I agreed.

It wasn't long before I was being asked to preach at other churches. I wrote my own sermons of course, but my mother typed my notes on her typewriter until I learned to type myself. Most of the time, I preached in Baptist congregations, but occasionally I had opportunities to speak to other denominations and to inter-denominational groups.

* * *

During the five and a half years Brother Bill served as pastor of Crescent Park Baptist Church, 1,304 people joined the church, and 55 young people made commitments to Christian vocational service—including three of his four sons. I was the first of the 55.

When it happened, my call was about one thing only—hearing and responding to God's leadership.

2 – Evangelism Conference

Three months after my call to ministry, Brother Bill and his associate invited me to join them on a trip to Dallas for the annual Baptist General Convention of Texas evangelism conference, a statewide meeting for ministers and laypersons.

The purpose of the conference was to fire us up with passion for winning the world to Jesus—to inspire us and send us home with a renewed commitment to fill our churches with new believers.

The evangelism conference was anything but a series of dry lectures. The goal was emotional impact, inspiration, and fervor. It was like a rock concert for people who didn't dance, drink, or tolerate loud music. It was a booster shot for Christian commitment.

A key element of the emotional impact was a crowd of thousands, all on the same page in terms of belief, ready and waiting to be touched by the presence of God. The conduits for God's message and power were threefold: soul-stirring Christian music, short talks (testimonies) by lay persons, and powerful preaching.

On the last night of the conference, before an audience of 7,000, two lay speakers shared their personal stories in preparation for the main event—a sermon by one of our most famous pastors.

First up, there was a professional baseball player who described his conversion at a Billy Graham crusade, speaking so convincingly and so earnestly about the significance of Jesus in his life and how truly wonderful it was to be a child of God.

Next was a man dressed in the white uniform of a prison inmate who related his story of finding Jesus while behind bars. As he spoke, he was overcome with emotion, humbled by the way God's forgiveness had set him spiritually free. As he finished his talk, he laid his head down on the podium and wept.

These testimonies primed the audience for the climactic sermon delivered by Dr. W.A. Criswell, pastor of the First Baptist Church of Dallas. Dr. Criswell's reputation preceded him, not only as pastor of the largest church in our denomination, but as a powerful speaker. That night, he preached with enormous conviction and gravitas, delivering a message that left an indelible mark on me: To be a successful man of God, you need a willingness to confess your own sins, a deep compassion for the lost, and an earnest commitment to the service of our Lord.

With tears streaming down his cheeks, Criswell asked all the ministers and missionaries in the audience to come forward, which they did. Then he asked the rest of us to bow our heads and to lean on the back of the chair in front of us. There was something extraordinarily connective in this act as we all began to pray, and some even fell to their knees, weeping.

As the prayer time ended, the assembled choir began to sing "Hallelujah, Hallelujah, Hallelujah."

I heard Criswell say that confession of sins was crucial for a man of God. I heard him stress that a strong commitment was essential. But what struck me most was his declaration that we needed to have compassion for people who do not know Jesus.

The message of the two-day conference was unmistakable: Evangelism was a way of life, a sacred calling, a mission we all embraced wholeheartedly—reaching out for Jesus, sharing his message, building his army of love and faith, and helping people from all walks of life and all religions to convert to a childlike trust in Jesus that would lead to rebirth. Nothing was more important.

I accepted this message as absolute truth, and I would spend decades believing it, practicing it, and doing my best to bring others into the fold.

3 – Permian High

Named after the Permian Basin—the oil-rich geological formation that underpins the Midland-Odessa area—Permian High School's claim to fame is a football program that has generated numerous titles, including six state championships. The team's championship run in 1988 led to the bestselling book, movie, and television series, *Friday Night Lights*.[1]

My call to ministry and early preaching in and around Odessa led to dramatic changes in my life at Permian High. A few months after the evangelism conference, near the end of my junior year, at the suggestion of one of the school's guidance counselors, I ran for Student Council president. In my speech before the student body of 2,000, I told my fellow students that my Christian faith was the most important thing in my life and explained that my commitment to Christ would shape me as their leader.

Just before the last change of classes on the day of the school election, students sat in their classrooms listening for the announcement of the results over the school's public-address system. I had won the election! I was the new student council president. As the bell rang to leave class and I stepped into the crowded hallway, within seconds, I realized my life at school was irrevocably changed. I was no longer just another face in the crowd. Everyone was saying hello and congratulating me. It was hard to squeeze through the crowd and make my way to my next class. Suddenly, everyone seemed to know and like me. It felt remarkably good.

More opportunities and rewards began coming my way. After hearing my campaign speech, the head of the speech department persuaded me to join the school's competitive speaking team. Several weeks after the student council election, I competed and won first place in oratory in the West Texas regional high school public speaking contest in El Paso. And I was elected president of the Christian Student Union, a non-denominational group that conducted voluntary religious services on campus each Wednesday morning.

As my opportunities and responsibilities increased, I connected the dots back to my obedience to God—my willingness to do whatever he called me to do—as did adult church leaders who began to hold me up as a model for what could happen when a teenager was fully committed. God was honoring my commitment in ways that were surprising to me, and I began to look forward to the unanticipated blessings of each new day.

I preached somewhere almost every week that summer in West Texas towns like Big Lake, Monahans, Notrees, and Lamesa.

On weekdays I worked for a fence company. I spent my days in front of a radial saw, cutting 20-foot-long boards to picket length. One morning, I was talking with a co-worker, Steve, about committing his life to Jesus—I was still attempting to obey the call to evangelism I had heard so many times. Steve was towering and muscular, a champion high school discus thrower in the state. I had no idea how he would respond to what I had to say, but he listened intently, and next thing I knew—we were kneeling in the yard of the fence company as he prayed to give his life to Jesus. Steve was my first convert.

In the fall, I began a relationship with the girl who would become my wife. The first time I ever saw Linda was when she strolled into our freshman history class in a yellow sleeveless dress balancing a foot-high stack of books. She was one of the most popular girls in school—tall, beautiful, and smart—a straight "A" student. We had shared one date in our sophomore year, but sparks didn't fly. Now, as our senior year began, our paths crossed frequently and this time, there was a connection. A critical part of that connection was our shared faith. Linda had experienced a spiritual awakening of her own during the previous summer. Throughout our senior year we were inseparable, and she became my partner in just about everything I did.

Just before Thanksgiving, I preached to a citywide, inter-denominational, Christian youth rally in Odessa. The rally was patterned after a Billy Graham crusade service but was targeted at teenagers. I led a committee of high school students in planning the event. Linda was in charge of publicity, and Brother Bill secured the support of ministers across the city.

Some 1,200 people—almost all high schoolers—showed up on a Saturday night at the county coliseum. Like Billy Graham, I preached about sin, forgiveness, heaven, and hell. I preached about the love of God, and presented Jesus as *the* way, *the* truth, and *the* life. And I invited anyone who did not know Jesus to accept him that night. At the end of the service, 50 teenagers came forward to make commitments to Jesus. Ministers from a wide variety of denominations were present to talk with each person who came forward— answering questions, assessing each decision, and most importantly—praying with each individual who had walked the aisle. When it was all over that night, I knelt behind the stage to thank God for our success.

My faith was providing values, purpose, and direction. My values were set by the teachings of Jesus: Love God with all your heart; love your neighbor as yourself; tell the truth; be kind; go the extra mile. My purpose was following the will of God as revealed to me in the Bible and in the direction I personally felt from God—the still small voice, the way circumstances unfolded, and the opportunities that seemed to appear out of nowhere. My direction was to pursue my education as a Christian minister, then to serve God wherever he might lead me.

I didn't have a thousand lives to give to God. But with the one life I had, I was dedicated to serving him. By the end of the summer after my senior year in high school I had preached 78 times in 11 cities.

---

[1] H.G. Bissinger, *Friday Night Lights: A Town, a Team, and a Dream* (Boston: Da Capo Press, 1990).

4 – Falling Back

My parents offered no input or opinions on college, so at 18, all I could do was rely on the ministers at my church and my high school counselor—all of whom made suggestions and offered to open doors as needed.

My counselor encouraged me to attend Baylor University. Baylor was the largest Baptist university in Texas but was not an option I would consider since I had been taught that Baylor was theologically liberal. Were I to attend Baylor, I would *de facto* become a liberal.

That was all the warning I needed.

Theological liberals did not believe the Bible was without error. In my West Texas Baptist world, the only thing worse than becoming a theological liberal was abandoning your faith. Essentially, to some Baptist ministers, theological liberalism *was* an abandonment of faith.

My minister of youth at Crescent Park Baptist, George Loutherback, was a graduate of Hardin-Simmons University, a Baptist school in Abilene, Texas. While he didn't pressure me to apply, he delivered an excellent sales pitch, and I ultimately decided on his alma mater, beginning classes in the fall of 1966.

HSU was an excellent fit. With fewer students than Permian High, a friendly campus atmosphere, and a solid Baptist identity providing a safe haven from theological liberalism, the school suited me perfectly.

One downside: Linda, enrolled in Odessa Junior College, was 167 miles away. We planned to spend our lives together, but we couldn't spend this part of it in the same town. She had wanted to join me at Hardin-Simmons, but her parents—not religious and not my biggest fans—had given her a choice. She could attend the largest university in the state, the University of Texas, which meant a world of opportunities for her. Or, she could stay in Odessa and attend the local junior college.

Her parents probably thought that if we were apart for a while, the relationship would fizzle. Linda, committed to our shared future, chose Odessa Junior College over sorority life in Austin—a life that would not lend itself to our young long-distance relationship. Linda and I continued to hope that she could later join me at Hardin-Simmons.

Despite living in different cities, we were committed to not dating other people, and keeping that commitment wasn't difficult. Not once did I meet anyone at Hardin-Simmons who could hold a candle to Linda. And I went home as often as possible on weekends.

I loved the positive atmosphere on the HSU campus and made lots of friends. I ran for Student Senate and won. I took my first college-level courses in religion that fall, and I joined the First Baptist Church of Abilene where I felt very much at home.

About halfway through the semester my dad informed me that he was struggling with my covering my expenses. Though I picked up part-time work to help, it wasn't enough. At first, I was convinced there had to be a way to stay, but there wasn't, so I resigned myself to going home.

In the blink of an eye, my first and only semester at Hardin-Simmons was over, and before I knew it, I was back in Odessa, back at Crescent Park Baptist Church, back under my parents' roof, and back in my old bedroom.

For the previous two years, I had experienced a steady flow of events that placed me in the spotlight, brought admiration from people around me, and made me feel I was winning, achieving, and succeeding. This steady progress made it easy to believe that God was at work in my life, and that he was moving me forward because he had something special in mind for me.

I had been taking giant steps up a ladder of achievement. But now, suddenly, the ladder was feeling shaky. And for the first time since my call to ministry, I seemed to be moving down the ladder instead of up.

Odessa Junior College was the only institution of higher learning in my bustling West Texas hometown better known for its oil rigs and its love of high school football. When I arrived on campus in January of 1967, the comparison to Hardin-Simmons University was striking. No one seemed happy to be there, and initially, I was no different.

One positive aspect of moving home—Linda. We were together again. And together, we would prepare for something bigger and better that God had in store for us.

Over time, I settled into a new routine and took advantage of what was available. I quickly found courses and instructors that piqued my interest and inspired me. My first ever speech course laid a foundation that I would rely on throughout my career. There was English literature, taught by a brilliant professor, who awakened me to the works of Melville, Faulkner, and other great writers. And psychology was a revelation. Taught by an eccentric but exceptional professor, I found the subject matter fascinating, and it would remain a passion for the rest of my life.

I got involved with the Baptist Student Union on campus and was elected president for the coming year. And that summer I preached revivals for the Texas Baptist Student Department across the state of Texas.

As my sophomore year began Brother Bill was in my corner and thinking on my behalf. He decided this would be a good time for me to gain some ministerial experience with a small, part-time pastorate.

In some denominations, pastors are assigned to local churches by a bishop. Not so in Baptist life. Each church picks its own pastor—a process involving an elected search committee that reviews multiple candidates and selects one to preach "in view of a call," after which the congregation votes on whether to accept or reject the candidate.

Brother Bill was a mover and shaker. Soon he found a church that needed a pastor as well as financial support from a church like his. It wasn't long before I was in conversation with the Western Hills Baptist Church. Linda and I were now engaged, so she joined me in my conversations with the church.

Western Hills Baptist Church was located on the west side of Odessa, outside of city zoning, in the kind of neighborhood where one house might be clean and neat, but the next might have an old, partially disassembled car in the front yard. On one of our first drives to the church, Linda and I saw a big-bellied man outside his house, standing in his underwear, dumping a bucket of dirty liquid in his yard. It was like a scene from a hillbilly movie.

Making matters worse, the church property was anything but upscale. The street wasn't paved, the grounds weren't landscaped, and dilapidated buildings were precariously perched on top of stacks of concrete blocks.

Despite what appeared on the surface as significant socioeconomic differences, Linda and I connected quickly with the church's members and they connected with us. I was called to be their pastor and began my new position in October of 1967, then a sophomore in college.

Now that I was a pastor, the next step would be ordination, which for Baptists means an official recognition that the minister has been set apart for service to God and is fully qualified to perform all aspects of ministry.

Any Southern Baptist Church can ordain a minister, and while many Southern Baptists place importance on ministers completing college and seminary, a young minister could be ordained whenever his church felt he was ready, regardless of how far along he was in his education.

Before an ordination service, a group of ministers and deacons form an ordaining council. One of the steps of ordination is to appear before the ordaining council to be questioned. The council would be looking for three things: evidence of a true Christian conversion, a convincing description of a call to ministry, and sound theological positions on key doctrines.

I was a little nervous about going before my ordination council. I was 19 and had no formal theological training. But I shared my Christian testimony of walking the aisle to receive Jesus as my savior at the age of nine, talked about my call to preach, and answered their theological questions. My answers generated lots of good discussion and the meeting lasted for two hours. The ordaining council gave me a thumbs-up.

The next step was an ordination service held on a Sunday night at Crescent Park Baptist Church. That evening, I was surrounded by a community that embraced and supported my calling. For three years, since first preaching at the age of 16, people in my home church had been a source of constant encouragement. Now they were present to participate in formally setting me apart as a minister called by God.

All this added up to a profoundly moving service. The congregation sang their joy, Brother Bill preached a short sermon that impressed on me the gravity of being called by God, and he further challenged me to be true to my newfound calling. As I was asked to kneel in front of the pulpit, I felt like a divine spotlight was shining on me, embracing me, making me part of something larger than myself. And I felt humbled. With family, friends, and members of my home church and the church I was now leading looking on, deacons and visiting ministers filed by me one at a time, laid their hands on my head, and whispered a prayer or some encouraging words in my ear.

After the laying on of hands ceremony, I preached, passionately. Something profoundly spiritual occurred that night—everyone felt it. My ordination service would remain one of the most memorable and important experiences in my religious life. It was also a powerful reminder of the connection I felt with my church family. These were my people. I was one of them. We belonged to each other.

Now, I was ready. I could devote myself to my first pastorate.

My plate was full. I was taking a full course load at school, serving as BSU president, and pastoring the Western Hills Baptist Church.

Serving as pastor when you are sorely lacking in life experience isn't without its entertaining moments. Entertaining when I look back, that is.

I knew how to preach, but when I had preached all my stock sermons, I had to learn how to come up with three new sermons each week—a challenging, but manageable task. More pressing was my lack of pastoral training. Fortunately, Brother Bill mentored me every step of the way.

As I was preparing to do my first premarital counseling session for a couple whose wedding ceremony I was going to perform, Brother Bill offered a simple three-point, premarital counseling outline. "Talk about money, sex, and faith," he said. When the couple arrived for their session, I launched into my version of Brother Bill's plan, expounding on money management, sex, and faith as each related to Christian marriage. Midway through my monologue, the nervous groom-to-be interrupted, "She's pregnant." His statement left me speechless. I was in over my head. I wrapped up the meeting as quickly as possible and agreed to do the ceremony.

Fortunately, I didn't have many surprises like that first counseling session. Most of the time, I felt up to the task and was charging full speed ahead. By the time I had served as pastor for six months, the Odessa newspaper ran a story on our church in the religion section, reporting that we had done remodeling work on our buildings and that 27 people had joined the church bringing the total membership to 85.[2]

On June 23, 1968, Linda and I were married. It was the summer after our sophomore year at Odessa Junior College. Six hundred people attended our wedding at Crescent Park Baptist Church. I was 20. Linda was 19. The youth choir sang, the hand bell choir played, and it was a joyful day. We were a pair of idealistic, task-oriented achievers, and we planned to reach for the stars.

---

[2] "Tim Sledge Serves 85," *The Odessa American*, April 12, 1968, 12.

5 – Promised Land

In 1969, Billy Graham was the world's most famous preacher, drawing record-setting crowds to massive arenas in cities across the U.S. and overseas. Some said he wasn't the most famous preacher in the world—he was the most famous person in the world.

Founded in 1860, Wheaton College, located 25 miles west of downtown Chicago, was Billy Graham's alma mater. Only one year earlier, tens of thousands of Vietnam War protestors had battled police in Chicago during riots that were televised and watched by the whole nation. But Wheaton College, set in a quiet suburban village of the same name, with its manicured lawns and tree-lined streets, was a world away.

Wheaton was the Promised Land. Not only was Wheaton the most renowned evangelical Christian college in the country, but in those days, the town itself was the Jerusalem of evangelical Christianity, and the area was the home of nationally known Christian organizations like Youth for Christ, Tyndale House Publishing, Christianity Today, Greater Europe Mission, and the national radio program, The Chapel of the Air.

An older couple at Crescent Park Baptist in Odessa—our spiritual grandparents—had heard the former president of Wheaton College speak at a retreat and knew him as a casual friend. Convinced that Wheaton was a perfect fit for Linda and me, they confirmed our interest in the school and made some phone calls on our behalf.

A representative of Wheaton came to our house in Odessa to interview us, an action that underscored the highly selective nature of the school's admission process. We were asked questions intended to demonstrate that we met the Wheaton's admissions criteria—a vital Christian experience, moral character, personal integrity, past participation in extracurricular activities—and of course, strong academic standing and good references from Christian leaders.

Weeks passed. When our decision letters finally arrived, we were elated. This would be a path beyond the limited scope of my West Texas Southern Baptist world—into the mainstream of evangelical teachers, writers, and leaders I had only read about. Not only were we optimistic about our future in ministry, but now we were moving to Chicago—the third largest city in the nation. This was going to be a very different life.

We had one problem. No money. Our parents weren't providing any financial help, and one year at Wheaton for the two of us would cost around $30,000 in today's dollars.

As an act of faith, we made our plans to move to Wheaton, Illinois, and start classes in the fall of 1969—with absolutely no idea how we would pay for the move, a place to live, or tuition. When it was time to head north, still without funds, we loaded our belongings into the largest U-Haul trailer we could rent, and trusted that God would provide.

The night before we were to leave for Illinois, we attended Wednesday evening services at Crescent Park Baptist Church. Brother Bill had told us to see him after the service, and at its conclusion, he handed us three checks. Three couples in the church had donated money to help us get started—a total of $5,000 in today's dollars. More than half the money had come from our surrogate grandparents, who had introduced us to Wheaton, and the rest from two other couples. We were enormously grateful to the three families, but we saw a larger process at work: God had led, and God had provided.

The 1,200-mile trip was long, and our U-Haul was so heavily loaded that it made our car swing violently left and right if we exceeded 50 miles an hour, making the three-day drive even more arduous.

Once we arrived, we used the money given to us not only to rent an apartment, but to pay our initial fees at the college. The financial aid office helped us qualify for student loans and grants, and another service at the school assisted in finding part-time jobs.

Faith reminded us that God was behind all the help we received. When you are following God's leadership, he provides what you need—that's what we believed, and it was what we were experiencing.

Wheaton was a place where Linda and I grew tremendously. The intellectual climate was challenging. Religion classes were small and personal. The faculty were experts in their field. Whereas at Hardin-Simmons, the textbook for my Old Testament class was written by Dr. Samuel J. Schultz, at Wheaton, my Old Testament professor *was* Dr. Samuel J. Schultz. And at the end of the first year, finding myself sitting just a few feet away from Billy Graham as he spoke in the Wheaton College chapel, I had to pinch myself!

A Wheaton professor recommended me for a minister of youth position at The Church on the County Line, a small, non-denominational congregation in Hinsdale, Illinois. I was thrilled at the opportunity. This would be my second paid ministry job, and we needed the money urgently.

Hinsdale is an upscale Chicago suburb, and my role was to lead a weekly Bible study for the church's teenage youth group. As the weeks went on, I developed a special bond with the young people. Our weekly discussions were lively and meaningful.

One Sunday morning, I noticed a poster on the church's bulletin board announcing a meeting sponsored by the John Birch Society. Not only were many members of this church very conservative in their religious beliefs, but they were dramatically so in their politics. I decided to avoid any political discussions—including discussions about the war that was raging in Vietnam.

Like many other college students, I was opposed to the war in Vietnam. As a full-time college student now in my junior year, I wasn't subject to the draft. While my deferment meant I didn't need to be a conscientious objector, I had decided if I were ever forced to enlist, I would refuse. The more I studied the teachings of Jesus, the stronger my belief that a follower of Jesus should never participate in war—any war. Years later, I realized that my youthful view on this topic was too idealistic, and I changed my position. But then, I believed it was wrong to participate in war, period.

In one of our weekly Bible study sessions in June of 1970, a young man in the group asked me the question I was dreading: "How do you feel about the Vietnam War?" I had already decided that if asked this question, I would answer truthfully. So, I judiciously explained my position. I elaborated on my convictions. I told them I believed Jesus taught that we shouldn't fight in wars. The youth group was very quiet as I made my case, and what followed was a healthy, open discussion on the topic.

A week or two after this incident, Linda and I traveled home to visit our families. Shortly after arriving in Texas, the phone rang. It was one of the lay leaders back in Hinsdale, a very kind man who was supportive of my ministry. He was calling to tell me that the church was having financial difficulties and could no longer afford a minister of youth. My position had been terminated. However, he assured me, the church would pay my full salary for the remainder of the summer. This made no sense.

"Is this about the youth group discussion on the ethics of war?" I asked. He sighed and replied, "Yes, it is. One of the dads of one of the teenagers is a naval officer, and other members have strong feelings about the war."

I wasn't surprised, but I was disappointed. And acting like the whole thing was the result of a shortage of funds was disingenuous. Worse, in my view, I had just been kicked out of my church family because I took some of the teachings of Jesus too seriously.

What also hurt: I wasn't allowed to return and say my goodbyes to the teenagers, which seemed unnecessarily cruel. Close bonds had been formed, and I was left without closure. This wouldn't be the last time I would experience being suddenly cut off from a community to whom I was ministering—people I cared about, people who cared about me—and not permitted to see them again.

After our departure from The Church on the County Line, Linda and I found a congregation we loved. Located in Chicago, 25 miles from our home in Wheaton, Circle Church was an innovative community that gathered in the Teamsters Union building on the south side of the city. During worship services, we could see and hear Chicago's famed elevated trains as they rumbled by, visible through a wall of windows near the top of the two-story room where we worshipped.

With a Sunday morning attendance of 200 to 300 people, Circle Church stood out with its five ministers, including one African American and one Asian American. The senior minister was David Mains. He remains one of the most creative and fascinating ministers I have ever met.

I quickly came to appreciate the striking diversity of the congregation—all ages, all colors, all socio-economic levels—from the inner city as well as the suburbs. On a given Sunday, the music might be contemporary with guitars or Bach performed by a string quartet. Each week, with his sermon, the minister put forth a "suggestion for life response," a short, simple, written statement—something we could do to put what we learned from the sermon into practice.

Circle Church felt like home. It was a place where everything I believed was being practiced. In an article about Circle Church published a decade later, David Mains explained:

> We deliberately located Circle Church in the hub of a wild mix of neighborhoods. Across the expressway loomed the University of Illinois Circle Campus, one of the world's largest medical centers; to the rear of our building stretched Chicago's famous west side black ghetto; Skid Row was a couple of blocks north, and a small, Greek commercial district thrived eight blocks east. Circle [Church] was a beehive of activities: modules met on art, communications, music, outreach, and urban interests. A drama group wrote and produced several full-length plays. Our musicians gave professional-quality concerts. Prayer, social action, evangelism, and small groups were all finding beautiful expression. Many of our members moved into the Austin community which then had the second highest crime rate in Chicago. Our people responded to the urgent needs around us with a legal clinic, a youth program, social workers, counselors, the beginnings of a medical clinic, and dreams of an alternative school program.[3]

Circle Church was a model for church renewal—a concept that involved nudging the church toward positive change in ways that it could, in turn, do a better job of meeting two important objectives. First, the church needed to lead people who were not yet believers to faith in Jesus (evangelism). Second, the church needed to help Christians grow in spiritual knowledge as well as in their day-to-day obedience to Jesus (discipleship). Church renewal embraced the concept of effecting real change in peoples' lives and sought to enable believers to grow into spiritual maturity so that faith became more than appearance, more than words, a true and authentic commitment to changed behavior. Church renewal was the new paradigm for my future ministry.

David Mains replaced Billy Graham as my role model.

---

[3] David Mains and Philip Yancey, "My Greatest Ministry Mistakes," *Leadership: A Practical Journal for Church Leaders*, Volume 1, Number 2 (Spring, 1980): 15, 18.

6 – Seminary Training

W anting to stay connected to my Southern Baptist roots, I returned to Texas for my seminary training. In 1971, the average size of one of the 187 seminaries accredited by The Association of Theological Schools was 175 students. With an enrollment of 1,920 [4] students, Southwestern Baptist Theological Seminary in Fort Worth was the largest evangelical seminary in the world.[5]

Despite the large size of the school and the fact that the seminary president like to refer to it as a preacher factory, I found my place. By the end of my first year at seminary, I had decided to major in pastoral care. I was becoming especially interested in what faith coupled with the help of psychology could accomplish. The head of the pastoral care department, Dr. C.W. Brister, saw potential in me. He seemed to appreciate the insights I shared in class comments and papers, and near the end of my first semester recommended me for a youth minister position at a church in Memphis, Tennessee.

Linda and I visited the Union Avenue Baptist Church on a weekend, it was an excellent match, and I landed a full-time job for the summer months. Union Avenue Baptist was an inner-city congregation with a weekly attendance of 600, a high percentage of college graduates, diverse income levels, and an influx of younger families since the new pastor had arrived a year earlier.

Pastor Lee Prince gave me tremendous support and latitude, allowing me to start several new ministries. I organized a call-in youth help line called Dial-a-Teen, staffed entirely by teenagers on Friday and Saturday evenings. The ministry's phone number was advertised by virtually every TV and radio station in the city, and youth from across the Memphis metropolitan area called in to discuss their problems with our teen volunteers.

I was busy every waking moment that summer, and I enjoyed every minute of it. As the summer ended and we prepared to return to Fort Worth, I was surprised when the pastor offered me an open-ended position. I would work part-time during the school year and come back full-time in future summer months. I accepted.

For the next two years, Linda and I lived in Memphis during the summers. When seminary classes were in session, I flew alone from Fort Worth to Memphis for one of two visits each month, and for the second monthly visit, drove the 1,000-mile round trip to Memphis so Linda could accompany me.

Four years before I began working in Memphis, Martin Luther King, Jr. had been shot and killed in the city. National Guard troops had been called in to restore order when rioting occurred. Some of the teenagers in the youth group remembered military tanks rolling through the streets after Dr. King's death. Memphis was still simmering with racial tension, and I found myself playing a private game each time I flew into town. I would see how long it would take before witnessing some visible evidence of racial tension. Sadly, it never took more than 30 minutes.

Our church wasn't integrated, but the youth volunteers answering Dial-a-Teen calls—at my direction—invited everyone who called, regardless of ethnicity, to visit our youth group events.

One summer night, two African-American girls came to a swimming party held at the home of one of the girls in our group. They been invited to the party by our Dial-a-Teen staff and had accepted the invitation.

During the event, I was called into the host's house to pick up the phone. The caller, the father of two girls in our church who were enjoying the party, was furious. "I heard you have some n-----s at the swimming party," he fumed. "No, but we do have two young ladies who are black at the party," I replied with calm defiance. My response made him even more livid. He arrived shortly afterward to pick up his daughters.

I was glad that our pastor was known as a liberal-minded promoter of positive race relations, but despite his genuine lack of prejudice, Pastor Lee Prince felt that our church wasn't ready to be integrated. Union Avenue's Child Enrichment Center was a highly regarded preschool program that included pupils from many families who didn't attend our church. In June of 1973, an African-American mother brought her child to apply for admission to the preschool. She was turned down. The incident didn't go unnoticed. *The Commercial Appeal*, the city newspaper for Memphis, published an article that leveled an accusation: "Union Avenue Baptist Church, which is considered one of the more liberal Southern Baptist Congregations in the city especially concerning race relations, has been accused of refusing to admit black children to its Child Enrichment Center." The accusation was true.

The article continued, "News that Union Avenue was being accused of racial discrimination was surprising. Mr. Prince has been very active in efforts to seek cooperation between black and white Baptist pastors."

And word had been passed along about our Dial-a-Teen invitations to our youth events: "The church also has a youth program that is directed toward getting black youngsters to participate in youth projects. These programs have been active only for the last few months, sources said."

The complaint had been filed by the National Association for the Advancement of Colored People. Mrs. Maxine Smith, the executive secretary of the NAACP was quoted, saying that the complaint was being studied and that some type of action would be taken. Word was that the NAACP was threatening an organized protest in front of our church.[6]

An emergency deacons' meeting was called to discuss how the church would respond. As the deacons gathered in the church's choir rehearsal room, the emotional tone was tense. The older deacons seemed most upset and passionate about what was happening. In their view, segregation was not something that needed review. I was shocked at their anger and vitriol.

As each of the deacons joined the discussion, not one mentioned what the Bible taught about race. There was no mention of "What would Jesus do?" No discussion of changing the preschool's admission policy.

I heard at least one threat of violence by one of the older deacons—a threat targeted at any protestor who might cause trouble at our church. Cooler heads prevailed, and the official plan was to go forward with the worship service. As long as the protestors stayed outside, the situation would be manageable. If they came inside and disrupted the service, it wasn't clear what would happen.

When the meeting ended, I was utterly deflated.

Several years later, when Lee Prince felt the time was right, the church did integrate. For him, it was a matter of when, not if. But that day I struggled to accept that the lay leaders of our church didn't look to the teachings of Jesus if it didn't suit them. Instead, they followed their cultural norms. They wanted to keep dark-skinned people out, so they did. And those who disagreed didn't stand up to them. These deacons, serving in a role that I respected, were just like everyone else, and possibly, less tolerant than many of the citizens of Memphis who were gradually beginning to move beyond the bias of skin color.

* * *

In April of 1974, as I was completing my master's degree classes, I was accepted into the seminary's Doctor of Ministry program—a relatively new degree program that focused on practical ministry skills and was a perfect fit for me. My doctoral classes would begin in the fall. I knew I wanted to devote full attention to my studies, so I gave the church notice that I was leaving at the end of the summer.

Leaving Memphis for the last time on a hot August day in 1974 was bittersweet. I felt a mix of pride and melancholy. I would miss the interaction with the congregation and the youth. I felt good about the work I had done at Union Avenue, and both my personal life and ministerial career had been strengthened by the support from Pastor Lee Prince.

Rolling westward on Interstate 40, my grief at leaving Memphis peaked as the massive structure of the Mississippi River Bridge came into view. Memphis was fading behind me in my rear-view mirror. The music playing on my car radio heightened my feelings of sadness. Just then, there was a commercial break and I heard the following words: "Teenagers, got a problem? Need help? Call Dial-a-Teen, 272-1631." It was one of our commercials—a public service spot that ran both on radio and TV.

Just as I was crossing the river that marked the western boundary of the city, it was as if God had spoken. The message was perfectly timed, and to me it said: "Tim, you made a difference here. You started something that will continue though you are leaving. Go in peace."

One month into my doctoral studies, my dad suffered a heart attack. I rushed to Odessa, making it in time to visit him in intensive care, but he was unconscious and on a ventilator. He died the next day, just weeks before what would have been his 68th birthday and his death was a crushing blow.

Despite issues caused by his struggle with alcoholism, there was so much he gave me that I cherish to this day—most significant was his belief in me and my ability to achieve anything I set my sights on. I like to think that in his last days, my dad had come to a place of true sobriety and peace. He had been delivering sermons as a lay preacher at a local rescue mission. And just before he died, he had been going to the home of a blind African-American man to read to him. One of the most wrenching conversations after my dad's death was with that man, as I gave him the news of my father's passing on the phone. His response to me: My father had been a good friend to him, and he would miss him so much. My faith assured me that my dad was in a better place.

As I returned to my doctoral classes, I was determined to learn all I could about how to help people overcome their problems—not just with prayer and Bible teaching, but with the tools of counseling and a focus on emotional health. But the most important paper I wrote that year was not about pastoral care. It was a paper titled "Renewal in the Local Church" in which I described my emerging philosophy of ministry, an approach rooted in my experiences with Circle Church in Chicago.

Church renewal included a backward look at the New Testament church as a model for what the church's spiritual core should be, and a forward look at cultural changes that beckoned the church to evolve in its methods. Church renewal also meant that Christian conversion was just the beginning, not the end and sum total of a Christian's personal experience with God. Conversion meant transformation of one's ongoing daily life. I wanted to lead a church where actions and decisions were truly driven by the teachings of Jesus. I wanted to lead a church that transcended cultural norms.

Church renewal would begin with a journey inward that was about becoming more self-aware and more open to the presence of God—at both the personal and congregational levels. The next step would be a journey outward that called for effective ministry and evangelism outside the walls of the church. My paper on church renewal served as a blueprint for what I hoped to facilitate in my first full-time position as a pastor.

I finished my on-campus doctoral work in spring of 1975.

Finally, after eight years of college and seminary classes, at the age of 27, I was ready to fulfill the commitment I made to God as a teenager: "Wherever you want me to go, I'll go."

---

[4] 1972-73 *Fact Book*, The Association of Theological Schools, Pittsburgh.

[5] Dan Martin, "SWBTS Celebrates 63rd Year," *The Fort Worth Star Telegram*, March 14, 1971.

[6] Beth J. Tamke, "Union Avenue Baptist Accused of Discrimination," *The Commercial Appeal*, June 30, 1973, 12.

7 – New York

I began looking for a full-time position during my last semester of doctoral studies. My prospects seemed bright. I had plenty of experience, having served as a youth evangelist, pastor, and inner-city youth minister. I was well educated. Linda was the ultimate preacher's wife—smart, with strong people skills, and dedicated to the cause. And I was blessed with an impressive list of people who were happy to provide references.

Despite all I had going for me, churches weren't lining up to hire me. After preaching at my home church in Odessa during my seminary years, a congregant said, "You sound like an intellectual." Translation: You don't sound like you're from around here anymore, and what you're saying isn't what we're used to hearing. My sermons were still simple, straightforward, and clear. I avoided theological jargon. But after years of education, my words reflected greater awareness of the nuances of life and faith.

My marketability would have been enhanced if I had been 10 years older, had shorter hair, and approached ministry like the pre-higher-education version of myself. I didn't look like, think like, or sound like what most Southern Baptist search committees were seeking.

In the Spring of my on-campus doctoral work, I noticed a flier on a seminary bulletin board announcing that the Baptist Convention of New York would be conducting interviews on campus looking to fill ministry positions in the tri-state area—New York, New Jersey, and Connecticut. Southwestern Seminary students didn't seem anxious to move to the northeastern U.S., but to Linda and me—New York beckoned. Following an encouraging interview on campus, we were invited to visit the Bergen Baptist Church.

Bergen Baptist was an unlikely option for a preacher from West Texas—a small Southern Baptist congregation in North Bergen County, New Jersey—just 16 miles from the George Washington Bridge that connects the Garden State to Manhattan. The church's 110 members were an impressive bunch, mainly transplanted Southerners in executive positions, commuting daily into the city or to offices in New Jersey, but this congregation was smaller than most where I had preached in recent years, and definitely smaller than what I envisioned for my first full-time pastorate.

As Southern Baptists, we often talked about the importance of missions—taking the message of Jesus to new places and building churches in areas new to our work. Metropolitan New York, in our view, was a vast mission field. And the possibility for growth at Bergen Baptist Church seemed limitless. Coupled with the lure of the area itself, I knew this was the right move.

The Bergen Baptist congregation voted to call me as pastor.

My philosophy of ministry had been delineated in my doctoral paper on renewal in the local church, and that was the direction in which I began to lead.

20

On a personal and an organizational level, church renewal was first a journey inward. For individuals, this meant becoming more self-aware, more knowledgeable about faith, more committed, and more in touch with God. For the congregation, the journey inward included examining how well we were executing the tasks God had called us to perform and being willing to initiate changes wherever needed to make the church more relevant to a modern world.

A successful journey inward would result in a journey outward—ministering to people outside the walls of the church in daily life, and, as opportunities arose, sharing faith so others could believe in Jesus.

One month after becoming pastor, the church approved my recommendation to begin a six-month journey inward built around sermons, retreats, and an 18-week discipleship group. The discipleship group was my doctoral project and a trial run of a process I planned to repeat and integrate into the life of the church. Based on the New Testament teaching that every Christian is called to be a minister, the purpose of the discipleship group was to help laypersons discover their spiritual gifts and to sense a call to Christian ministry—not as professional ministers, but as lay ministers in day-to-day life.

I had come to believe, there was another important ingredient for a healthy life of faith and ministry—psychological self-awareness. Sometimes, life in Christ could be seriously impeded by unresolved mental health issues. So, in addition to studying basic theological concepts and working on the daily disciplines of Bible reading and prayer, the discipleship group participants' journey inward included a psychological personality test with follow-up exercises and discussions that aimed to increase self-awareness. Winning new converts was imperative, but helping Christians become faithful disciples of Jesus—psychologically self-aware disciples—was also essential. And, disciples like this would be better equipped to win new converts.

By the time the discipleship group completed its final meeting in April of 1976, we were ready to begin our journey outward. To help launch the journey outward—which meant reaching out to people beyond our closed circle of Southern congregants—I preached a sermon sharing my long-held convictions that we were under God's mandate to let people know that meaning in this life and life after death come through Jesus Christ and only through Jesus Christ.

However determined we were to share our message, being a Southern Baptist in the metropolitan area of New York City could be challenging. Despite the prevalence of our denomination in the South, and our being the largest Protestant denomination in the U.S., we were "Southern" and we were "Baptists," neither of which commended us to people in New Jersey.

In my sermon, I stressed that we could make all kinds of excuses about how hard it was to win converts in New Jersey, but we were compelled to move beyond excuses. We had to learn to share the good news in the daily course of life—in our encounters with business associates, neighbors, and friends. And while we needed to live Christ-like lives, exemplary living alone would never be enough. We had to spread the message of the good news about Jesus, and that included inviting others to respond.

I reminded my congregants that Southern accents or not, our faith was based on the Bible, and our reliance on its message gave credibility to all that we believed. We had no reason to be ashamed of our faith and could be confident and proud of what we believed and what we could share with others.

And soon, we began to see success in our outreach efforts.

One day, a rugged looking man walked through the doors of my office wanting to talk. My conversation with Vic marked the beginning of a series of successful efforts to reach adults in our community who did not know Jesus.

Vic ran a local construction company. He had been unfaithful to his wife. She found out, took the kids and left, and he was devastated. That day in my office, Vic prayed to invite Jesus into his life. In the testimony he shared just before I baptized him, he said that prior to making his commitment to Jesus, "I really wasn't the nicest guy to know. There wasn't too much I hadn't gotten into between drugs and running around with women and messing up my life." Now, he was entering the baptismal waters as a changed man!

When Vic's wife, Cheryl, came to see me, and she too prayed to receive Jesus as her savior, I was thrilled. In her baptismal testimony, she said, "My life has never been this happy or this meaningful."

Compared to the rest of our members—corporate executives and their families—these two were rough around the edges, but our congregation welcomed them with open arms. This was what we were supposed to be about—reaching people where they were and as they were, regardless of whether they spent their days in an office or at a construction site.

A year or so after Vic and Cheryl joined our church, we welcomed Wendell through our doors, a middle-aged executive whose wife had committed suicide only days before. She had gone into their garage, started the car, and asphyxiated herself.

The next week I went to visit Wendell and learned that he had been an executive at a nationally known company before losing his job. I expressed my deepest condolences for his losses, reaching out to him as a minster and a friend. In that meeting, he prayed to ask Jesus to become his lord and savior.

At his baptismal service, Wendell shared his testimony with the congregation, describing the loss of his job and then his wife. He said he had hit bottom emotionally by the time he showed up at our church. But now, with Jesus in his life, he proclaimed, "Things have changed dramatically. I've put my faith in the Lord." It was easy to see that he was looking forward to a bright future in his new spiritual walk.

It wasn't long before Vic, Cheryl, and Wendell became friends. Vic and Cheryl helped Wendell through the grieving process and single-parenting his daughter. Though they lived on the same street, if not for the church, they were unlikely to have ever spent time together. But thanks to their newfound faith, they formed genuine bonds. This was why I became a pastor, I told myself. This was real Christianity. We were helping people turn their lives around and make uncommon connections that transcended common barriers.

In the following months, there were more adults who came to know Jesus as their savior. There was the Italian guy who owed a gambling debt to the Mafia. After his conversion, he testified, "God has taken my life from a chaotic mess and straightened it out into one of loving my fellow man and my family." There was the Jewish guy who became a friend. I didn't press him; I just shared, a little at a time, until he eventually decided to give his life to Jesus.

For me, bringing people like Vic, Cheryl, Wendell, and others into the Christian fold was what my calling was about. This was precisely why I was so far from home—helping people establish a personal relationship with God, and—as a result—find the strength to face whatever life handed them.

Our church was beginning to grow, but that also meant it was changing. We were no longer focused on Southern transplants; we were becoming a more community-based church. As I led the congregation in this new direction, some of our members were not happy with our new course. Expressing his anger, one deacon let loose a stream of grievances directed at me when he said: "I'm ready to raise hell about this! I stepped back to analyze your ministry and found you were concentrating on new Christians and the down-and-outers with nothing for the rest of us." He and his family left the church.

Fortunately, not all the members shared his views. But it was increasingly clear that some members saw the church as a "payment for services rendered" kind of operation. If new converts didn't give as much financial support as long-term members, then why should they get so much attention? I couldn't find a Bible verse to support that view, and I was coming to understand that regardless of how much the Bible talked about the importance of winning new converts, long term members weren't always excited about reaching the unreached. I was learning that one of the greatest obstacles to growing a church could be existing members who liked things as they were.

Gradually, the tone and direction of the congregation changed. When I arrived in 1975, Bergen Baptist was an island of Southerners. Six years later, many positive changes had occurred—the most important was that the church's membership became more community-based and diverse; eventually, less than half the members were transplanted Southerners and our ministries included a dozen different nationalities and ethnicities.

Not only had we reshaped who we were, but we had also accomplished multiple objectives. We refocused the deacons, deepening their understanding of church growth and ministry. We set up a weekday preschool—under Linda's guidance—administered by a paid director who was a member of the church and a New Jersey native. And we had developed an active youth ministry with a volunteer leader.

Our membership and budget giving were up by more than 40% over the previous year. While these numbers were outstanding, it had been necessary to lose some members to shape our new identity. In terms of total membership, we were just slightly ahead of where we had started six years earlier.

But our balance sheet of life experiences was well in the black. Our family had grown, and we had found an extended family in our congregation, and sometimes, in those who weren't church members but were touched by our ministries. Our son, Jonathan, was born in February of 1976, seven months after our arrival in New Jersey. Prior to his birth, Linda had been teaching English as a ministry to a group of Japanese women who were not members of the church. Following Jonathan's arrival, Linda's students provided us with homemade Japanese food every day for a week. Welcomed with equal joy, our second son, David, came along four years later. With each child, our church family was there to celebrate, and we never wanted for a babysitter.

And our Christian fellowship was wider than our local congregation. One year, as chairman of the Metropolitan New York Baptist Association's Youth Committee, one of my duties was overseeing a winter retreat for teenagers from metro area churches. Held in Stroudsburg, Pennsylvania, the retreat's site was perfection, like something out of the movies—a snowy wonderland with downhill slopes for sledding and a frozen pond for ice skating. Attendees reflected the ethnic diversity of New York City, and with this diversity, was a depth of harmony, unity, and joy.

From day one in New Jersey, we delighted in where we lived. There were the neighbors on our street—the ex-priest and his wife who introduced us to our first New England lobsters one lovely weekend in Connecticut, the former Iranian judge who had escaped to the U.S. after the fall of the Shah of Iran, and the niece of the president of Liberia who had fled her country when her uncle was killed in a coup d'état in 1980.

And there was Manhattan, always offering some delightful experience: a Broadway play, a visit to Chinatown, a view from the top of the Empire State Building, or a slow ride around the island on a Circle Line cruise.

It was amazing how quickly and irrevocably our world had expanded since we left West Texas, but a pastorate of 100 members was a small church, regardless of how much we achieved. And in the metro New York City area, despite the tremendous outreach potential, less than one tenth of one percent of the population were Southern Baptists, and the average size of an Anglo Southern Baptist congregation was around 100.

With no large Anglo churches of my denomination in the suburbs of New York nor in the entire Baptist Convention of New York, I saw the limits of what I could achieve as a Southern Baptist pastor in the Northeast. Despite the accomplishments, opportunities, and experiences, I was growing restless. After serving as pastor of Bergen Baptist Church for six years, it was time for something new.

8 – Farming Town

Living in the metropolitan New York City area was an experience like no other, and with all its diversity and dynamism, there were times it felt more like home to me than the segregated South. I often wondered if I could ever leave the area without being terribly bored. But now, despite my fear that nowhere else could compete, I felt it was time to move on.

In the summer of 1981, rather than flying to a denominational conference in Los Angeles, I flew from New York to Phoenix, rented a car, visited with a minister friend, and then motored across the western side of the state to L.A. I had always wanted to see Arizona, and on that road trip, I fell in love with the state's wide-open desert, expansive sky, and a few of the state's 194 mountain ranges. When I returned to New Jersey, I asked my friend in Phoenix to recommend me to a church in the Grand Canyon state.

I was recommended to the First Southern Baptist Church in Buckeye, Arizona, a small farming town, 35 miles west of downtown Phoenix. One of its key selling points: This town was on the verge of experiencing tremendous growth as the Phoenix suburbs moved westward.

Four months later, when Linda and I first visited Buckeye at the invitation of the pastor search committee, though the desert and surrounding vistas were beautiful, the little town was... well, not beautiful. And from what I could tell, it would be a long time before the rural town's population of 3,100 would be shifting into an explosive growth mode.

I was formulating ways to politely tell our hosts we weren't a good match after all, but as the weekend unfolded, Linda and I couldn't help but be impressed by the people we met—kind, thoughtful, genuine, and unpretentious. And the desert has its own kind of persuasive power, in some ways, not unlike my hometown in West Texas.

Surprising ourselves, we decided that Buckeye would be a good next step. At first glance, it seemed like the edge of nowhere, but we decided it was actually somewhere special—especially for our family life. When the church extended a call, we accepted.

In November of 1981, Linda and I arrived in Buckeye, Arizona, with one preschooler, one toddler, five rooms of modest furniture, and of course, boxes and boxes of my books. We knew how to find the good in any place we lived, but upon our arrival, we could not have found anywhere that would have been a greater contrast to New York City.

It wasn't just population size that made our new home so different, it was the cultural differences, and they were many—everything from nicknames ("Toad" and "Rat") to food (venison and bear at the church potluck) to wild rumors (devil worshippers meeting nightly in the desert).

At the time of our move, Jonathan was five and David was one. We found a house in a developed community with an acre of property and amenities we had not enjoyed before—a backyard pool where the boys could swim, a covered patio with a brick grille for cooking, and a nearby irrigation canal where I could jog with our Springer Spaniel at my side.

On the surface, Buckeye was an unlikely choice for me. I was a city slicker; being the pastor of farmers and cowboys didn't appear to be a reasonable fit, but one thing about me bridged the gap—my preaching. Baptists, regardless of their lifestyle, always loved good preaching and that was my gift.

I still preached evangelistic sermons and sermons that focused on purely spiritual topics like how to have a daily quiet time or how to build spiritual intellect. But I also preached practical sermons on how to improve one's life, with topics like starting over, breaking a bad habit, getting through trying times, and discovering your own potential. The Buckeye congregation liked what they heard.

For me, Buckeye became a school in pastoral care. Not long after our move there, I was called to the burn unit of a Phoenix hospital to visit a college student. His vehicle's gas tank had exploded when he was hit by a drunk driver, and he was left severely burned over most of his body. The first time I saw him, he was propped up in a vertical position bathed with lights to maintain his body temperature. He couldn't speak. His ears were gone as was part of his nose. He was in and out of consciousness.

Nothing in my seminary training or ministerial experience prepared me for standing beside him, trying to connect and comfort him, unsure that he could hear or understand what I was saying. I watched the young man endure tremendous suffering as I visited over the next few months. Eventually, after receiving a $20 million settlement and enduring a multitude of plastic surgeries, he pressed forward with his life.

There were other experiences of standing close to tragedy. I remember speeding to a family farm to drive a deacon's wife to the Phoenix hospital where her toddler son had been taken. His head was run over by the back tire of a tractor. The mother was brave, but I felt her terror and her struggle to comprehend what had happened. Remarkably, her son survived.

I vividly recall rushing to the emergency room to see one of our high school students. He had skipped classes, spent the day outside of town drinking beer, and on the way back into Buckeye, his car struck and killed a woman riding a bicycle. He was still drunk when I talked with him in the hospital—alternating between laughter and tears. I was disgusted, but I also felt sympathy for him as I witnessed his waves of awareness at what he had done.

One of the most heartbreaking funeral services I ever officiated involved a 51-year-old grandfather and his 2-year-old grandson. Three generations were aboard a twin-engine plane piloted by the grandfather when there was a problem on take-off from their ranch. Only the 30-year-old son survived. The loss he would have to grieve—his father and his son—was so profound I could not even imagine it.

In my six years as pastor at Bergen Baptist, not once had I officiated a funeral service. Here, it seemed that I presided over a funeral once or twice a month. Not only were many in our community older—leading to predictable age-related deaths—but our church was the largest in the community, so I was often asked to conduct services for individuals outside our membership.

When ministering to people who are facing life's most difficult tragedies, and doing so with genuine empathy, there is something that seeps out of you—drains you—imperceptible in intensity compared to what those you are ministering to are feeling, but, nevertheless, for the minister, significant.

Another kind of pastoral stress is neither severe nor acute, but chronic. It is the drip, drip, drip of hypersensitivity, unreasonable expectations, and childishness of some church members. And, it is the challenge of living up to every member's expectations for their pastor—his priorities, his strengths, even his personality. Over time, these persistent issues can be more draining than the periodic dramatic episodes.

One source of the drip, drip, drip was the church business meeting. Baptist churches operate as a democracy. Congregational business meetings are held to approve the annual budget, elect lay leaders to various positions, vote on starting new ministries, and to address other routine matters. Any church member can be recognized and allowed to speak in one of these meetings. Consequently, a business meeting is often the place where certain members—usually the same individuals over and over—revel in the opportunity to stand up and talk at length about what is wrong with whatever is being proposed. The Buckeye church had more than the usual share of long-winded naysayers.

Complicating the decision-making process, some individuals bring personal issues—family of origin issues, authority figure issues, issues around money—to each business meeting in a way that generates a stubborn resistance to making changes, spending money, or starting anything that has never been done before. The Buckeye church had its share of those congregants as well.

In a church business meeting, the minister is expected to be Christ-like in his responses, with an emphasis on kind and gentle—no matter how silly or irrelevant a speaker's comments might be. But if the pastor doesn't know how—or is afraid—to give a firm response to a long-winded talker or a crazy idea to move the discussion forward, the result will be a paralyzed congregation instead of a progressive, growing one. Handling these chronic objectors requires deftness and skill, and Buckeye gave me lots of practice.

Another evaluation point has to do with how a pastor can be pigeonholed into one category or another. In Baptist life, church members would describe their pastor as either a "good preacher" or a "good pastor," but rarely both. A good preacher could capture and hold their attention during services—inspiring through his words and his leadership. On the other hand, a good pastor was more approachable, more warm and fuzzy—visible out and about in the larger community, expressing compassion and support for individuals.

I cared about each person in our church, and I developed many close relationships in Buckeye. Nevertheless, I fit in the good preacher category. My predecessor, on the other hand, was a good pastor. He excelled at visiting the sick—at the hospital or in their homes—and was equally skilled at giving attention to the emotionally needy. A few of the older members of the church frequently criticized and compared me to him, insisting that I didn't make enough pastoral visits. Though I thought I was visiting when and where I was needed, perhaps they were right. Maybe I could do better.

On one occasion, I was urgently informed by one of my critics that a man who worked at a gas station near the church was in need of a hospital visit. Wanting to prove my willingness to visit anyone who needed me—this patient wasn't a church member and had expressed no interest in seeing me—I complied with the request. I reasoned that the man might be in a dire situation. Maybe he needed someone to talk to and pray with him as he faced a medical crisis. With little information but hoping to do some good, I made the 45-minute drive to the hospital on the west side of Phoenix. I sat down next to the man's bed. I expressed sympathy for his illness and probed discreetly about his condition. He replied with some chagrin, "I have a habit of keeping a toothpick in my mouth all the time, and somehow, I swallowed my toothpick."

I had no sense of making a meaningful connection with the man during the visit—just a sense that he was a little embarrassed about why he was in the hospital and a little confused about why I had come to see him. After visiting the man hospitalized because he swallowed a toothpick, surely, I had now proved my willingness to make hospital visits—regardless of the reason.

Finding myself in a small, rural farming community yet to experience the predicted boom in population growth, I looked for creative ministry opportunities that might be available to a church of our size.

In 1983, I visited the office of our local cable television office where I proposed broadcasting Christian programming on the local religious access channel. Our discussions—and our options—progressed over several months. Ultimately, the cable company surprised us by offering to install a transmission line from our building to theirs—at no cost to us. Within a few months, we had made a sizeable investment to buy the necessary equipment and were producing four different TV programs that went out on our own cable channel in our little community. I wrote and presented a daily devotional program. One of our church members broadcast her own talk show. Another congregant created an exercise program. And we also televised our Sunday morning services.

I welcomed any opportunity to broaden the influence of my ministry. I spoke for statewide Baptist events for teenagers and college students, and I continued to write for national Southern Baptist curriculum periodicals targeted at teens, something I had started doing when working as a minister of youth in Memphis. Linda was also finding ways to make an impact beyond our church's ministries. She was the director of the Buckeye Elementary School gifted program, a board member for our state Baptist children's services organization, and a writer of Southern Baptist children's curricula.

Though our schedules were full, sometimes hectic, our life in Arizona was an interlude with less worry about what was on the evening news and more time for family activities. Although Buckeye was a desert town, it felt like an oasis; those years were among the most fulfilling for our family. We were happy. Our boys were happy. In some ways, Buckeye was parked in an earlier era, and less complicated than life in the big city. Driving to work each day, I couldn't fail to admire the beauty of the surrounding farmlands, desert, and mountains, and I told myself how lucky I was to live in such a beautiful place.

But intermissions are temporary respites, and that's how Buckeye was beginning to feel. I wasn't fulfilling my potential, and I hadn't given up on having a larger impact. Halfway into my third year in Arizona, I decided that I wanted to lead a church with more potential for growth. And as I was contemplating my next step vocationally, part of my planning included reviewing my strategy for ministry.

I had been influenced by Billy Graham's evangelistic model in my early years, but it had become apparent that mass evangelism wasn't the best way to reach and retain converts. The church renewal movement, introduced to me by Circle Church in Chicago, brought the focus back to local churches, and inspired a wider vision for what innovative congregations might look like. But a question, both spiritual and pragmatic, remained unanswered: How do you lead a church to grow—not only in the quality of its ministries, but in the number of people it reaches?

Church growth was becoming a specialized field of study that focused on answering that question, and a fresh group of researchers were writing on the subject. The church growth movement, like the question it sought to answer, was both spiritual and pragmatic, stressing the imperative of leading new converts to faith in Jesus while also exploring the nuts and bolts of organizing for numerical growth.

I made myself a student of this new movement, attending church growth conferences in California where many of the movement's leaders were located, and reading every church growth book I could find.

9 – Main Event

The pastor search committee of the Kingsland Baptist Church had begun its work in December of 1984 with more than 120 pastoral candidates submitted for consideration. By the following March, the committee had narrowed the search to 10 individuals who were invited to respond to a questionnaire and provide references. I was one of the 10.

In his letter of recommendation, Dr. C.W. Brister shared kind words about me. He included phrases like "dynamic leadership qualities," "quiet, convincing faith," and "persuasive spiritual direction." He described me as "conservative in theology, warmly evangelistic, and committed to the very finest in leadership, worship, and pastoral care ministries in the local church." I was fortunate to have such an ardent supporter.

After reviewing my references and other information I provided, two members of the search committee came to hear me preach in Buckeye in May. The following month, Linda and I were invited to Houston. After meeting with us on a Saturday, members of the search committee came to hear me preach the next day as the guest speaker at another Baptist church in the area.

Following what was later described as a period of "long and intensive prayer and waiting upon the Lord for a sense of his direction," the search committee unanimously voted to invite me for a weekend visit in mid-July when I would preach in Kingsland's morning worship service in view of a call to be pastor of the church.

The church was in Katy, Texas, a rapidly growing suburb on the west side of Houston—a locale that would place us closer to our extended families, offer access to a noteworthy school system, put us back in a city environment, and provide an opportunity to focus on church growth. Kingsland Baptist Church had the growth potential I was looking for, and the church was seeking a pastor to lead them from a small congregation to a larger, more organized, more inspiring, and more influential force in the community. Everything pointed to that goal being achievable. Katy was a rapidly growing suburb of Houston. The church's existing buildings occupied only one-fourth of its 14.5 acres of land, which meant plenty of room to expand. Importantly, only eight years old, the church was organizationally young enough that attempts to implement change wouldn't be countered by decades of tradition.

The congregation had 560 members with an average Sunday morning worship attendance of 300. The vocations of the nine members of the search committee were representative of the congregation: accountant, bank president, elementary school teacher, homemaker, regional school district administrator, carpet company owner, regional service manager for a national electronics company, and the vice president of a construction company.

As part of my due diligence, I had interviewed the church's only previous pastor and asked him why he left the church. He told me he had looked toward the next 10 years, realized he would be tasked with leading multiple fundraising and building programs, and decided he would be more at home in a quieter, more reflective environment.

In response to the search committee's request, I provided references from people who had known me over the course of my life. The committee compiled a summary of the comments received from my references and shared it with me. Under positive traits, my references had written: "very good preacher, always well prepared, ability to get people involved, flexibility in ways to reach people, personal concern, growth oriented, intelligent, truthful, fair, up-front, hard worker, and creative ideas." I couldn't complain about any of those affirmations.

The references described Linda as "loyal, very personable, caring, an excellent teacher, committed to ministry, loving, warm, exuberant, compassionate, supportive, and an asset to Tim." They were correct.

The committee also asked my references to share concerns about my leadership. These comments included: "may appear stand-offish because of his quiet nature," "frustration with people who expect to be coddled," and "loathes playing the game." These observations were also on target.

In a questionnaire from the committee, I was asked what I least enjoyed in ministry. I wrote, "relating to disgruntled individuals who feel they should set my priorities and write my agenda."

In response to another question, I described the kind of church I wanted to pastor: a church that was ready to obey the command of Jesus to reach people not already committed to him, a church where my family and I could plant our roots, a church that was not a stepping stone to get somewhere else, a church that understood I was there for the long haul.

The search committee provided me with a notebook of information about the church that included its constitution. One thing I carefully checked was the description of the role of deacons. Traditionally, in Southern Baptist churches, the deacon body was a governing board. No major decisions or changes could be made without their approval.

I was part of a current mindset of Baptist ministers who viewed deacons not as overseers of the church, but as partners in ministry.

After reading the church's constitution and noting that the focus of the deacon body was on supporting the pastor and ministering to families in the congregation, I was satisfied that I would be comfortable with the deacons' role at Kingsland Baptist Church.

The notebook also contained the results of a survey of what the congregation was looking for in a pastor. The results, in order of priority, were: character, an ability to deal with financial issues, administrative skills, preaching, leadership, teaching, equipping others to lead, evangelism, counseling, and visiting members and prospects.

The relationship between a pastor and a congregation is, in some ways, like a romantic relationship. When two adults first meet with an eye toward a closer connection, each one puts their best foot forward and shares freely with the other. In addition, the two individuals may consciously or unconsciously alert one another to issues that could create stress.

My early interactions with Kingsland Baptist Church were no different. I saw and heard much about the church that I liked; they saw and heard much about me that they liked. And, we each, in different ways, revealed areas where stress might occur. I was open in expressing that what I least enjoyed in ministry was relating to disgruntled individuals who wanted to set my priorities for me. They told me that reaching unchurched people was number eight in their list of 10 priorities for their pastor. But neither the committee nor I noticed these implicit warnings. We were in the romance stage, focused on what we liked about each other.

Two weeks before our visit with the congregation, the church newsletter included my answers to the committee's questions about my ministry philosophy and strategy. The core of my beliefs had not changed since my high school years. I began my answer with what was foundational: "The Bible is without error and is the authority for everything we do. Everyone is a sinner and receiving Jesus as savior is the only way to fix this problem."

Then, I described my sense of responsibility for casting a vision for the church and inspiring the congregation to adopt that vision as its own. This vision would be crystallized into a simple statement of purpose by which all activities and programs of the church would then be measured. And this vision would require a sacrificial commitment from me and from each congregant.

As is usual when Baptist churches invite a pastor to visit in view of a call, my whole family participated in the events during the weekend visit to Kingsland in July of 1985. A photo was published in the church newsletter before our visit, and we looked like the perfect minister's family—the beautiful spouse who loved being a pastor's wife, two winsome, blonde-haired boys, now five and nine years old, and me. Not only did we look the part, we were exactly what we appeared to be—a strong, loving, and affectionate family.

The search committee arranged multiple events for our visit, allowing us to meet church members before Sunday services. The result of our interactions: We were excited at the prospect of returning to Texas to a congregation of enthusiastic, warm-hearted, and educated people who wanted their church to grow.

I preached on Sunday morning. Linda and I returned that evening for a church-wide question and answer session. Following that, the church voted on a motion to call me as pastor.

I had asked the search committee to include what would become the church's new statement of focus in the written motion calling me as pastor. Simply stated, it was a commitment to live in obedience to the Great Commission—Jesus's command to make converts and build disciples. It was a commitment to church growth. This was one more way of making sure the church wanted to be a committed fellowship of believers who were ready to make other-centered, community outreach a priority.

The congregation accepted the commitment I was asking them to make and voted overwhelmingly to call me as pastor.

The search committee chairman later wrote that when I gave my acceptance of the call to be pastor that evening, "there was an overwhelming sense of the presence of the Spirit of God in the room."

When I was called to serve as pastor of the Kingsland Baptist Church in August of 1985, I was certain I had found the perfect place to minister, exactly the right spot. I was 37 years old and the average age in my new church was 38. I had years of experience under my belt, and my philosophy of ministry had been well thought out. I was committed to leading a church to grow numerically and in Christian maturity.

Considering the path I had traveled thus far, I felt well equipped for the task ahead. I felt solid in my foundations, my progress, and my vision for the future, influenced and shaped by so much and so many: the public ministry of evangelist Billy Graham; my Odessa pastor, Brother Bill; my course work at Wheaton College; the Chicago church renewal leader, David Mains; my seminary education in pastoral care and the mentoring of Dr. C.W. Brister; the insightful preaching example of my Fort Worth pastor, John Claypool; the teaching of contemporary church growth strategists; and my years of experience in ministry. I was confident in my role as a change agent who understood how to lead and what to do next.

Here, at Kingsland Baptist Church, I would be able to bring all my education and experience to a position of leading a congregation to the highest levels of evangelism and discipleship. All my years of education and ministry had been leading to this.

I couldn't wait to get started.

10 – Priority Driven

T he congregation of Kingsland Baptist Church welcomed our family with open arms. We had come to just the right place at just the right time. God had led me to the perfect set of circumstances for leading a church to grow.

In the early months of my pastorate, the congregation and community responded to my leadership more positively than anywhere I had previously served. I felt grateful, optimistic, and empowered.

As I settled into my new pastoral home, I concentrated on my primary focus—preaching. I was diligent in crafting my sermons to be simple, practical, and inspirational. I remained conservative in my theology, but my sermons had become more positive in tone.

In September, one month after my arrival, I began a sermon series called *Don't Give Up on Excellence*, in which I encouraged believers to push beyond the minimum requirements in all important aspects of life. I challenged congregants to avoid creating their own second-best life by doing nothing with what they had been given, or by pursuing the wrong priorities, or by adopting a less than desirable attitude. I offered biblical examples of how God could turn life's second best into a door to excellence. I challenged the congregation to a life of positive thinking—energized by faith in God.

Each of these sermons was biblically based and focused on teaching practical skills for daily life. And the response was exactly what I hoped for. We printed 5x8-inch placards with the words "Don't Give Up on Excellence" and handed them out each week. Based on feedback from congregants, the placards quickly made their way to office desks, refrigerator magnets, and student notebooks.

The congregation liked what they were hearing each week, and at the close of each Sunday service there were positive comments, enthusiastic handshakes, and lots of smiles.

Later that year, I preached a "how to" sermon series that started with a sermon on how to receive the gift of eternal life, then moved in a more pragmatic direction with sermons on handling anger, finding inner peace, and building a happy home.

In each of my sermons, I was working toward one or more of three ongoing objectives: challenging members to full commitment to their faith, reminding them of God's ever-present love and care, and developing practical skills for successful, fulfilling living.

Following what I had picked up from Pastor David Mains in Chicago, each of my sermons also included Suggestions for Life Response—practical ways that attendees could act on what they heard from the pulpit, printed on a separate sheet in the worship bulletin so they could be carried and referred to throughout the week.

For the first time, I was pastoring in a place where outstanding preaching could have a major impact on building a larger congregation.

Ten years earlier, my attitude as a Southern Baptist preacher in New Jersey was that of an optimistic shoe salesman on an island of barefoot locals. But the reality was that regardless of what I might preach, New Jersey's population wasn't very interested in a Southern Baptist Church. In its own way, Buckeye, Arizona, wasn't much different. When someone loved my preaching, there just weren't many people to tell.

In Katy, Texas, for the first time in my ministry, I was pastoring a congregation where those who loved my preaching knew plenty of other interested people they could invite to the church. And that's what happened. My audience began to grow.

But outstanding preaching and an expanding community weren't all that was needed for dramatic numerical growth to occur. Action and change were required. So, I set about examining everything the church did, and asking how it was helping or hindering our ability to reach more people—even if it was just some pragmatic change that was needed.

One of the first adjustments I made at Kingsland was in the church office. The secretary who answered the phone was a gruff woman who seemed bothered when she took calls. This had to stop, immediately. I directed our minister of education to relieve the woman of her receptionist duties. I wasn't asking that she be fired; I simply wanted a pleasant, polite, and helpful person to answer the phone. The minister of education resisted. I held firm. I asked him to assign the task to a secretary already working for us who was perpetually cheerful. Reluctantly, he complied.

Ensuring that an appropriately upbeat person answered the phone was a small modification, but an important one. Every aspect of our church needed to convey a friendly attitude. Every contact with our church—from a quick phone query to walking through our doors—needed to be a warm and welcoming experience.

No institution or organization is exempted from politics; the secretary relieved of phone duty was married to a deacon named Merrill. He was a kind, soft-spoken man, but it was always risky to do something that might alienate a lay leader in the church—it was like planting a land mine.

Another early and significant change involved computer technology. During my pastorate in Arizona, I began to realize how much more efficiently we could work if we could automate some of our administrative and outreach tasks. Two years after the first IBM personal computers went on sale, I persuaded the Buckeye church to buy one. I taught myself how to set up a database software application, and I developed a customized program to track church attendance, prospect contacts, and financial records. I called the application "Smart Church."

During my first year at Kingsland Baptist, I obtained approval to purchase multiple computers. We set up a local computer network and began using my Smart Church software. In the following months and years, I noted what worked and didn't work in the software, making improvements as needed and shaping the application into an important tool for church growth.

Soon we were using Smart Church to create weekly Care Sheets. These were printed reports providing Bible Study leaders and deacons with information that helped them recognize downward trends in attendance—flagging individuals to be contacted, providing addresses and phone numbers, and prompting the leader to make a call or a visit.

We took other simple steps toward growth. "Visitor Only" signs were placed in front of a selection of our best parking spaces. Additional signs provided easy directions to our welcome center, staffed by a team of volunteers. They were trained to offer a warm greeting and point the way to a Bible Study class or worship service.

To follow up with first-time visitors, we needed to know who they were and how to contact them. Gathering even a few personal details from a visitor on the first Sunday they came could be difficult, so rather than single out first-timers, we began asking everyone who attended worship services to sign in. Naturally, visitors were more likely to complete a quick form if everyone else was doing it.

In each Sunday morning worship service, a staff member or lay leader would walk the congregation through filling out a page that was provided with the worship bulletin. This served as a record of attendance, and also included space for prayer requests and notes to communicate requests to church staff.

All the information we collected went to the appropriate lay leaders and to our Smart Church software, which then generated attendance reports, contact prompts, and a variety of other resources for outreach and ministry.

The most immediate use of the Sunday sign-in information? Every Sunday afternoon, I made a personal telephone call to each family who visited us for the first time that morning.

Kingsland Baptist Church required change-oriented leadership to spearhead growth. Given the tendency to "do it the way we have always done it" in any church, if we didn't develop a strong leadership body—preferably one that included men and women—it would be easy for the deacons, by default, to fall back into their traditional Baptist role as a governing board rather than a partner in ministry.

The rigid requirements for election as a deacon in our congregation eliminated most of our adult members from consideration. If you were a man who had never been divorced, did not use alcohol, and consistently gave at least 10% of your income to the church, you qualified for a screening committee interview after which you might be placed on a deacon election ballot for the next congregational vote.

The result was a diaconate that tended to be more conservative and less open to change than the congregation as a whole. Too often, in other congregations I had observed, deacons seemed to view their primary role as guarding the status quo, which usually meant saying no to change—frequently changes that were critical to reaching people who had never made a commitment to Jesus.

I had my sights set on a leadership body that would truly lead, not just say no.

With the congregation's approval and support, I formed a group called the "Great Commission Task Force." The Great Commission refers to the post-resurrection command by Jesus to take his message to all the world, to "make disciples of all nations."[7]

The Great Commission Task Force, not the deacons, would be the key leadership group in our congregation—a growth-minded, non-traditional, open-to-new-possibilities group of men and women focused on helping our church find creative ways of reaching individuals who had not made a commitment to Jesus.

It was ironic that establishing an outreach-oriented leadership group required special effort; after all, the Baptist church was where I learned that reaching people for Jesus was our highest priority. One of the earliest examples of this was the passionate presentation of Baptist megachurch pastor W.A. Criswell at the 1965 Dallas evangelism conference. I was 16 years old when I heard him speak, and in the decades that followed, his message had been reinforced in countless sermons I heard from other Baptist leaders of renown.

Jesus commanded his followers to take his message to the whole world—starting in our own communities. The congregation of Kingsland Baptist Church had, at my request, included in the wording of my call to become pastor a specific commitment to reaching unchurched people.

I was convinced that I had the force of a command from God as well as a commitment by my congregation supporting my leadership toward prioritizing outreach. Now, the Great Commission Task Force would be working with me to implement this vision.

---

[7] Matthew 28:19.

11 – Prayer Force

To expedite our quest for expansion, we enlisted the top Southern Baptist church growth consultant to work with us. This alliance would extend over a period of several years as we developed and implemented a strategy for growth.

One of the most memorable pieces of advice we received from the consultant: "The main thing is to make sure the main thing is the main thing." Our main thing was evangelism—reaching people who had not committed themselves to Jesus.

But evangelism needed to be supported with the power of prayer, and prayer was crucial to every aspect of church life. So, one of the first tasks our consultant advised us to do was to create a prayer ministry. We accepted his challenge. The objective of the new ministry was to staff a prayer room 24/7 using church members as volunteers.

Our emphasis was on a personal relationship with a loving God who was always listening and always wanting us to tell him what we needed. We believed what Jesus said: "Whatever you ask for in prayer, believe that you have received it, and it will be yours."[8] But we also understood there were requirements that had to be met if our prayers were to be answered.

To receive God's response, we needed to ask, but we also needed to have enough faith. And, though not stated in the verse quoted above, we knew that the request had to be something that was within the scope of God's will.

Having a personal relationship with God through Jesus meant we could talk to God conversationally just like we talked to anyone else. But how could we talk to an invisible, silent conversational partner? That's where faith came in.

We trusted that God was listening to our every word. We believed that he answered through a still small voice, granting some subtle inner sense of what we should do or how we should see a situation.

If there was no still small voice right away, our task was to wait upon the Lord in faith. He would answer according to his own timetable.

We also believed we would *see* answers to prayer—that God could and would alter the course of events in the lives of individuals, churches, communities, nations, and even the world, if enough believers prayed with enough faith and enough consistency.

Intercessory prayer means praying for other people—interceding with God on their behalf—and that's what our new prayer ministry was about. The prayer room was a place for intercessory prayer, which was one of the ways we in the congregation showed our love for one another and for our community.

In a church like ours, you would routinely hear conversations like the following: "My sister's having cancer surgery on Monday. Emily, would you

pray for her?" "Yes, Sue, what's your sister's name?" "Her name is Julia."
Emily's intercessory prayer would sound like something this:

> God, please help Sue's sister, Julia, to feel your presence and
> love as she undergoes surgery on Monday. Surround her with
> your warmth and majesty, Lord. And if it is your will, I pray
> that you would use the doctors to successfully remove all the
> cancer… every cell of it. I trust that you can do all things, and
> I ask for an outpouring of your love and power on Julia.

The prayer ministry was a way of ramping up this normal, usually informal, process of making a prayer request to a friend or to one's Bible Study class. And we wouldn't be praying just for fellow congregants in our new prayer ministry. Members of other churches as well as people who didn't attend any church could also ask for our prayers.

We began recruiting volunteers to commit to one hour in the prayer room at the same time each week. We secured a phone line for the prayer room, and felt God was working right along with us when we were able to secure 492-PRAY as our number.

It wasn't long before most of the one-hour prayer slots had been filled. If we couldn't fill a late-night slot, we used a phone number rollover system to forward calls to the home of a volunteer who had agreed to handle calls for one night in the week, and to respond, regardless of the hour.

We leased a billboard that displayed our 492-PRAY number, and soon the phone started ringing.

Called-in requests were prayed for immediately. The volunteer taking the call would pray aloud with the caller. When the call ended, the volunteer would log the request so other volunteers who came to the prayer room in the following hours and days could continue praying for the request.

When not responding to a phone call, the prayer ministry volunteer would pray for all the requests that had been called in earlier and for other requests written on prayer cards that had been dropped in the offering plate during Sunday services.

A bulletin board in the prayer room displayed some of the more urgent requests as well as notes from individuals thanking prayer room volunteers for their prayers. Any prayer request that produced unexpected, dramatic results was shared on the board.

We didn't keep a list of prayers that had obviously gone unanswered, because we believed that if God said no, there was a good reason, and it was just as much a sign of his love as when he said yes.

After praying for someone, the prayer volunteer would frequently write a short note on a fold-over mailer we called a "Prayergram," which would be mailed to the person who made the prayer request.

The prayer ministry grew quickly. One of the things that made this new ministry so significant was that, unlike the prayer requests often shared in traditional prayer meetings, many of the requests received by the prayer room were personal and made in a way that required some vulnerability. It wasn't just the recipients of prayer who were helped. Those who prayed as part of this ministry felt empowered themselves and grew spiritually because of their time in the prayer room.

The Bible taught us that a spiritual war was going on all around us, and we saw those who served in this ministry as our prayer warriors. And there were some things these prayer warriors were asked to pray for constantly: our weekly worship services, our church staff, our ministries, and of course, our outreach efforts.

Standard practice in Baptist congregations included a Wednesday night worship service focusing on prayer. Singing was usually included along with a devotional talk by the pastor, sharing of prayer requests, and a time for prayer—either silent prayer or a series of individuals voluntarily praying aloud, one by one.

Sometimes the prayer requests were immediate and intense, but more typical was a request to "pray for Cousin Lou Ann who lives in another city and will be having foot surgery next week." Not that Cousin Lou Ann's foot surgery wasn't important, but Wednesday night prayers seldom involved personal vulnerability on the part of the individual making the request. More often, they targeted distant needs with no way of determining whether the requests were answered.

Occasionally, a prayer request for someone in the church who was going through a difficult time (and wasn't present) could be a "sanctified" way of sharing a tidbit of gossip, but that was rare. Well… maybe not all that rare.

As in most congregations, at Kingsland Baptist our Wednesday night worship services were poorly attended and suffered from little feeling of a strongly supported, purposeful event.

Now, with our new emphasis on prayer through the 24/7 prayer ministry, our Wednesday evenings could take on new meaning by being refocused.

Outreach seemed like the perfect fit. While refocusing our Wednesday evening slot on outreach, we could continue to offer a small prayer and Bible study meeting for those who needed a "Wednesday Night Prayer Meeting."

Under the new plan, church members were encouraged to stop by the welcome center on Wednesday evening and pick up a "Calling Card"—generated by Smart Church—that contained information about a prospective member, and then, with info in hand, make a phone call or a personal visit.

Cell phones were yet to arrive on the scene, but by installing multiple land line telephones in the welcome center, we made it easy for volunteers to make their calls while already on-site.

We also made available our own custom fold-over "Join Us" mailers in which a volunteer could write a short note to a church visitor. Likewise, our

"We Missed You" mailers were used for notes to those whose attendance was in decline.

As part of the Wednesday night outreach emphasis, Bible Study class leaders could pick up the weekly Smart Church Care Sheets alerting them to ministry contacts they needed to make. In similar fashion, since each deacon was assigned a group of member families to shepherd, Deacon Care Sheets were also available on Wednesday nights, alerting deacons to individuals in their family groups in need of contact.

Behind each of these computer-generated tools was our genuine desire to ensure that no one fell through the cracks as we sought to care not only for members, but for anyone who might walk through our doors.

We began serving a prepared meal on Wednesday evenings. Members could come, enjoy dinner, visit with their friends, participate in the various outreach activities underway, or, if desired, attend a scaled-down prayer meeting. Children, middle schoolers and high schoolers were offered age-graded events. Also on tap—our weekly adult choir rehearsal.

Much of what we were doing on our very busy Wednesday evenings was typical for a large Baptist church. We weren't actually a large church yet, but one of the keys to numerical growth was "acting like" the church you wanted to become. That's what we were doing. And we were also doing some unique, creative things to connect with potential new members, to minister to existing members, and to involve as many congregants as possible in the outreach process.

---

[8] Mark 11:24.

12 – Wholehearted Growth

In the first months after my arrival at Kingsland, I led the church to approve a plan to enlarge the worship center and add a new parking lot. Both projects were completed in the spring of 1987, and just in time. We needed the additional 128 seats and the 72 new parking spaces for Easter worship services in April.

With a record-breaking worship attendance of 689 people—an increase of 21% over the previous Easter—the timing was perfect. When we checked our numbers five months later in the fall, we found that we had added 215 new members in the past 12 months. I was delighted and expectant, foreseeing even more growth in the coming months and years.

Following my lead, the Great Commission Task Force recommended that the church approve fundraising for and development of design plans for a new building that would house a worship center, welcome center, prayer room, staff offices, and a music suite. The proposed worship center would seat almost three times as many people as the existing one. The congregation approved the proposal.

Our church staff was growing too. That same year, we added a new minister of education, an outreach secretary, a director of communications, and a new minister of music.

The minister of education, the one who was unhappy with my early telephone reassignment, left to take a position in another church. Our new minister of education, Rick Gregory, was a doctoral student at the University of Houston, and the sharpest church staff member I have ever worked with. Under his leadership, our rate of Bible Study growth increased to a level rivaling our growth rate for worship attendance.

We needed someone to manage data input and reporting using our Smart Church software, so we created and filled a new outreach secretary position.

When I asked for a volunteer to edit our weekly church newsletter, a stay-at-home mom who had been a member of the church for 10 days stepped up. Ellen was a bundle of energy, a person who welcomed any new challenge she was given, and she changed our homely little newsletter into what became an award-winning publication called *The Encourager*. After nine months as a volunteer, we hired Ellen for what became a full-time, paid position as director of communications. We began sending a community-wide mailing to thousands of homes in our area—two times each year. We added two leased billboards to our original 492-PRAY billboard. In front of our building, we added a new church sign with a message board that enabled us to communicate with people who drove by our property.

What had previously been one staff position—minister of music and youth—was now two positions. After months of searching, we called our new minister of music—a man who was rich in talent and motivational skills. And he was a fireball—full of energy and focused on glorifying God through his gift of music. Under his leadership, the choir sustained rapid growth and achieved new heights in the quality of the music they produced. It wasn't long before comments were rolling in from church members; each time the choir sang, so exquisite were their voices and the arrangements, we quite literally experienced chills. And, not long into his tenure, our talented minister of music added an orchestra to our Sunday morning services.

The heart of the building under design was a new, larger space for worship; and the Sunday morning worship service was the heart of who we were. Each week, wholehearted congregational singing, prayers, dynamic solos, and presentations by the choir and orchestra all set the stage for the focal point of the hour—the weekly sermon.

In Baptist churches, the pulpit is located at center stage, not left or right, to emphasize the primacy of the preaching of the word of God.

In smaller congregations, mediocre preaching could be tolerated if the minister was a walking bundle of encouragement, affirmation, and love in the church and community. In larger churches, like mine was becoming, there was no way the pastor could have one-to-one interactions with everyone. People skills were still important, but the spotlight was brighter on the Sunday morning sermon.

I saw my preaching role as the most important thing I did. It was my primary focus. I planned each series of sermons meticulously, usually months in advance. I gave our minister of music my sermon topics as soon as possible, which allowed the music and all other aspects of worship services to be coordinated.

And, in line with my belief in the Bible as the completely reliable sourcebook of our faith, I structured each sermon around one or more biblical passages, which I then linked to contemporary life. My goal was to explain what the passage meant, to talk about how it applied to everyday living, and to challenge my listeners to be motivated by this biblical truth during the week.

The congregation of Kingsland Baptist Church appreciated, valued, and complimented the way my sermons were clearly based on Bible texts. And my preaching attracted new faces to the crowd.

I preached plenty of sermons on traditional spiritual topics like the death and resurrection of Jesus, the meaning of faith, the power of prayer, finding the will of God, and sharing faith with non-believers. But I also preached about the struggles so common in any life: overcoming guilt and fear, coping with a troubled heart, and handling tough times.

No matter what my topic, in addition to making sure my sermons were biblically based, I wanted each message to be easily understandable and to carry a strong emotional impact. I knew I was hitting a home run when the entire audience was noticeably still and quiet as they listened.

Sunday morning worship was the most important hour of the week. We focused on who God is and who God wanted us to be; we celebrated our faith as a close-knit community; we sang, prayed, worshipped, listened, and learned with the Bible as our foundation and our inspiration.

In February of 1988, with a goal of $1.6 million, we began fundraising for the new building. The theme of our campaign was "Wholehearted Obedience." We hired a professional fundraiser whose first step was a one-on-one meeting with me during which I was instructed to motivate by example in giving sacrificially. I would need to make a giving pledge that was unquestionably a sacrifice, and I would need to share the specifics with the congregation.

I felt like I had been selected for a suicide mission—an important one—but Kamikaze-like all the same. But I was completely committed to my faith and to ministry—wholehearted obedience had always been my attitude. So, as uncomfortable as it was—I was up to the task.

Linda and I were already giving 10% of our pre-tax income. We agreed to give another 10% to the building program, which meant redirecting my monthly contribution to my retirement fund for the next three years.

While giving away three years of retirement contributions would be reason for most people to be concerned, I wasn't worried. For years, I had read articles in *The Baptist Standard*, our state Baptist paper, about pastors who retired after long and faithful service to a church and were given a house or a car as an expression of gratitude. I believed God and the church would take care of my future. And, Jesus had taught us not to worry about tomorrow.

As we prepared to launch the Wholehearted Obedience campaign, we organized a church banquet to start off the effort with a memorable event.

Following the fundraising consultant's guidance, during the banquet, I announced the percentage of income that Linda and I would be contributing to the building fund. I explained that one of the ways we were managing this was by using my monthly retirement contribution for three years. I was setting an example with a commitment to sacrificial giving, and I used my message that night to encourage, inspire, and challenge.

The banquet was a success. The excitement our congregation felt for our church's mission was palpable that night, and everyone was looking forward to an expanded facility where we could all worship together at one time.

In the days that followed, the congregation responded to the challenge given at the banquet by making their own sacrificial three-year commitments to the building fund.

I loved where I was and what I was doing. The organizational changes I facilitated at Kingsland—staff adjustments, administrative processes, expanded space, computerization—were bearing fruit. The church growth principles we were putting into practice were succeeding. I was fulfilling my dream of leading a church to grow.

13 – Panic Attacks

What a strange time in life to be hurting. For more than two decades, my dream had been to lead a church into dramatic growth, and now it was happening. Not only was our church growing rapidly, but my congregation was filled with people who loved me and supported my leadership.

I was 39 years old. I felt fulfilled. I believed I was living in obedience to God in my ministry. My family was healthy and happy. I was exactly where I had always wanted to be. I should have felt content.

But all was not well. Despite receiving help here and there through the years, I was in pain that I could neither articulate nor understand. I found myself gripped by something I had never experienced before—panic attacks.

Panic is a powerful foe, and fear of panic striking when you least expect can be nearly as palpable as the experience itself—an experience in which your heart pounds, danger feels imminent, and it's hard to think about anything but the anxiety of the moment.

So, what was happening? What was wrong? Why did I feel panic when I was sitting on the sanctuary platform before it was time for me to preach? This wasn't nerves; speaking didn't make me nervous. This was something else. I felt exposed and vulnerable.

And there were other times when panic surprised me. Sometimes it would wake me in the middle of the night.

I felt humiliated that I couldn't defeat my own anxieties.

As a seminary student, I had been shocked and disappointed when I overheard two professors—the school's most vocal advocates of the deeper spiritual life—chatting about the type of tranquilizer each was taking. Pretending "God is all you need" while privately taking anti-anxiety medications wasn't my cup of tea.

I stepped over to the more measured side of my seminary's curriculum, and became a pastoral care major, which meant that I believed in God plus counseling—even God plus medication—if that's what a situation called for. I emerged from seminary as a minister who taught people to trust God while being honest about their personal struggles.

Through my own preaching, teaching, and counseling, I had assured hundreds of individuals that seeing a professional counselor was both acceptable and advisable. In my view, following Jesus did not mean we would be problem-free, nor did it mean we could not seek other kinds of help.

However, getting help for myself was different—and tremendously difficult. Shouldn't I be able to manage my own problems? But sometimes, the panic made me feel like I was going to die. I was at a loss. I needed help.

Ultimately, my panic attacks forced me to practice what I preached.

The counselor I went to see was a woman who appeared to be at least 50, maybe older. She had the look of someone who smoked a lot and ate little—slim, but not in a way that looked healthy. She smiled warmly as she extended her hand to shake mine, motioned for me to sit, and then began by introducing herself. "My name is Marie and I am a recovering alcoholic."

My heart sank. All I heard was "alcoholic," loud and alarming. For a moment, it was hard to pay attention to anything else she said. How could an alcoholic help me? It was as if the word "recovering" meant nothing—but the word "alcoholic" meant everything. Alcohol had hurt me, hurt my family, and marred many good experiences and memories as much as I had tried to keep them in some clean, separate space.

Through the years I maintained my commitment never to touch alcohol, and I found that rigorous adherence to my Baptist way of life gave me an additional, powerful reason to say no to drinking. Gradually, over time, I had gained a more reasonable view about moderate alcohol use, yet at a core level, I still hated the way it caused so much loss and pain.

So, when the counselor introduced herself as a recovering alcoholic, it was hard to avoid connecting her with the pain alcoholism had inflicted.

I had considered the idea that alcoholism was a sickness, but I couldn't buy into it. In my view, those who consistently drank to excess and to the detriment of themselves and their families were making a choice. I was unable to trust a counselor even if the word "recovering" preceded the word "alcoholic?"

Despite my initial resistance, somehow, I began to share with the counselor. In a way, her distance from the world I inhabited helped me to be more open as I poured out hurts, failures, and fears. And I wept, releasing pain that had been dammed up for decades.

When I left the counseling session, initially I felt lighter. Relieved. But it wasn't long before I returned to my preoccupation with her alcoholic history. I could not focus on the fact that she was "recovering."

My panic attacks continued, but I didn't return for any more sessions with Marie. I told myself it was because she didn't share my spiritual values. I knew that recovering alcoholics could recognize just about anything as their higher power. In my view, there was only one higher power, and that was Jesus.

I picked up a book on panic attacks and taught myself some coping techniques. I was able to manage a little better, but the panic attacks did not disappear. I looked for patterns and found none. The attacks occurred at random times and places.

I started seeing a second counselor, a Christian therapist whose philosophy was to focus on changing negative behaviors rather than digging for underlying causes. He was also a Baptist minister, and I was comforted by our shared spiritual values. I talked freely with him about my panic attacks.

As part of our work together, I was hooked up to a biofeedback monitor that measured skin temperature as well as other biometric indicators. I worked on learning to relax by consciously raising the skin temperature at my fingertip. I would feel better for a few days after a session, but the panic attacks did not stop.

My medical doctor prescribed tranquilizers, but this posed another layer of problems. Although I understood that people sometimes need medication for emotional problems, I wasn't ready to join their ranks. I felt shame, and it was hard not to liken myself to the anxiety-prone seminary professors I overheard years earlier. Now I was judging myself, thinking, "I'm a pastor. Every week I preach to others about how to handle life, but I'm not doing a good job of handling my own."

Whatever inner turmoil I was experiencing, at least I was not ineffective. I was still helping people. I was still inspiring others and being there for them. But the panic lay just beneath the surface. I felt like I was operating with an open wound in the palm of my hand. I could grasp and lift, but not without the possibility of an unpredictable surge of pain.

14 – Treatment Center

When I lived in Buckeye, I never realized that my home was an hour away from one of the nation's leading alcohol and drug addiction treatment centers. I found out when I received a call letting me know that my cousin Mike was a patient there. We had been close as kids, but we had been out of touch for more than 20 years.

I visited Mike at The Meadows in Wickenburg, Arizona, as he worked his way through detox and into a process of rigorous self-examination, honesty, and recovery. After treatment, Mike actively participated in Alcoholics Anonymous, and found not only sobriety, but also a new philosophy of living and a new passion for life.

This time, Mike and I did stay in touch, and in his sobriety, I found him to be an incredibly honest, loving, and insightful friend. We became more like brothers than cousins.

A talented salesman who reminded me of my father, Mike was now a wholehearted advocate for recovery—not only in terms of overcoming addictions, but also in the sense of recovering from addiction-related emotional pain. And he wanted me to go to The Meadows to attend a five-day program available to ministers, with no fees except for room and board. The Meadows wanted to acquaint ministers with their program to promote referrals of church and community members. Mike also knew that I was an adult child of an alcoholic and believed I would experience some significant personal growth if I went to The Meadows.

For years, Mike tried, using all his persuasive powers, to sell me on the value of a visit to The Meadows, but I never bought it. I was completely resistant to the idea. I wasn't an alcoholic. That was my father's issue. So why on earth would I need to visit a treatment center for any length of time, even a few days?

* * *

The 1980s saw a growing number of books published on adult children of alcoholics. I read my first of these books while living in Arizona, and despite the self-analysis I had done as part of my seminary studies in pastoral care, the assertion that children of alcoholics suffered *predictable* damage from their early experiences was a revelation to me.

Through my reading, I learned that an adult child is an individual who acts like an adult while still a child, and then, as an adult, continues to deal with unresolved childhood issues. And I learned that growing up with an addicted or abusive parent was most often the causative factor.

I continued to buy and read books on adult children of alcoholics after becoming pastor at Kingsland and noticing the proliferation and popularity of these books as well as articles on the topic, I decided to schedule a sermon series on adult children of alcoholics.

I found biblical texts and principles that addressed many of the issues common to adult children and began outlining the sermon series. I scheduled a start date, several months away, and continued working on the content for the sermons. Then, I had a brainstorm: Why not go to The Meadows for five days—the program Mike had been telling me about—to get material for the sermons?

It might seem odd, but what prompted me to decide to go The Meadows wasn't my panic attacks nor the knowledge that I might have issues in my life that were characteristic of adult children of alcoholics. I was going to the treatment center to learn more about the topic that was soon to be the focus of my preaching.

* * *

In March of 1988, my five days at The Meadows turned out to be far more about me than about acquiring insights for a series of sermons.

With swankier buildings—and guests who weren't there as a last-ditch effort to literally save their lives—The Meadows would have felt like a resort rather than a treatment center. The facility was surrounded by low mountains, an expanse of desert, and the beauty of the saguaro cactus. Overhead, the sky was an impossibly brilliant sea of blue.

A group of 30 people gathered in the clubhouse next to the pool. There, we watched a video about alcoholism. As the video played, I glanced around the room. I was aware of being anxious. I had no idea what I might be asked to do, and I didn't like not being in control. But I also felt excitement. Something positive—something I couldn't anticipate—might be on the horizon.

The first morning of the program, I was assigned to an in-patient therapy group consisting of six or seven people plus the group facilitator.

As the session began, the facilitator stated his name, made a few introductory comments, and then asked us to introduce ourselves. We went around the room, as one after another, each person said their first name, followed by "I'm a recovering alcoholic and drug addict," or "I'm a recovering sex addict and drug addict," or "I'm a recovering alcoholic and I was an abused child," or some other self-description of multiple types of brokenness.

There were two of us yet to speak, and I was next. As each participant had spoken, I felt more certain I was in the wrong place. What was I doing here? How could these sick people possibly help me, a minister? I was sure they would expect me to be able to give them answers. But then I thought: "What if they don't like me *because* I'm a minister?"

All eyes turned to me. My heart was pounding. I took a breath and started to talk. I don't remember much of what I said, but I told them I was an adult child of an alcoholic, and that I was hurting. I was struggling not to cry.

The last person to speak was also a minister. His second marriage was ending in divorce. He too was in pain, tearing up and speaking haltingly. At least I wasn't the only person of faith in the group.

As I observed the man who facilitated our sessions, for all his skill and emotional intensity, I quickly understood that he was not a spiritual person— at least not by my definition. I was pretty sure that he wouldn't be recommending that anyone pray to receive Jesus as a solution for their problems.

As the discussion and exercises unfolded, one person was given an object shaped like a banjo and used it to beat a three-foot spongy cube while screaming, "I hate you, I hate you." This was like no group session I had ever experienced. I wanted to run.

An hour into the meeting, all I could think about was how messed up these people were. Now I really wanted out. But I stayed.

As the session continued, I was struck by the extraordinary honesty with which the participants were sharing their struggles, problems, and failures. This clear invitation to share in such an open and honest way was unlike anything I had ever witnessed. Giving voice to unguarded revelations was equal parts terrifying, compelling, and contagious.

Maybe it was time for me to stop acting like everything was okay.

* * *

As I listened to the other group members tell their stories, I gradually realized that even though their lifestyles were dramatically different from mine, what I was hearing sounded familiar. I wasn't an addict myself, but I was dealing with similar emotional issues.

I soon had to admit that I was gaining much more than material for a series of sermons. I had found a place where individuals—including me—could share their emotions and struggles without risk of judgment or rejection.

With two intense group meetings daily, insights were coming fast and furious. I was gaining a better understanding of my own emotional pain, and, as I listened to the honest sharing of the alcoholics in the group, I was coming to better understand my father's struggles.

One important insight for me was the discovery that shame had been a companion my whole life. I felt shame for the times my father came home drunk, shame for the times he was drunk and didn't come home, shame for the times his car was parked crooked in the driveway, shame for his urinating on the bedroom floor, same for his DWIs—shame, shame, shame.

It was as if I had been standing waist-deep in a body of water, tasked with holding 20 balloons beneath the surface, each one some source of shame. I had managed to master this skill for years, presenting a pleasant face while straining to keep the balloons under water where they couldn't be seen. But this demanded tremendous effort. No wonder I felt depleted. No wonder I felt panicked. No wonder that as I began to let the balloons go, I felt enormous relief.

My childhood was more about fear, lack of control, and shame than I had ever wanted to admit. Shame lived in those balloons I struggled to press below the surface. So much of it wasn't my own. And I would have to let it go—all of it.

Somehow, I had overcome shame's attacks on my self-confidence, but I had failed to stop shame's grip on my emotional life. Intellectually, I had accepted that God was loving and full of grace, but I still had difficulty feeling grace in the deepest part of me. I could lead others to experience God's acceptance and love, but I struggled to fully experience it myself.

What did I really know about depending on God? In some respects, hadn't I largely been depending on myself? Wasn't I convinced that whatever I was going through, I was the one responsible for keeping it together?

What was happening at The Meadows felt like spiritual growth. But how could spiritual insights come from such unspiritual people?

Maybe some redefinitions were in order as I found myself being helped by people who, on the surface, had nothing to offer me, but were in fact offering tremendous support.

I had been foolish to assume that the Houston counselor—the recovering alcoholic—could not help me.

And I had to ask myself why I had not, in all these years, been able to find this kind of help at church.

The final day of the program at The Meadows happened to fall on my 40th birthday. It was a milestone, not about my 40 years, but rather, the remarkable insights gained in what was a turning point and a new beginning.

Little did I know how profoundly those five days would impact my life.

15 – Vulnerable Preaching

The topics for the adult children of alcoholics sermons had been finalized before I left for Arizona. In fact, we had mailed flyers for the series to thousands of households in our community.

The sermon series began on March 20, 1988, less than two weeks after my return from The Meadows. The series was named *The Gift of Freedom: Adult Children of Alcoholics – A Biblical Perspective*. Each sermon was based on different verses from the eighth chapter of the book of Romans, and each of these sermon texts supported a principle of recovery and emotional healing.

Topics for the first two weeks were "Discovering Self-Esteem" and "Controlling Compulsiveness." In these sermons, I included mentions of my own painful childhood experiences as well as my panic attacks. I was purposely making myself more vulnerable in the pulpit than I had ever been before.

The response was overwhelmingly positive.

The third sermon, delivered on Easter Sunday, was titled "Overcoming the Fear of Joy." It focused on the feeling of waiting for the other shoe to drop and not being able to experience joy in the present moment. Easter was the perfect day for this topic.

On that Easter Sunday, we counted 978 people in attendance. One year earlier, Easter had drawn 689. During those first three weeks of the sermon series, we had 286 first-time visitors.

In the fourth sermon, "Help for People Who Grew Up Too Soon," I described how children growing up in dysfunctional families often respond by acting like adults. This was an especially personal topic for me.

After that sermon, the religion editor of the *Houston Chronicle*, the city's newspaper of record, interviewed me. The following Sunday edition of the *Houston Chronicle* included an article that started on the front page of the Lifestyle section and continued onto the next page. It was full of details on my personal journey as an adult child of an alcoholic, as well as my struggle with panic attacks, and my recent visit to The Meadows.[9]

So much for keeping my problems to myself. Not only was I now vulnerable to my congregation, but to the whole city. In the coming years, my newfound openness and vulnerability would become one of my greatest assets and, in at least one critical instance, my greatest liability.

After the article appeared, the floodgates opened. Worship services were attended by individuals and families from other parts of Houston and from other denominations. Church members and visiting attendees began to share hurts in a way I had never experienced. By becoming vulnerable myself, I had implicitly given permission for others to expose their stories of emotional pain.

I was discovering just how many Christians were acting the part of a changed life while silently hurting, and unable to find a place to talk. In the following years, I couldn't count the number of times I would hear the words "I've never told anyone this before…"

I had unintentionally pulled back a curtain that was hiding a secret in the church, not just in my congregation, but in every congregation I would visit in the ensuing years.

* * *

Along with the sermons, I had decided to provide a small group opportunity to offer the kind of support I had experienced at The Meadows.

I felt confident that the model and techniques I had observed were excellent preparation to both develop and lead recovery support groups in the church.

Each group meeting would deal with the sermon topic from the previous Sunday, with the focus not on addiction, but on emotional healing.

I hoped we would have enough interest to kick off one or two groups, but I wasn't sure if anyone would show up. The plan was for me to lead one of the groups, and depending on the numbers, Rick, our minister of education, could lead a second group if needed.

A few days after the first sermon in the series, 60 people came for sign-up night. Almost half of those who came were not members of Kingsland Baptist Church.

We immediately changed our game plan to accommodate everyone who wanted to participate. Rick would lead two of the groups, I would lead three, and a member of our church who was completing training as a professional counselor would sit in on my group each week, as an apprentice, and then, later in the week, lead her own group.

We were quickly up and running with six groups which we called Face to Face Groups. Meeting once weekly during the 11-week series, participants were provided with an interactive guide based on the week's sermon topic. The guide included a daily reading assignment and questions requiring some careful thought and written responses.

After hearing the Sunday sermon and working through the lesson for the week, group members came to the meeting primed for meaningful sharing. Like my group at The Meadows, these support group meetings were intense and powerful—every single week—and hardly anyone missed a meeting.

* * *

As the sermon series progressed, I preached on seven more topics essential to healing and recovery:

- "Perfectionism and Procrastination"
- "How to Be at Peace with Your Past"
- "The Advantages of a Turbulent Past"

- "Release from Shame and Guilt"
- "It's Okay to Be Yourself"
- "Forgiving the People Who Have Hurt You"

The last sermon in the series, "The Stamp of Approval," addressed the pain of never receiving a "blessing" from a parent, and how one could find a sense of affirmation in other ways.

Perhaps it wasn't surprising that in the weeks and months following my time at The Meadows, as I opened up about my own challenges, as I faced my own emotions, as I began to share more deeply with others who were struggling, I became less anxious and more comfortable with things we cannot control.

And then one day, I realized my panic attacks had stopped.

---

[9] Cecile Holmes White, "Adult Children of Alcoholics Seeking Help," *Houston Chronicle*, April 15, 1988, Lifestyle Section, 1-2.

16 – Older Brothers

The people of Kingsland Baptist Church sensed that something was different in me, and that difference was drawing new congregants as our reputation began to shift and grow. We were becoming a refuge to people who were in pain and a welcoming place where they could find help.

As believers, we had been taught to act as if Jesus had "fixed us" when privately, many of us knew that we still felt broken. I had given believers permission to stop pretending by taking off my mask, confessing my struggle with panic attacks, and talking about some of my emotional wounds.

My new message was that we each need to embrace the pain of the past so we can let it go. We each need to find selected safe people with whom we can talk about our emotional injuries. We each need help in understanding how past traumatic events have affected us, and we each need to learn new patterns of thought and action.

My five days at a treatment center had awakened me to the power of support groups as a way facilitating this type of recovery and growth. In an article I wrote for *Growing Disciples* magazine nine years after going to The Meadows, I described a support group as "a small group of people who agree to meet together once a week to be honest with each other about their struggles, to encourage one another, and to seek God's help in becoming all he wants them to be." I explained that the attitude in a support group as: "We are here to help you work on your personal growth. We too are struggling. We have learned that growth takes time." I described the growth journey as one in which we "often take one step forward and two steps back, but when we fall, we get up and keep walking ahead." And I added, "The support group environment has a way of pulling people into a powerful current moving toward wholeness."[10]

After our first round of groups in the spring of 1988, as we moved toward the summer months, we wondered if this had been a one-time phenomenon. Had the first six groups met the need? Was anyone else interested?

As it turned out, we were only beginning. Once we announced the summer schedule, not only did we have more people participating than in the spring, but again, half of them came from outside our church. Christians were coming to our groups describing years of commitment to their savior, but too little relief from their emotional pain. Our work in the support groups was clear. We were helping people to create deep and positive change in their lives.

Although most of the congregation seemed excited that we were reaching emotionally wounded people, some weren't happy about the new emphasis.

The openness and vulnerability I displayed was unsettling to some in the old guard—those who knew me before my experience at The Meadows. I had upset the status quo. I expressed what they perceived as "weakness." I had fiddled with the view that being a Christian meant you had solved your problems and were always strong. I had, by my actions, implied that they too might need to look themselves in the mirror.

And, although I made it clear that I didn't think everyone came from a dysfunctional family, some congregants felt threatened. It was as if, suddenly, a new standard for self-awareness was on the table. It wasn't enough to pray to accept Jesus as your savior. It wasn't enough to expand your learning of the Bible. It wasn't enough to improve your life of prayer.

A new challenge was being issued, a challenge to be introspective about the impact of your childhood on adulthood. For some, this challenge meant remembering painful experiences that had been purposefully locked away for decades, and possibly never examined at all.

And now, those who were broken and willing to talk about their struggles became the heroes, seeming to displace the position of those who knew their Bible inside and out and held the longest tenure as believers.

We heard complaints from some of our long-time congregants as they referred to the *support group people*. "Their kids don't know how to act in church," we heard. "The support group parents don't volunteer in the nursery like other parents," they said.

Petty complaints aside, wasn't this exactly what was supposed to be happening? Wouldn't Jesus rejoice at a broader group of people taking comfort in what the church has to offer? Weren't we called to make ourselves uncomfortable so that we could reach people in the name of Jesus?

The idea of feeling discomfort with the growing number of people who came to us openly expressing their pain seemed at odds with the core of who Jesus taught us to be—welcoming and accepting. Nevertheless, some members of the church were convinced we were getting off track. We were moving away from our mission. We were no longer the church as they had always known it.

To me, we were moving closer to what the church had been in its earliest days, the very meaning of faith, and the very practice of the principles Jesus gave us—a place of healing, a new start, a truly loving community.

My interpretation of the pushback at the time was this. Those who resisted our changing stance wanted something else from the church. They simply wanted the church to take care of them. If this club wasn't taking good care of them, they felt it entirely within their rights to complain. It was like the deacon in New Jersey who said, "I'm ready to raise hell about this! I stepped back to analyze your ministry and found you were concentrating on new Christians and the down-and-outers with nothing for the rest of us."

This phenomenon has a name, *the older brother syndrome*, and derives from Jesus's parable of the prodigal son.[11] When the prodigal son returns after squandering his life in rebellious living, his father throws a party and to celebrate his homecoming. The prodigal son's older brother had never rebelled and did not share in the joy of his brother's return. His resentful attitude could be summarized as: "I've been faithful, and no one has thrown a party for me!"

Initially, I didn't realize we were on a course of creating a second congregation within our church, a congregation for prodigals who were trying to come home. This left some in the existing congregation feeling like the older brother, believing they were no longer receiving the attention they deserved.

Despite the older brother resistance, I knew there was no turning back. I began to refer to our church as a healing place for hurting people.

In my *Growing Disciples* article, I described support groups as a way of communicating who should feel welcome in church: "The church is for anyone who is in pain. We are here to help. The church is not here simply for people who either have it all together or can appear to have it all together. The church is also for people who are hurting so much that the hurt cannot be hidden."[12]

In June of 1988, following the first round of Face to Face groups, the annual meeting of the Southern Baptist Convention took place in San Antonio, Texas. While attending the convention, I ran into an editor friend for whom I had written curriculum materials in the 70s. I told him about my recent sermon series and our support groups. It was a serendipitous moment. Our Baptist Sunday School Board—where he worked—was planning to publish resources on Christian recovery. One year later, he wrote that he had recommended me as "the ideal writer and possibly the only Baptist writer really equipped to help a church start such a ministry." Our conversation eventually led to my writing *Making Peace with Your Past*, which was published in 1992.

We continued to build on our healing focus, starting a Sunday morning Bible Study class for adults in recovery. When I would walk down the hallway on Sundays as Bible classes were dismissing, I could see a striking difference in the recovery class and our traditional classes. Passing by a traditional class that was ending, I saw socializing and smiles. People might be laughing. They might be talking about the next big football game or an upcoming social event.

But passing by the recovery class, I saw people hugging. I saw people tearing up. I saw eyes locked in deep conversations. I saw people who were growing and changing. This was what I had spent my entire life wanting—this kind of connection, this kind of ministry, this human expression of God's love.

And while I still loved every member of Kingsland Baptist Church and considered many long-term members close, personal friends, I was beginning to feel more at home with the men and women who were learning to talk about their broken places, their struggles, and their healing.

---

[10] Tim Sledge, "Why Churches Should Offer Support Group Ministries," Growing Disciples (January February March 1997), 45-47.

[11] Luke 15:11-32.

[12] Tim Sledge, "Why Churches Should Offer Support Group Ministries," 45-57.

17 – Breaking Ground

At one minute after midnight on New Year's Day, 1989, we broke ground to begin construction of our new building. Six months earlier, with over a million dollars in member pledges to the building fund, the congregation had voted a unanimous approval of the final architectural plans, giving a green light for proceeding with construction.

The early morning groundbreaking was a great way for our congregation to celebrate the beginning of a new year. Everyone was excited at the prospect of one space large enough for us all to worship together each Sunday.

By any measure, our growth efforts were succeeding. Three months earlier, in September, our Bible Study attendance reached a record high of 810, and to accommodate our growth, we added a third Bible Study hour, giving us three worship services and three Bible Study hours on Sunday mornings.

I began the year with a theologically-oriented sermon series on *Paradoxes of the Christian Faith*. The series focused on aspects of faith that have no either-or resolution—concepts that can only be understood as both-ands. For example, one sermon explored the concept that God knows whether you will choose to accept him before you decide, yet you still exercise your free will when you make your decision. Another message examined the concept that salvation is a gift from God and simultaneously a costly commitment.

In March, I began another recovery-oriented sermon series. The previous series, a year earlier, had captured the attention of Houston—not just Katy—and had put us on the map as a healing place for emotionally hurting people.

Now, I had been commissioned by my publisher to write a second book, an evangelical Christian version of the 12-Steps. Using Bible passages as the basis for each message, I would preach 15 sermons that painted a picture of Christian renewal and personal recovery from compulsive behaviors. Advertised in another community-wide mailing, the title of the series was *Twelve Steps: A Biblical Perspective – Attitudes, Actions, and Changes*.

A recurring theme in the series was the concept that brokenness leads to surrender, and surrender leads to renewal. These were spiritual concepts that any believer could relate to—regardless of their interest level in recovery.

Along with each week's sermon, I wrote an interactive guide for group members to use that week. I then led the weekly pilot group, which gave me good feedback for fine-tuning what I was writing. Five years later, *Moving Beyond Your Past*, was published, based on these sermons.

Our support group ministry—now in Round Four since we had offered groups in the previous spring, summer and fall—was our most innovative and noteworthy ministry, though it wasn't the only reason we were growing. Our church's growth was fueled by multiple ministries—our worship services, the youth and children's programs, the music ministry, and other successful ministries, all of which were praised and appreciated.

But the support group ministry continued to generate controversy. Responding to my oft-used statement that our church was a healing place for hurting people, one established member said, "I'm not a hurting person, and I don't like being identified with a healing place for hurting people." I guess he had forgotten that Jesus, speaking of his own ministry, said, "It is not the healthy who need a doctor, but the sick."[13]

When leading a church to grow, you learn to tune out the static and listen for the music of forward movement. Whatever you do, someone won't like it, and that's usually static. But when it comes to measuring growth, the "music" is in the numbers used to gauge what is happening—numbers not valuable in themselves, but valuable because of the positively-impacted lives they represent.

During the *Attitudes, Actions, and Changes* sermon series, we broke another worship attendance record with 1,091 present on Easter Sunday.

---

[13] Mark 2:17.

18 – Quiet Courage

Four months after our New Year's Day ground-breaking ceremony, we hosted our *I Love My Church Banquet* at a local hotel ballroom. This was an annual event—a time for food, fellowship, and inspiration.

Each year, I made sure I had an arsenal of funny stories that allowed me to make one of our leaders in the audience a character in each joke. It was good-natured roasting that generated lots of laughter—one lady commented that she lost all her mascara—and made us feel like a close-knit family in a place where we could laugh at ourselves.

After my round of jokes, I would shift into the mode of inspirational leader and launch into a motivational talk. On that April evening in 1989, the subject of my talk was "The Middle of the Race." I spoke about the excitement of beginning a race and the extra surge of adrenaline that helps cross the finish line, then explained how the middle of a race can be the toughest part.

We could now see the outline of our new building complex as the structural steel beams rose into the sky—and it was obvious that the new complex was larger than all our existing buildings. We could see our dream becoming reality, but we were in the middle of a race.

On Sundays, members might find nails in the parking lot and construction dust in their Sunday School classes. A door they usually entered might not be there anymore; it could be hard to find a seat in the sanctuary. And I was issuing regular, carefully-worded encouragements to keep those building fund donations coming.

I described the middle of a race as the hardest stretch, but I pointed out that it was a good time to reaffirm our identity as a people of conviction, a community with a dream. I recast my vision for the church, and I reminded the audience how much the church needed their support, prayers, and donations. I ended the banquet sermon with a call to wholehearted commitment—a challenge to finish the race.

I didn't realize that night how hard the race was about to become for me.

Two months after the banquet, life was humming along. Our attendance and membership numbers were climbing. The recovery support groups were offering meaningful—even life-changing—help. Our massive new building now had a roof and the exterior walls were being closed in. I was riding high.

And then I got the call. It was the kind of call I received before my father passed away. This time, I headed to Odessa to be with my mother before she died on May 22, 1989. I was there by her bedside when she passed, and I was overwhelmed with grief, but she had suffered so much with no relief in sight, and that made it easier to let her go.

I knew my mother had been proud of me, and I felt I had been a good son, but I wondered if I had somehow failed her. I wondered if I could have done a better job of sharing what I had learned about emotional healing. I wondered if her illness had grown out of the deep well of unspoken sorrow she must have borne living with my father.

* * *

When I was 18, I met one of my dad's cousins for the first time. As he related an anecdote about my father, he remarked, "That happened when your dad was married to Shirley." Seeing my expression of shock and bewilderment, my cousin apologized immediately. "I'm so sorry. I thought you knew." But I didn't know.

I never could muster the courage to tell Dad I knew about his first marriage. The topic was guarded by an unspoken rule of silence.

When my dad died, nine years after I had learned of his first marriage, I felt anxious about bringing up the subject with my mother—I wasn't even sure she knew about it—but I finally asked her why no one had ever told me about Dad's first marriage. Her reply was simply, "I thought you knew about that." It wasn't something she wanted to talk about.

Several years after my mother's death, I asked a friend who was traveling to Amarillo, the city where my mother and dad met, to do me a favor and stop by the courthouse to look for divorce documents. Maybe Shirley had lived in Amarillo too, and if divorce documents could be found, they would shed light on my father's first marriage.

I was curious. Who was Shirley? How long was my dad married to her? Did I have half brothers or sisters?

My friend returned with more than I expected. My father's first marriage had lasted almost 20 years, there were no children, and Shirley was the one who filed for divorce in December of 1946, citing my dad's abuse of alcohol as the reason. Their divorce was finalized on February 6, 1947. And my parents were married on February 23, 1947, just over two weeks later.

Not only did my friend find the record of my father's divorce, but another legal document was even more unnerving. It was a petition for annulment of marriage, filed by my mother—three days after marrying my dad. If the fact that she tried to annul the marriage wasn't enough, the content of the document was even more troubling. In the petition, my mother stated that my dad had persuaded her to drink to the point of intoxication, something she had never done before, and then convinced her to marry him while she was under the influence.

A courthouse clerk's notation on the bottom of the document, dated months after it was originally filed, indicated that my mother hadn't taken the final steps necessary to execute the annulment, and the time limit for doing so had expired.

What I was aware of before this document appeared was a bare-bones set of facts. When my parents married, my dad was 40—tall, blue-eyed, movie-star handsome. My mother, only 25, was pretty and quiet. They met in Amarillo; the wedding ceremony took place in New Mexico. And they were married for 13 months before I was born. That was all I knew. Until now.

I had asked my friend to visit the courthouse to get information about my dad's first marriage, never expecting to learn the shocking truth about how he and my mother had started their marriage, and how my mother had almost ended it three days after the wedding.

In all the years I had known her, my mother always diligently followed rules, never did anything morally questionable, and I cannot remember anyone ever saying a bad word about her. As I tried to put myself in her shoes, I could only imagine that she must have felt a massive amount of shame over the circumstances of her marriage.

I was deeply saddened. If only I had known before my mother's death, maybe I could have helped her diminish the shame of how her marriage began. I could have told her that what happened was in the distant past, and no longer mattered. I could have talked to her, put more puzzle pieces together for both of us, and tried to better understand the reality of her life. Instead, I was left with questions that could never be answered.

The closest thing my mother ever had to a support group was a women's Sunday School class. While it was a source of love and encouragement, it certainly didn't provide a means to address, understand, or come to grips with the issues related to my father's alcoholism and the depths of her shame.

She had listened to the tapes of my *Making Peace with Your Past* sermons. She seemed surprised at how much my father's alcoholism had affected me. We talked about it, but she could only go so far.

My mother would never know the insights of one-to-one psychological help. She would never know the relief of releasing secrets and addressing grief, shame, and anger as one can only do with the help of a therapy group or a counselor. I deeply regretted that I had not been able to help her in the same way I had helped so many in my church.

* * *

In her youth, my mother had won awards for penmanship. A bookkeeper for a company in Odessa, she had continued to work as long as she could through the rheumatoid arthritis, even when the disease and the medicines she took for it had affected her fingers, hands, toes, knees, ribs, skin, eyes, and lungs. Her doctor said it was the worst case of rheumatoid arthritis he had ever seen. Though my mother suffered terribly, she seldom complained. And her ledgers—even when her fingers were gnarled by arthritis—still displayed her elegant and symmetrical handwriting.

At the time of her passing, my mother was 67 years old. Though she had been diagnosed with rheumatoid arthritis at the age of 51, my sister and I never got a clear answer as to exactly what caused the disease in her lungs, required the use of supplementary oxygen for the last decade of her life, and ultimately brought her to a premature end.

On that final day in the hospital, I watched my mother's breathing gradually slow and become more irregular. I sat close to her as she took her last breath in the same local hospital where my father had died 14½ years earlier.

Thinking of her suffering and her death, even today, brings me to the edge of tears. She didn't deserve so much pain. She had always done everything she could to love me, support me, and protect me.

Kingsland's minister of music and one of the best soloists from the choir made the trip to Odessa to sing at my mother's funeral.

We had the graveside ceremony before the church service, at the end of which my sister and I, along with our families, tossed handfuls of dirt on her casket once it was lowered into the grave. All of us—including her four grandchildren who loved her so much—were weeping. We had sustained a terrible loss that each of us must face eventually, but that fact has no impact when it happens to you.

Back at the church where I had grown up, I delivered the funeral sermon. It was one gift I could still give my mother. I spoke of her virtues and her meaning to me. I spoke of what her life could teach us about faith. I spoke of her gentle nature, her steadfast belief in me, and her persistent ability to not give up. "Even quiet people can have a powerful influence on the lives of others," I said. And I added, "You don't really know who a person is until you see that person face the storms of life." My mother had passed that test with flying colors. She was an exceptionally courageous woman, and to me, a model of quiet courage.

One of the values of faith is the unshakeable conviction that this life is not all there is. I wanted to believe I would see my mother again; I did believe I would see my mother again. Speaking to the audience and reassuring myself I said: "For the Christian, death's victory is temporary."

When I returned to Katy, I was flooded with kindness. Expressions of sympathy from the congregation were many and heartfelt. The woman who had gone to Odessa to sing at the funeral had heard me talk about the ice box cookies my mother used to make. She found the recipe, baked a batch, and delivered them to me.

Three months after my mother's death, in August of 1989, we conducted our first support group retreat. Its theme was "Choices: Then and Now." This first recovery retreat, like all the others that followed, had the feeling of a family reunion—not a dysfunctional family reunion, but an atmosphere that was open, accepting, loving, and healing. For me, this was especially important in the wake of my recent loss.

If only my mother could have participated in something like this.

19 – Encouragement Center

Despite the "middle of the race" challenges faced in the months that followed the banquet, as individuals and as a congregation, we all pressed forward. The congregants gave faithfully and sacrificially to help pay for building costs. Our numbers and enthusiasm continued to grow. Soon, we could see the finish line

We sent out a community mailing announcing the opening of our new Encouragement Center. The mailer described the new sanctuary's fan-shaped design (making every one of the 1,400 seats a good seat), our state-of-the-art sound and lighting, and our accommodations for a 140-voice choir and a small orchestra.

We began using the new worship center on September 24, 1989. My "inaugural" sermon was "Creating an Encouraging Environment."

The final addition that had allowed us to move in was the arrival of the pews at around 10 p.m. the night before. Church members helped the pew company's crew with installation into the early morning hours. I was there, laboring alongside them. As we finished the last of the pews, I was exhausted, but elated. Our congregation shared dreams. We worked together with purpose. We were truly a community.

For the first time since I had been pastor of the church, we could seat everyone in a single Sunday worship service—a welcome relief from preaching three times every Sunday morning, but more important was the powerful sense of fellowship, inspiration, and energy we could now share.

The official opening of the Encouragement Center came two weeks later, on October 1st. We designated it "Celebration Sunday." The founding pastor of Kingsland spoke briefly, and I preached a visionary sermon titled, "What You See Depends on Where You Stand." It was indeed a day of celebration.

Finally, with our whole congregation worshipping together, our church felt like the large church we had, in actuality, become.

And our growth surged—that October, our worship attendance was up 45% over the same month of the previous year. Our old sanctuary could seat about 500 worshippers. As advertised in the mailing, our new Encouragement Center was designed for nearly three times that, but I was already wishing we had made it even larger.

20 – Too Close

Our support group ministry continued to grow. Over the next few years, we added more groups addressing more issues, and saw more people being touched by the expanding scope of our efforts. Increasingly, when I was around these "recovery people," I felt like I was in the New Testament Church—simple, confessional, honest, and powerful.

We settled in to a schedule of offering a new round of support groups each September, January, and June, with one support group retreat in the summer and one in December. In addition to the retreats, the rounds of groups and our weekly recovery Bible Study class on Sunday mornings, we added a weekly open meeting structured like a 12-Step gathering where walk-ins were welcome to participate.

Thursday night became recovery night. We started the evening with a meeting of the support group leaders. Then we moved on to a large group recovery talk by a counselor or some leader in recovery. That meeting was open to anyone who wanted to come but was mainly attended by those who were present to attend one of the support group meetings that immediately followed.

It was in the small group meetings—lasting two or more hours—that the intense, personal, and grueling but productive work of dealing with issues of emotional healing and recovery took place.

Early on in our support group ministry, we realized we were going to need volunteer leaders to help us meet the demand for all those who were interested. So, we started a program to train lay persons as support group leaders. Their first step: participating as a member of a Making Peace Group. Their second step: participating as an apprentice to a group's leader during another Making Peace Group.

I had learned that the most important principle for leading a support group was demonstrating the behavior I wanted to see in the group—being open about my own struggles as the child of an alcoholic. Each time I kicked off the first meeting of a group, I retold my story with absolute honesty, expressing my own vulnerability.

Inevitably, the group members followed my lead and began sharing with the same level of honesty I modeled. I was finding I had a gift for leading these groups, but part of the formula was very simple. Participants gave as good as they got; they would share at the same level as the leader, whoever it was.

As group members talked about their deepest hurts and struggles over a period of 11 weeks—each group was comprised of six to eight men and women including the leader—the bond that formed was unlike anything I had seen in any kind of group.

Our support group leaders' meetings were similar in their emotional openness. Even as leaders, we shared enormously personal aspects of who we were and what our struggles were—with one another. Many times, our leader meetings took on the tone of one of the support groups. As leaders, we helped each other.

I understood a key hazard of counseling—transference—a process in which the person receiving counseling can transfer feelings toward another person to the counselor—often in a way that leads to a connection with the counselor, one which mimics some other significant relationship such as that with a parent. Consequently, I knew that my role as a group leader could foster strong feelings of attachment toward me by a group member.

As it turns out, I may have been intellectually prepared for the sharing that occurred in our group sessions, and likewise the attachment someone might form to me, but I wasn't as prepared as I thought I was for the deep emotional bonding that I might feel, nor how profoundly its intensity might affect me.

When you serve as a pastor, almost everyone treats you a little differently. They edit what they say around you. Some go so far as to act as if you are the eyes and ears of God. It's an isolating aspect of the role that I never liked, and because of that, I always—with varying results—encouraged people to be themselves around me.

Something about the atmosphere of our support group ministry lifted me out of my usual semi-isolated state. I felt more like a "regular" human being around the support group leaders and members. They respected me as their leader, yet I didn't feel set apart; instead, I felt like one of them.

In one of our early rounds of groups, a woman who was close to my age, a recovering alcoholic who talked freely about her sobriety, became the apprentice for a group I was leading. It was the support group ministry that had brought her and her family to our church.

Though she had done a great deal of work in 12-Step groups before coming to our church's recovery ministry, like everyone else, she had begun by participating in one of our Making Peace Groups. Following that, for 11 weeks, she worked closely as my apprentice. Her years of personal recovery work and her outgoing personality made her a natural in a therapeutic environment and a great candidate for becoming a support group leader. In the months following her apprenticeship, she became part of our leadership team.

Over time, our friendship deepened.

As a minister, though you may be treated in a way that isolates you, the opposite is also true. Many will treat you like a trusted family member and share a spiritual intimacy unique between pastor and congregant. The closeness that is established often bypasses longer, more usual timeframes to establish trust.

I was used to close pastoral relationships with women as well as men. A minister may find himself in the position of being the only man in a room full of women—at a weekday Bible study, in Vacation Bible School, or helping set up tables and chairs for the next event. You get used to it. You handle it. It grows out of trust and, for the most part, is a good thing for God's work.

But I wasn't handling the attachment that was forming with my one-time apprentice like I usually did —particularly as she displayed the disarming honesty that is characteristic of many recovering alcoholics. At some level, she probably reminded me of my father, but a version of him willingly seeking to grow in recovery and emotional wholeness—like my cousin Mike.

There was something else. Something that felt new and different. She treated me like a normal person—a difference that was, in a way, about no difference at all. And it was a powerful experience. The more she opened up about her real self, the more she challenged me to do the same.

I found I was enjoying my conversations with her—nothing special— whatever we might chat about in the usual course of seeing each other at events related to the support group ministry.

Where were the alarm bells I had cultivated and perfected? Why didn't I pay attention to the warning signs? Why didn't I acknowledge what was happening? I had a lifetime of protective systems in place to prevent even the slightest violation of the moral code I preached and lived by. One of the most important elements of that code: Avoid even the appearance of sexually inappropriate behavior. But there was no sexual behavior.

What was happening to me? Nothing, I kept telling myself. I had said no to temptations that beckoned many times in my years of ministry. I would not falter now. I wouldn't even appear to falter now. The boundary line regarding sexual missteps was crystal clear.

Leadership, a journal for professional ministers, conducted a survey of ministers reporting that almost one in four had engaged in a sexually inappropriate act at least once in their ministries.[14] I knew this was a real danger. For me, the line wasn't just sexual intercourse; it was far more stringent—no suggestive language and no inappropriate touching. The utmost care had to be taken—including being careful about even finding oneself alone in a room with a woman. And if you were counseling a woman in your office, it was best that your door had a window. If there was no window, keep the door cracked.

The prospect of any impropriety derailing my life as a minister was terrifying, cementing my resolve to not only avoid moral compromise, but any possibility of the appearance of moral compromise.

In addition to my commitment of fidelity to my wife and obedience to my faith, I was fully aware that any sexual indiscretion would cost me my job. While I couldn't imagine it, if I ever did indulge in any such impropriety, my conscience would prompt me to immediately confess it and resign.

What I wasn't as alert to as I should have been was the slow development of emotional intimacy that eventually causes you to wake up one day and say to yourself, "I really care about this person."

Though the motives of my apprentice and my own were innocent, that is precisely what happened in our case. We were frequently on the phone, just talking. Ever disarming, she would ask me something every time we spoke that no one else was asking. It was a small thing, "Are you happy today?" It was a question that expressed a concern that I appreciated greatly.

My wife cared for me deeply and was unquestionably concerned for my well-being, but I wasn't used to someone cutting through all the busyness of my life and paying attention to me in such a simple yet fundamental way as asking, "Are you happy today?" And it was easier to hear it from someone who wasn't entwined with the routine aspects of my daily life, which is part of the seductive power of any kind of affair, whether emotional or sexual.

I was entirely transparent with Linda about this growing friendship, or so I thought. I told her my apprentice and I had become friends. We went out to dinner together, the four of us, Linda and myself with my friend and her husband. I was trying to stay accountable, and I wanted my friendship to sit squarely in the acceptable zone. Yet the relationship continued to deepen, and as it did, I kept telling myself that it was not inappropriate. We were simply good friends sharing a connection through a ministry we both loved.

Once or twice a year, I went on a solo retreat to a friend's beach house in Galveston for long-range sermon planning. While I was there, my friend called me. She wanted to know the address of the beach house. She wanted to come see me. She told me what she wanted to do when she got there.

It was an alarming wake-up call. I didn't tell her my whereabouts. I could no longer deceive myself. And I could no longer pretend that the relationship hadn't gotten out of hand.

As soon as I hung up the phone, I called Jerry Brown, the counselor in Colorado who had helped with a career assessment several years earlier. I told him the story. I asked what I should do. He told me to tell Linda, and to seek counseling immediately—the two of us, together.

When I struggled to explain to Linda what was happening, I had a difficult time getting her to understand. "You told me she was your friend," she said. "I already know about that." When I finally succeeded in making the nature of the relationship clear—that a serious bond had formed and that I had slipped into an emotional affair—Linda was devastated.

I hadn't wanted to admit what was going on. I hadn't wanted to call it what it was. I was so focused on the "do not touch" rules that I never broke, I had convinced myself that everything was okay. I was wrong. I had to take responsibility for what had happened. Though we had never crossed a physical line—our relationship was all talk and expressing feelings—it was still wrong. The fact that I had refused to take things to a physical level felt like a victory in one sense, but overall, I had failed my wife, my marriage, and myself.

Linda and I began counseling with a husband-wife team. I held myself accountable for what took place, and asked Linda to forgive me. At first, I insisted that the woman and I could still be friends, but with clear limits on how often we talked and what we talked about. That wasn't a workable plan. The only solution was for us to stop all interactions, which we finally did.

Processing the situation I had allowed to develop was hard—different from anything I had been compelled to work through before because of the central role I had played in what took place. At first, I was defensive, and then the guilt was terrible. The need to make amends was pressing. Seeing Linda suffer—she felt betrayed, and with good reason—left me feeling helpless.

And then there was my deep loneliness. Despite the realization that I had been wrong, I grieved the loss of a friendship that had somehow broken through years of isolation and connected with me, the person, not the minister.

I had to fight through my feelings. I had to do whatever it would take to keep our marriage strong, our family intact, and my ministry moving forward.

Had I ever entered into a physical affair, there would have been no question as to what I should do vocationally. I would have resigned as pastor.

Prior to this experience, I'm not sure I even knew what an emotional affair was. Receiving instruction on physical boundaries had been very black and white, but this? This was fuzzy. How could a minister—how could anyone—discern the dividing line between "just enough" emotional connection but not too much? Was crossing the line the only way I could have learned this lesson?

Working with our marriage counselors, I decided that the knowledge of this event was not something to share with my congregation.

In the 12-Step fashion of making amends, I asked the woman to forgive me. Harder and more humbling, I asked her husband to forgive me. Both were gracious and offered their forgiveness.

The counseling sessions were grueling, but we made progress. In addition to the weeks of counseling sessions, it took months of difficult conversations, silences, and tears to rebuild trust with Linda. She told me later that in those days, she worked harder than ever to be the perfect wife—in every way. But the problem we were working to overcome was a result of my imperfections, not hers.

Linda and I stayed at it—sometimes caught in the rhythm of two steps forward and one step back—and eventually, we reached a place of healing. Slowly, we moved back into our more normal focus on the challenges and joys of marriage, parenting, and leading our church. My emotional affair was no longer an open wound, but it did leave a scar on our relationship.

Although I was fighting wrenching personal battles, life continued as usual around me with a steady stream of church activities necessitating my attention, engagement, and leadership—sermons needing to be written and delivered, individuals requiring guidance and help, plus the ramping up of a multitude of tasks associated with the business of church growth. The pace and diversity of responsibilities served, in some ways, as a welcome distraction from my troubles. Those same responsibilities were also a reminder of all that I had put at risk, including my belief in myself.

I had placed my marriage and my ministry in jeopardy—something I could never have imagined. I had made life more difficult for another couple—also unimaginable. Although I asked for and believed that I received God's forgiveness, I felt deeply disappointed in myself. Now, despite a lifetime of faith, my own behavior had to be added to my collection of *exceptions to the rule of faith*.

I developed a new internal warning light. "Watch out for inappropriate emotional intimacy." I learned to appreciate the emotional closeness in our groups while keeping a careful watch on my own feelings to avoid problematic attachments.

Theoretically, groups such as ours could have been segregated by gender to avoid inappropriate emotional connections. However, a gender-segregated approach would have been less effective. The inclusion of both men and women was one of the elements that made group interactions so powerful, and often contributed to the level of change that occurred in the lives of group participants. I had seen this dynamic play out time and time again.

For example, if a woman has been the target of rage from her father while growing up, she might find herself in a group with a man who raged at his children. As our sessions would proceed, by listening to the woman, the man better understood the pain he was causing his children. Similarly, by listening to the man, the woman could better understand—not justify—the inner turmoil that may have fueled her father's behavior. And by understanding her father better, she began to have more power over her own emotional pain

Without sharing what had happened to me, I began alerting support group leaders to the danger of inappropriate emotional entanglements. Hopefully my experience could help others avoid the same problem. In the facilitator's guide for my second book, *Moving Beyond Your Past*, I included an explicit warning about the danger of inappropriate relationships developing from the sense of emotional intimacy that naturally occurs in the course of support group meetings. And though I did not mention my own experience, I offered specifics on setting boundaries to avoid exactly what had happened to me.[15]

Though I found my way back, I couldn't help wishing that such a clear warning had existed for me.

---

[14] "How Common Is Pastoral Indiscretion?", *Leadership: A Practical Journal for Church Leaders*, Volume IX, Number 1 (Winter 1988,): 12.

[15] Tim Sledge, *Moving Beyond Your Past Facilitator's Guide* (Nashville: LifeWay Press, 1994), 8.

21 – Two Congregations

The writing was on the wall, as they say. It was not so clearly discernible as it is now, but it was there nevertheless. In January of 1990, two separate congregations were emerging within Kingsland Baptist Church. I've come to refer to them as *Congregation One* and *Congregation Two*.

Congregation One represented more traditional Baptist thinking. This audience loved sermons about purely spiritual topics like prayer, temptation, obedience, finding the will of God, and the second coming of Jesus. They were more likely to view a sermon as truly biblical if it started with the reading of a Bible text and was followed by a step-by-step explanation of the meaning of the text. For these congregants, a lifelong quest to learn more about the Bible was especially important.

Congregation Two included some long-term Baptists, but more characteristic of this audience were people who had come to the church because of our emphasis on providing help with day-to-day life issues. Many of the members of this second congregation had participated in our support group ministries—like the individual who wrote me an encouraging letter that summed how many had responded to our emphasis on emotional healing:

> I had prayed for years to find a church like Kingsland. I immediately felt at home and was so encouraged to see a pastor who let the people see he was human and vulnerable. I felt God's love, acceptance and support through his people, and that encouraged me to grow and heal. It did take some courage on my part and risk too, but I was so miserable and isolated that I was willing to try.

This individual had been drawn into our fellowship not only by the atmosphere of acceptance, but also by our recognition that becoming a Christian did not automatically make all problems disappear, and our support for the concept that self-care is healthy and normal. And the closing words, directed to me personally, affirmed what I was trying so hard to do: "Tim, thank you for allowing yourself to be real and showing how God can work in our lives." Letters like this meant the world to me.

While many of the members of *Congregation Two* had attended our support groups, not all of them had. In fact, there may have been more members of *Congregation Two* who had not been in our support groups. They were simply people who loved sermons that gave them practical help for daily living. They were interested in learning more about the Bible, but their main interest was, "Help me get through the coming week in a positive way."

While the *Congregation One* people wanted to grow spiritually, they delighted in hearing sermons that talked about topics they had heard many times before—like how Jesus had died for them, forgiven them, and promised them eternal life. Their focus seemed to be on reinforcing what they already believed. To some extent, this is a human trait, but it seemed more pronounced for this group.

Congregation Two was hungrier for new, practical information about how to live a successful and positive Christian life. If a sermon was interesting, inspiring, and connected with real-life issues, they were happy.

Attempting to respond to the needs of *Congregation One* and *Congregation Two*, I worked to provide a balance between the two types of sermons. Over time, I would alternate between more traditional and more practical topics.

The more practical sermons were still Bible-based but contained an increased number of references to psychological principles and other common-sense tools for managing life. The traditional sermons included practical life applications, but the topic was more clearly spiritual, and the sermon was likely to involve more step-by-step exposition of a Bible passage.

When I preached the more traditional sermons, members of *Congregation One* gave me thumbs up. When I preached more practical, how-to-live sermons, I received positive feedback from *Congregation Two*.

I had begun 1989 with the theologically-oriented *Paradoxes of the Christian Faith* series that focused on *Congregation One*. In my next series, I had preached the *Attitudes, Actions, and Changes* recovery sermons with a focus on *Congregation Two*.

In the following months, I continued my attempt to balance spiritual and practical topics. I preached a series for *Congregation One* on praising God that included four sermons: "God Is Great," "God Is Good," "God Is Love," and "God Is Dependable."

Then I preached a series on balanced living with a focus on *Congregation Two*, including "How to Be on Fire for the Lord Without Burning Out," "Balanced People Have Rhythm," and "How to Be Balanced Without Being Boring," among others.

Then it was back to *Congregation One* for a series on sin, righteousness, and temptation, followed by a series on building healthy friendships for *Congregation Two*.

Church members, like everyone else, are more complex than any binary categorization like this, and the responses to my sermons were multifaceted. Some sermons connected with both groups, and some individuals did not fit neatly into either *Congregation One* or *Two*. Nevertheless, both congregations were in place, and over time, had an increasing impact on the life of our church.

22 – Growth Pattern

The architects who designed our Encouragement Center had estimated its seating capacity at 1,400. In the spring of 1990, on the first Easter since our Encouragement Center had opened, worship attendance was 1,578, up from 1,091 the previous Easter.

Easter Sunday is the most attended service of the year for any Christian church. It is also the most challenging Sunday of the year for the pastor since it will attract the largest number of people who don't attend on a regular basis. These individuals are likely to have mixed feelings about showing up, sitting still, and listening to a sermon, which means that Easter Sunday services need to be short and especially interesting due to the high potential for an impatient, restless audience.

Our 1990 Easter service was significant not only because of the record-breaking attendance, but also because the tone of the service was not typical for the holiday. My sermon series on balance was in progress, and "The Balance of Life and Death" was my sermon topic.

I poured out my heart as I preached that day. I asked the audience to examine themselves. And in addition to the usual reasons for coming forward at the end of the service, I invited people to look deep inside, let go of any spiritual pretense, and come to the front of the sanctuary to pray if they felt moved to do so.

Normally, a Sunday morning invitation at the end of the service lasted four or five minutes. On an Easter Sunday, it was likely to be even shorter. On this Easter Sunday, the invitation lasted 20 minutes. I was taken aback and very moved by the response. Twenty-six people joined our membership. Others came forward during the invitation to unburden their hearts in prayer. Our church newsletter reported on the service a few days later.

> Folding chairs were placed in four aisles to make more room. The double doors were propped open and extra pews and chairs were arranged in the foyers upstairs and downstairs. Every space was full.

> It soon became apparent that this was not just another wonderful and record-breaking service at Kingsland. Through the testimony of song by choir members, soloists, and the congregation, the witness of baptism, and a powerful message of the crucifixion and resurrection, hearts were softened.

> When the invitation began, the difference was even more apparent. The work of God's Spirit was evident as people immediately responded to the call for obedience and

commitment. The front of the Encouragement Center soon filled with people making decisions. Pastor Sledge and deacons counseled with individuals as they came forward. Ushers brought chairs to the front. There was never a lull in the twenty minutes of invitation.

The congregation had an overwhelming sense that God was at work in our church that day. Our church was not simply growing. Our congregation was spiritually alive! God was present and at work among us. That's how the congregation saw it, and that's how I saw it.

And that day, *Congregation One* and *Congregation Two* were merged into one unified group.

* * *

The following summer, our ministerial staff and several of our lay leaders attended a church growth conference in California. It was an illuminating experience for all of us, especially the lay leaders. The conference speaker warned that the power of tradition could be a major barrier to church growth. He explained that a growing Baptist church has more in common with a growing non-Baptist church than with a traditional Baptist church.

That made sense for many reasons. For one, growing churches—regardless of denominational affiliation—are open to change. Traditional, non-growing churches, typically, are not.

As we moved the church into successive, ever larger size categories, we had to guide the congregation through a recurring rebirthing experience. For example, we were advised that most churches below 1,000 in weekly attendance have usually not made up their minds who will lead—the laity or the paid staff. In other words, larger churches needed to be directed more by the decisions of professional staff than volunteer lay leaders.[16] But lay leaders do not let go of power easily.

The growth we discussed at the conference wasn't just a dream—it was in progress at Kingsland. Our attendance in Bible Study and worship had more than doubled in four years. Since I had become pastor, our Sunday morning schedule—the number of Bible Study hours and worship services we offered—had changed three times. Now, we were ready for another change, from one Sunday morning service in the Encouragement Center to two—two Bible Study hours and two worship services, the same schedule as when I came to the church, but this time with our larger worship facility and expanded educational space.

I had been placing an emphasis on the Great Commission for several years. The Great Commission is the command of the resurrected Jesus to take his message to the whole world: "Go and make disciples of all nations, baptizing them in the name of the Father and of the Son and of the Holy Spirit, and teaching them to obey everything I have commanded you."[17] The "whole world" started in our own community.

In October of 1990, I challenged members of the congregation to make a three-year commitment to read the Great Commission every day, and to follow the daily reading with a simple prayer: "God, show me my place in making the Great Commission a reality in my community." I wanted each and every church member to be thinking about reaching unchurched people—each and every day.

Individuals from *Congregation One* and *Congregation Two* came forward at the end of both morning services that Sunday, standing in front of the congregation, making this promise public—300 people made the commitment!

Like other Baptist churches, we measured the success of our obedience to Jesus's command to reach unchurched people by the number of individuals we baptized each year. Over the next 12 months, we baptized 127. An official letter from the Southern Baptist leader tasked with tracking baptisms informed us that we had been ranked 153rd for local church baptisms out of 38,000 churches in the Southern Baptist Convention.

I was proud of what we were achieving. Our church *was* living in obedience to the Great Commission.

* * *

We were making significant gains, but we suffered our share of losses as well. In May, Rick Gregory, having finished his Ph.D. at the University of Houston, resigned to become the vice president of a Baptist university in our state. In September, our minister of music resigned to fill the same position at a larger church in another state. We were now searching for three full-time, ministerial staff positions: minister of education, minister of music, and minister of preschool and children.

Given our size, growth rate, and high visibility, our staff was especially attractive to other churches and Christian organizations. And serving on the staff of a growing church like ours was stressful—multiple building and fundraising campaigns, frequent changes in the Sunday schedule, new policies, new procedures, and a constant need to recruit a larger pool of volunteer leaders.

We were now larger than 99% of all protestant churches in the U.S., and that meant we could expect that only around 5% of the ministerial pool in our denomination would be qualified to serve at Kingsland. Finding qualified personnel would be one of the church's greatest challenges and one of my greatest sources of stress in the months to come.

---

[16] Carl George, Meta-Church Cluster Conference, Charles E. Fuller Institute, Los Angeles, September 25-27, 1990.

[17] Matthew 28:19-20.

23 – Ocean View

In March of 1991, our Easter attendance was 1,750, up from 1,578 the preceding year. Kingsland Baptist Church was making an impact on the west side of Houston. Our community was growing rapidly, but the church was growing faster. In terms of percentage growth, Kingsland Baptist Church was growing more than three times as fast as the Katy community.

Our Smart Church software was now tracking attendance for all classes and small groups in the church. The software's reports revealed that during the 52 weeks prior to that Easter Sunday, 4,306 different people had participated in at least one event at our church.

To sustain our growth, it was crucial that our key lay leaders stay in growth mode as well. We needed shared ownership in a challenging vision for the next steps we would take in expanding our church.

In August, we conducted our first annual leadership retreat, an event attended by our ministerial staff and 44 lay leaders. The event started on Friday evening and ended after lunch on Sunday. It was unusual to have the staff and so many church leaders absent from a Sunday morning worship service, but that reflected the importance we placed on leadership development.

During the retreat, I shared three goals for the congregation: The first was purely spiritual: I wanted us to experience a renewed openness to the presence and power of God. The other goals were more tangible: I wanted us to find and use creative methods to reach the unchurched in our community—with one creative method already targeted—building a network of home Bible Study groups. And I wanted us to implement a system for identifying, developing, and training new lay leaders in our congregation.

In September, we implemented another change in our Sunday morning program. Each of our two Sunday morning services would now provide a different style of worship. One service would be more traditional with a full choir, an orchestra, and hymn singing. The interim minister of music and I would dress in coat and tie. The other service would feature a musical praise team including six singers, guitars, and drums. Rather than traditional hymns, we would sing choruses—newer songs characterized by more current language and musical style than traditional hymns. The dress "code" for the contemporary service was casual.

Change and growth were becoming the norm for our congregation.

That fall, as I had done with varying levels of consistency since high school, I was documenting my thoughts, feelings, and spiritual ups and downs in a journal. I wrote about my personal life as well as my ministry—noting joys, fears, and challenges.

My journal included notations on current thoughts and events as well as written prayers for my wife, sons, and myself. My prayers included gratitude that Linda and I were now in a good place. And I was thankful for her new opportunity for ministry—the church had voted to make her the interim minister of preschool and children. I wrote prayers asking for strength and wisdom to be an excellent husband, father, and pastor.

I journaled my progress, frustrations, and sometimes, exhaustion and discouragement. At the core of my faith was the idea that I, like every other believer, needed God's help. Each day, I needed to "let go and let God." Over and over, I found myself writing and saying a prayer I had learned at The Meadows in 1988, "God, I can't. You can. I'm going to let you."

I also journaled about the stress I was feeling as I worked with multiple search committees to fill our three empty ministerial staff positions. Instead of looking for a new minister of education, we had decided to search for an associate pastor, whose responsibilities would include supervising our adult Bible Study program. Our search for a minister of education thereby became a search for an associate pastor. Blake, our current chairman of deacons, was also the chairman of the associate pastor search committee. In his mid-forties, he was a substantial man—well-dressed, precise in every sentence he spoke, and serious-minded about any role he filled.

Blake had served as the chairman of the pastor search committee that called me to Kingsland, and as I had gotten to know him better, I was struck by how different we were. He had originally aimed for the ministry and graduated from our denomination's most liberal seminary, while I had attended the most conservative. When called upon to lead in prayer or speak to the congregation, spoke in a deep, somewhat affected, formal voice as if from an earlier era.

Blake's commitment to Jesus was unquestionable. His sincerity was genuine. Despite our differences in approach, we were friends. His family had invited my family into their home many times. They always treated us like members of their own family, and we felt honored by their hospitality.

During the associate pastor search process, I became aware that Blake was interested in the associate pastor position himself. He was a brilliant seminary graduate working in an impressive secular job. However, in my view, as intelligent and talented as he was, he wasn't the right person for the job—not for our growing, innovative church.

I felt I needed to address the situation immediately—before it gained momentum among the members of the search committee. It was an awkward set of circumstances I could never have predicted. What was the best way to deal directly, but delicately, with the individual managing a search when he was hoping to snag the position? How could I do it without hurting him? How could I manage it without political fallout?

I talked to Blake. Gently—at least I thought it was gently—but firmly. I explained that we needed someone with previous experience as a full-time associate pastor or minister of education, criteria he did not meet. I cushioned the blow to the best of my ability, but I told him I was not willing to consider him for the position.

My words stung harder than I anticipated. Not only did he respond in anger, but he sent me a letter in which he resigned as chairman of the associate pastor search committee and from his four other leadership positions in the church, including the diaconate.

I disliked such confrontations, but I knew that leadership sometimes required navigating what appeared to be no-win situations. I also understood the potential liability—for myself—any time a key lay leader was angry with me. Despite Blake's immediate and unfortunate response, I knew I had done the right thing, even if it meant that another leadership land mine had been planted. But I was sorry I had hurt Blake, someone I considered a friend.

A few weeks later, Blake suffered a heart attack. I took no pleasure in his health crisis. We were at odds, but we were brothers in Christ. When I went to visit him at the hospital, I wasn't sure what his response would be. As soon as I entered his room he brightened and said, "Hello friend."

As I sat down beside him, he took my hand in both of his and held it, clasping with his usual strong grip. We prayed together. He seemed like a very different man from the one who had resigned just a few weeks earlier. He said, "I have some changes to make." I replied, "One day at a time."

I was thankful for what appeared to be healing in our relationship.

Eventually, with a new chairman, the associate pastor search committee narrowed its focus to one man, Nelson. In September of 1991, I traveled to Los Angeles to meet with him, and we talked in more detail.

One of our conversations remains an especially clear memory for two reasons. First, we were sitting on an outdoor bench with a spectacular view of the Pacific Ocean. We discussed the responsibilities his job would entail: a split between one-to-one ministries (visitation, counseling, weddings) and organizational leadership (adult Bible Study, outreach, deacons). The split in responsibilities reflected the fact that we needed two new staff members—an associate pastor and a minister of education—but we couldn't afford to fill both positions just then, so he would be doing double duty for a while.

The second reason I retain such a clear memory of our conversation is this. I used the opportunity to make it clear to Nelson how much I would depend on his loyalty if he became our associate pastor. I explained to him that his focus would be on building close personal relationships as well as comforting and counseling individuals. This would enable me to focus increasingly on leading the whole congregation.

While I had no intention of ceasing—in any way—to engage with individual members, this was a modification of the present staff structure. The nature of Nelson's potential role, his increased involvement with individuals and my necessary steps back, would give him the power to hurt me.

I knew the criticisms that were sure to come. Given the purposeful division of labor between us, I could reasonably anticipate that some members would say I didn't care enough about them and was no longer ministering sufficiently to individuals in the church. And members of *Congregation One* would no doubt complain about the breadth of innovative changes we would continue to institute. But I accepted this as a normal part of the ongoing transition to becoming an even larger church.

Stressing the importance of loyalty, I explained that it was essential for me to be able to count on him. Nelson responded positively to every aspect of our discussion, and indicated he was interested in joining our staff.

With strong references positioning Nelson as a team player, I returned to Houston, gave my thumbs up, and we moved on to the next step: inviting him and his family to meet our church family.

In November, Nelson came to meet the congregation of Kingsland Baptist Church. The church newsletter had introduced him to the congregation before his visit, reporting that a pastor he had worked with said, "People love him and relate to him easily. He draws people to him." Another pastor reinforced the message with this: "He has a listening ear. If you are considering him for pastoral care work, he would be wonderful."

With my encouragement and backing, Kingsland Baptist Church voted to call Nelson as our new associate pastor.

Two weeks later, another candidate came to town, this time a potential minister of music. Rodney had been serving in his current church for 12 years. The search committee that had found him described him as a dynamic and sensitive leader who was good at encouraging hurting people. They commended him to the church as a man with "a powerful gift for preparing God's people for worship, praise, and spiritual growth." The church agreed with the search committee's recommendation and voted yes. Now we had two new full-time ministerial staff members.

I breathed a sigh of relief. Two slots filled with one more to go.

24 – Bethlehem Boulevard

Bethlehem Boulevard was a nativity scene on steroids—a half-mile long movie set with live camels, cows, sheep, and a cast of hundreds. We organized teams for recruiting, costume design, sewing, construction, audio, traffic, and more.

This was a new ministry—an implementation of one of the goals I had shared with church leaders at our summer leadership retreat: to find and use creative methods to reach the unchurched in our community.

On the day after Thanksgiving in 1991, we started construction of the set. We worked all that day and the next—usually days spent with family or shopping. From then on, we worked every weekend until opening night in mid-December, engaging an energized and enthusiastic group of volunteers—some church members and some people who were just getting acquainted with our congregation. Building and assembling the sets could use anyone willing to roll up their sleeves and help—men, women, and teenagers. It was "get out your tools" time, and I was right in the thick of it, alternating between building and supervising.

We sent a community-wide mailer to advertise the event, for which we charged four dollars per car, purely to cover our costs.

When a car pulled up to the entrance to Bethlehem Boulevard, they were given printed materials that included an invitation to attend our upcoming Christmas Eve services as well as an open invitation to visit our church anytime. And, each vehicle that passed through our half-mile good news road was given a tape to play as they slowly rolled along. If a car wasn't equipped with a cassette player, we loaned them one.

As each vehicle passed from one vignette to another, they would not only see, but also hear the story of Jesus with a changing musical background and sound effects. First was the manger, complete with lambs and cows—as the audio tape described how Jesus was born to a virgin in Bethlehem. Next came the wise men and their camels, with the narrated description of their long journey to find the Christ child.

What followed was one living scene after another—a crowd listening to Jesus teach, another group watching him heal the sick, and another with Jesus blessing a gathering of children. As each vehicle passed the midpoint of the show, a DaVinci-like tableau of the Last Supper—second story level—came into view as the narrator spoke the words Jesus uttered when he shared the bread and lifted the cup.

The next scene was hidden from view until fully in sight. It was three empty crosses with an extra sound track—playing through a powerful outdoor audio system—the sound of a heavy hammer driving nails into a cross. You could hear it all up and down the boulevard.

Finally, our guests drove past a beautifully lighted empty tomb with a large stone set to one side as our narrative tape proclaimed that Jesus had risen from the dead and now offered eternal life to all who would receive him.

When the event was over, and we tallied the numbers, we were amazed and delighted to know that almost 7,000 people had experienced Bethlehem Boulevard over the course of three nights. It would become one of our most visible and enjoyable ministries.

This was an avenue for sharing the true message of Christmas with our community, and it was successful in another way—involving hundreds of volunteers, both members and non-members. Working together on the project was a unique and entertaining opportunity for people who were thinking about joining our church to get to know us better.

And so successful was this ministry that in the following years, we grew to an average annual attendance of more than 10,000—with Houston television stations including video of our event on the 10 o'clock news—and our volunteer force of cast and crew eventually grew to 1,000.

* * *

Kingsland Baptist was gaining publicity beyond our local community and even beyond Houston. Articles about our support group ministry were appearing in national Southern Baptist periodicals. I was being asked to share my story, and the story of the important work we were doing in our support groups, and as a result, a new audience was emerging for me, personally. In the preceding months, I had spoken on support groups and emotional healing at conferences in Houston, New Orleans, Dallas, and Tulsa. My schedule was ramping up, but I was good to go. I was a man on a mission.

After Bethlehem Boulevard in December, I made a quick trip to Nashville, Tennessee, to speak to the national meeting of the Southern Baptist State Directors of Family Ministry. I shared my family of origin story. I was purposely transparent. I made myself vulnerable. I believed this openness to be a necessary ingredient for achieving a connection with the audience and providing context for the value of what our support ministries could achieve. But I was beginning to notice that reliving the reality of my childhood, over and over, was emotionally draining.

After speaking to the group, I journaled:

> Each time I tell my story, it's hard. I feel I am exposing myself. I feel that some people may not understand, but they may never say so. On the other hand, after I had finished speaking, I sat down at a table with three ministers. One of the men told me that his wife was currently having panic attacks. Another told me that his daughter was getting a divorce, and that her husband had abused her. And, later, another told me

that incest had occurred in his family of origin.

I flew back to Houston. A week later, I returned to Nashville to make the same presentation to another group, the Southern Baptist State Directors of Discipleship Training. After that event, I received a letter from Avery Willis, the program leader of the denominational office that was preparing to publish *Making Peace with Your Past*. He wrote, "Your presentation at our December meeting with the state directors was super! I've had so many people mention the effect that you had on them. I believe this is the beginning of a wonderful relationship as we seek to minister to the brokenhearted and broken people of the world."

Then, he shared a surprising impact my book was already having, "By the way, the assistant editor who has been working on your manuscript is being profoundly affected by it. He is discovering why things went on in his family like they did… I believe that is going to be the testimony of many, many people." He was right. In the ensuing years, as I would travel to different cities to speak about *Making Peace with Your Past*, it became routine for people to introduce themselves to me and say, "Your book changed my life."

25 – Bedroom Wall

When I received the call, my heart sank. A 16-year-old boy from our church had shot and killed himself. I immediately drove to the boy's home. A dozen people were standing outside holding each other and crying. Multiple police cars and an ambulance were parked out front.

I went inside and sat down in the living room. It was partially dark. The boy's body was still in his bedroom upstairs.

Several women from the church were sitting on the couch. They were attempting to comfort the boy's mother. One of them told her, "God allowed this to happen so something worse would not." I said nothing. "Something worse?" I thought. "Like what?" I made a mental note to provide corrective input to the parents later, but now wasn't the time.

The boy's parents were in shock. They talked then cried and talked then cried some more. They saw no warning signs, they said. It was a night like any other. The father had gone back to his office after dinner, the boy's teenage sister had been babysitting outside the home, and the mother had returned from one of our Home Bible Study meetings to find her son dead in his bedroom.

I asked two of the investigating police officers if there was any way this could have been an accident. Both answered no, with defeat in their voices, as if to say, "I wish that were the case."

For the first hour or so, the victim's parents tried to convince themselves that their son's death was an accident. But later in the evening, the medical examiner spoke to the boy's father. There was no longer any question. The boy had put a shotgun to his mouth and blown out the back of his head.

The hours that followed saw a steady stream of arrivals and departures—family, friends, and church members.

I eased the parents into the kitchen when it was time to remove the body. I watched the EMTs bring the boy down the stairs. He was strapped to a board with a clear plastic bag wrapped around his head. He had blood on the front of his neck, but his face was unharmed. He was wearing workout shorts, and someone had tucked his hands into his waistband, so they wouldn't dangle as he was carried out.

Before the police left, they advised that the blood-drenched carpet be removed that night, or the smell would be unbearable the next morning. We were told about a service that provided this type of cleanup, but we couldn't reach them. We did the only thing we could. We took care of it ourselves.

Our minister of youth stepped in, enlisting the help of three members of our church to clean the bedroom that night. The boy's bedspread was covered with brain tissue and stained red. One area of the carpet was a pool of blood some 15 inches in diameter. A section was cut out and removed, but that revealed significant staining on the wooden floor underneath. The four volunteers scrubbed to get up as much of the blood as possible.

And there was more to deal with: bits of human tissue scattered throughout the room and blood splattered on the ceiling above. On the walls were posters displaying Bible verses, including these:

...but the one who stands firm to the end will be saved. Matthew 24:13

For God so loved the world that he gave his one and only Son, that whoever believes in him shall not perish but have eternal life. John 3:16

...for everyone born of God overcomes the world. This is the victory that has overcome the world, even our faith. 1 John 5:4

I can do all this through him who gives me strength. Philippians 4:13

At least three of these messages seemed tragically untrue that night. One, promising eternal life, offered some consolation to the boy's family, friends, and me. We could all hope that whatever pain had driven the 16-year-old to end his life, he was now in heaven with God.

As the police finally cleared out, one of them shook his head and remarked, "I sure am sorry."

I nodded. I certainly felt the horror of the moment—I had a teenage son almost the same age—but I couldn't allow myself to react as a father. I was needed as a minister. My own emotional reaction would have to wait until I was back at home. My aim was to provide a calming presence. I offered no easy answers but found ways to comfort. I was acutely aware that there was nothing I or anyone else could do to stop the emotional pain but being there with the grieving parents mattered.

I left the family's house at around one in the morning.

The next day, I went to visit the family again for several hours. Our church was now large enough that I didn't know everyone, and I hadn't been personally acquainted with this couple before the death of their son. Even so, it was clear that these were loving parents and caring people. But they were numb. In shock.

Trying in vain to process what was happening, I could not begin to imagine how they felt.

The teenager's father made a comment that he thought his son had been shot through the side of the head—maybe it was an accident after all. I asked him if he remembered what the medical examiner had said the night before. His reply: He couldn't; so much had happened, the details were fuzzy in his mind. How could anyone be expected to remember a conversation in the minutes or hours after his child had taken his own life? Besides, the first stage of grief is denial.

As we talked I learned more of the backstory. The boy had been working at a part-time job that he disliked. He had been cut from the tennis team. There was a yearbook staff position at school that he wanted and didn't get. Apparently, shortly before taking his life, the teenager joked to another student about finding a machete and ending it all. One of his close friends said she had been concerned for several weeks; he hadn't been acting like himself.

Warning signs are always easier to see after the fact.

On the previous Sunday, I had preached a sermon on "What to Do When You Have to Walk on Water," which was about dealing with challenging life situations. As I visited with the parents, the boy's mother referred to the sermon and said she was trying to apply it to what was happening to her.

I knew that just being there was helpful, yet I felt helpless. I knew that the hope we found in our faith was all-powerful, yet I felt powerless in the face of so profound a tragedy. If my sermons helped, I was glad. But it seemed like so little.

At the funeral, the casket was open. The boy looked perfect. No wounds were visible. Our minister of music sang a song titled "When Answers Aren't Enough." This was certainly one of those times. Whatever answers we might struggle to find would never be enough.

When I was 20 years old, the father of a girl I knew in school had killed himself. During the funeral service, no one acknowledged the suicide in any way, not even indirectly. The minister performing the service acted as if the man had died of natural causes. This lack of acknowledgement created a sort of vacuum—an emotional black hole that seemed, in my view, to hinder any meaningful processing of grief. Everyone in attendance had to be thinking about what happened. But the minister was ignoring what had occurred as if that would somehow help, and it didn't. Instead, his disregard for the facts loomed like an impenetrable wall between the mourners and the minister, and thus the opportunity to bring us together in dealing with the enormity of our confusion and hurt became an opportunity missed.

What I took from that experience were important lessons: A funeral service serves to comfort family and friends, to help them say goodbye, and to begin the process of working through grief in a real, healthy way. And to facilitate that process—I decided—it is better to make some reference, even if small, to the actual circumstances of a person's death rather than pretend they didn't exist. Even if it was challenging to walk this tightrope—honoring the truth when a death was suicide—I felt compelled to stick to my rule.

I followed my rule in leading the services for this suicide victim. In speaking of the boy, I talked of his fine qualities, what a wonderful person he was, and his knowledge of the truth. Though I approached the facts of his death obliquely, I did not avoid addressing them altogether: "He was a person who, for a short time, had gotten into a pattern of thinking that was not like him. He had chosen a permanent solution for a temporary problem."

I lovingly challenged his parents to have courage and to lean on their friends. With so many teenagers at the service, I felt it was critical to speak directly to them as well. I told them that we all have times when we don't think straight, and when that happens, it's important to not make any big decisions, to talk to someone else, and to look to God. I said, "If he could speak to us now, I think he would say to his family, "I'm sorry." I think he would say to his friends, "I made a mistake. Don't do what I did."

I expressed my belief that he was now with God, and that God was helping him grow beyond the confused thinking of the days before he ended his life. And then I spoke to everyone present about the importance of not blaming themselves for what had happened: "None of us is perfect, but, even if we had acted perfectly toward him, we would still be asking, 'What could I have done differently?' Don't let yourself drown in the if only's. If there is something that you would change about how you related to him in his last days on earth, use that knowledge today and tomorrow and for the rest of your life, but do not be drowned by the if only's."

I ended my remarks with a reading from Romans 8, a New Testament passage which promises that nothing—including death—can separate us from the love of God. For the closing song, we all joined together in singing "We Are One in the Bond of Love."

No one could have said or done anything to wipe away the family's pain but being surrounded and supported by a loving church fellowship did make a difference.

I could not wipe away the scenes I had witnessed, much less silence the questions. I stood in a bedroom where a teenager blew his brains out. I saw the Bible verses prominently displayed on his walls. His parents were like any other two people who love their children—imperfect, as we all are, but good, caring, and responsible people. This was more than another *exception to the rule of faith*; this was a horrible tragedy.

As I wondered how this could happen, standard ministerial answers like "Maybe the young man never truly knew Jesus as his savior" or "Maybe he was out of fellowship with God" were wholly inadequate.

Responses like these were losing their value for me. In their place, I saw this as one more example of why mental health mattered, how psychological problems could override a religious commitment, and how faith alone wasn't always enough. I was reminded that my pastoral approach had to stay sensitive not only to the spiritual needs of the people I ministered to, but to their psychological needs as well.

Two Sundays later, my sermon was "How to Climb Out of a Black Hole." While the topic had been planned long before the suicide, it suddenly took on an air of greater urgency. That month, two church counselors began offering weekly grief support group meetings for teens for a period of six weeks.

I didn't try to provide a "why" for everything that happened to my congregation, much less the 16-year-old boy who took his own life. My role was to offer comfort, wisdom, and hope. So, that's what I did.

Two weeks after the funeral, I noted in my journal that I was emotionally and physically exhausted. What I was experiencing and privately expressing was the weight of my role as a pastor. My responsibility was to remain the voice of strength and courage. That was my job. That was my calling. But always finding a way to put in a good word for a God who allowed such tragedies was sometimes a heavy burden.

* * *

The minister of youth who led the cleanup of the young suicide victim's bedroom had come to Kingsland two years earlier. You couldn't be around him for 10 minutes without laughing about something. But he wasn't just funny and fun, he was deeply committed to his faith, and had a passion for leading young people to grow spiritually.

When he had accepted the church's vote to call him as minister of youth during a Sunday evening service, the congregation gave him a standing ovation. His arrival at Kingsland marked the beginning of a dynamic youth ministry that touched our entire community.

One of his additions to our youth ministry was an annual event called U-Turn. Groups of a dozen teens would meet in the homes of church members for a weekend, participating in adult-led learning events designed to help them grow as Christians. The concept: to deepen their commitment, and if necessary, to inspire a spiritual U-Turn.

On the Sunday evening of each U-Turn weekend, the entire church would gather for a worship service in which the youth who attended would share what they had experienced.

In the spring of 1992, the Sunday night U-Turn sharing service was especially joyful. Our minister of youth had done another great job of leading this life-changing, annual event.

But just as the service was about to end, I was handed a note: One of the boys who had attended U-Turn had killed himself that afternoon.

As much as I hated to destroy the celebratory tone that had been created by the youth testimonials shared that evening, I knew that if I didn't make the announcement immediately, news of the death would spread like wildfire from one person to the next before anyone even left the building.

I made the announcement. Then, I led everyone in a prayer asking for guidance and strength.

Putting the pieces together, the picture of what happened began to emerge. The 16-year-old had been in treatment for depression in a psychiatric hospital and was released early to attend U-Turn. Following the last U-Turn session on Sunday afternoon, he drove just outside the area where he lived, and shot himself in the head while sitting in his Jeep.

In the funeral sermon, I focused on his good qualities: his love of people, his big smile, his sense of right and wrong, his devotion to his family, and his gratitude for his spiritual life. But once again, I found myself in front of an audience of teenagers faced with addressing the suicide of one of their own. As much as my role required me to comfort the family, I couldn't lose sight of the need to speak to the youth—to insist that if they were troubled, things would get better—and to insist on life.

I talked about the power of one choice. I talked about the danger of giving up too quickly. I talked about overestimating the magnitude of our problems while underestimating the strength of our resources. I challenged everyone to say no to trying to carry the whole world on their shoulders.

At the conclusion of my sermon, I stressed that God might seem far away, but he is near. Not only does he provide hope and meaning for the life beyond, but he can help us with our grief right now.

For a funeral like this one, the best effort feels like it is never enough. Nonetheless, the boy's father wrote to thank me for my support, and for helping him realize that his son was safe in God's arms.

Spending a weekend of Bible study, sharing, and prayer all specially structured for teens was supposed to be uplifting—a source of guidance and strength. Our event was called U-Turn because its goal was to help adolescents turn their lives toward God and goodness. Yet this young man had made a fatal U-Turn after participating.

He was the second 16-year-old to commit suicide in five months. All I could do was point to depression and the premature hospital release. How else could I explain this young man's life-ending response to a weekend that had been life-giving for all the other participants?

This was one more example of why the church needed to be aware of psychological needs and to provide psychological tools—in addition to spiritual tools—for health and wholeness.

* * *

One week after this latest tragic death, I began preaching a four-week sermon series that had been scheduled for months—*Growing Through Grief*. Along with the series, we had also scheduled recovery groups focused on the grieving process. Sadly, they would be needed more than we had imagined.

For four years, our church had been conducting support groups that were spiritual in many ways, but a great deal of what truly powered them was work of a psychological nature. *Making Peace with Your Past* was filled with scripture references, and even invitations to profess faith in Jesus, but much of the group process was clearly psychological in its content and approach.

My book was about letting go and letting God take control, but it also dealt with understanding the psycho-social dynamics of one's family of origin. It was about gaining insights into issues like perfectionism, unhealthy shame, and positive self-esteem. It was about finding strength to understand and confront the negative events in childhood, feeling the pain, then getting on with a healthy and meaningful life.

Yes, group members prayed for one another. Yes, the principles we taught were biblical. But so many of the participants came to the group experience after a lifetime of studying the Bible, praying, and attempting to obey God, while never finding a way out of their emotional pain.

At times, I wondered if psychological help was more powerful than prayer and spiritual commitment, at least in some circumstances. After all, Bible verses posted on bedroom walls and the biblical concepts taught at U-Turn weekends weren't preventing teenage suicides. But I had to be careful. In my world, too much emphasis on anything but the Bible could result in a damaging label—liberal.

26 – Theological War

To evangelical Christians, the greatest enemy to a correct view of the Bible is theological liberalism, a movement that began in 19th century Europe and uses science, empirical evidence, and reason as tools for interpreting the Bible. Theological liberalism does not see the Bible as "without error." And as far as evangelicals are concerned, once you go down the "Bible contains errors" road, faith loses its clarity and certainty.

In the last decades of the 20th century, evangelicals argued that liberalism was the cause of declining membership and dying churches in mainline Protestant denominations. Simply stated, conservative churches were on the rise, while liberal churches were falling in numbers.

From a secular view, all Southern Baptists were extremely conservative. But differing positions on the theological spectrum did exist within the denomination, and the scene playing out around me reflected this reality.

By 1991, the most conservative among Southern Baptists had been stirring for more than a decade. Theological fundamentalists identified liberalism in our ranks and labeled it as a cancer to be excised before it metastasized and destroyed our denomination. And the primary location of the tumors had been pinpointed. It was in our seminaries.

The fundamentalists went on the attack. Their strategy, at each annual meeting of the Southern Baptist Convention was to elect a convention president whose leadership appointments would place conservatives on the boards of national denominational agencies—including our six seminaries.

Targeting seminary leadership was a critical aspect of their plan. First, gain control of a seminary's board of trustees. They, in turn, would put in place a conservative seminary president. He would then replace liberal professors with conservatives. Seminary students would consequently receive a more conservative theological education, and eventually, those in the pews would be hearing a more correct version of the Christian message.

Since board members served staggered three-year terms, the planned takeover required years for full implementation.

In the early stages of the conflict, though I didn't see myself as a fundamentalist, I instinctively identified with the more conservative side. I saw myself as squarely in their camp when it came to my theological beliefs, my education, and my strict adherence to biblical teachings. But over time, as I watched the struggle unfold, I became uncomfortable with the far-right group. Many of their leaders seemed angry, judgmental, and looking to point a finger at anyone who did not precisely toe the line.

Fundamentalist leaders on the national scene demonstrated a willingness to lie about their perceived adversaries. For example, the president of one of our seminaries was accused of having a problem with alcohol. But it was later revealed that he was a member of the American Temperance Society, making the accusation absurd.

The more I scrutinized the movement, the more I saw it as divisive and often superficial—a disagreement over labels. Gradually, I came to realize that while I was theologically conservative, as far as the denominational in-fighting was concerned, I was a moderate, or as the other side liked to call us—a liberal. I just wasn't part of the fundamentalist tribe.

The 1985 meeting of the Southern Baptist Convention in Dallas—with attendance registered at 45,519—was a watershed moment when theological moderates tried for the last time to stem the tide of a fundamentalist takeover. The moderates lost.

By 1991, with seven consecutive fundamentalist Southern Baptist Convention presidents in a row, the Southern Baptist war for control of the denomination was largely over at the national level, but it would take a few more years to get the board members in place to complete the terminations of "liberal" seminary presidents. Things were different at the state denominational level in Texas, where the moderates remained strong and largely in control.

I had, for the most part, tried to keep a low profile and stay out of the conflict, but my ministerial friends were theological moderates, and my focus on recovery and support groups made me suspect in the eyes of some. While my beliefs about the Bible were extremely conservative, using support groups to augment God's healing power—well, that might be something a liberal would do.

An example of how the tribal aspect of this theological conflict could make identifying advocates for each side a difficult task took place in October of 1991. I had started a three-year term as a member of Houston Baptist University's board of trustees, which was composed of several Southern Baptist pastors and a larger number of businessmen, including notable lay leaders from First Baptist Church and Second Baptist Church. Not only were these the two largest Baptist churches in Houston, but they were also two of the most highly visible churches aligned with the fundamentalist side in the national controversy.

During one of our board meetings, the university president announced that the school had been given a piece of land that hosted an active television transmission tower. Until the university could sell the property, it would be receiving revenue from cable companies that paid for use of the tower to transmit their signals.

As the board meeting proceeded, I asked what I considered a pertinent question. I wanted to know if there was pornographic programming on the cable channels that would be providing revenue to the university. Everyone knew the answer was likely yes. Nevertheless, laymen on the board from First Baptist and Second Baptist rose to the defense of the university president.

Plainly annoyed, one of them said with disdain, "There's unwholesome programming even on network channels. We can't refuse this gift because of some programming that might be transmitted by the tower."

A pastor friend sitting next to me jumped into the fray and took my side, questioning whether our Baptist university should make money, even indirectly, from pornography. Suddenly, laymen from the city's two largest fundamentalist Baptist churches appeared to think my friend and I were too "spiritual" when it came to acceptance of a financial gift.

The pastor of Houston's First Baptist Church, also on the board, had dozed off—the meeting followed a heavy lunch—but he awoke in time to see laymen he knew in a disagreement with my "liberal" friend and me. Not yet fully awake and not fully aware of what we were arguing about, the pastor made several comments siding with the laymen. A few minutes later, as the fog of his nap cleared, he realized what the conversation was about, and recognized his mistake, but it was too late to change sides in the discussion.

The irony couldn't have been lost on anyone looking at the situation objectively. Lay leaders from two churches leading in a nationwide movement to exert fundamentalist control of the Southern Baptist Convention were arguing for revenues from pornographic programming and doing so against two so-called liberal pastors who found it improper.

The university president ended what was becoming a heated discussion by announcing the matter was tabled until a later time.

After the meeting, the pastor of First Baptist Church—the one who had joined the wrong side of the argument as he awoke from a nap—invited my friend and me for coffee. This was a first. Over hot drinks and snacks, this gregarious, good-hearted man poured on the charm. Though he never stated it explicitly, his objective was clear. He didn't want the word getting out that he had spoken in favor of income from sexually explicit programming. It probably didn't matter. Who would have believed us?

Behind the scenes, I saw repeated examples of how churches claiming theological purity were subject to the same human failings and limitations as any other organization—including incidents of sexual misconduct ranging from inappropriate touching to extramarital and homosexual affairs. And when it happened in their own realm, they typically guarded their image and kept it quiet.

27 – Megachurch Steamroller

For the most part, our denominations' theological war was background static because so much was going on in my own ministry—navigating the needs of *Congregation One* and *Congregation Two*, starting new ministries, leading support groups, speaking, and now a new opportunity—teaching at the Houston campus of Southwestern Baptist Theological Seminary, a part-time assignment made possible by the fact that the theologically moderate president of the seminary had not yet been fired.

I began teaching two classes in January of 1992: "Pastoral Leadership in the Church" and "Pastoral Care of Persons in Crisis." This new responsibility required one afternoon a week away from my office, and some additional time for preparing course content and grading papers.

I loved teaching. My students were highly motivated. Class discussions were energizing. The classroom experience stimulated my thinking on issues of pastoral care in the church, and it gave me a chance to promote the value of support group ministries to a new generation of seminary students.

That same month, *Leadership*, a non-denominational journal for church leaders, dedicated a whole issue to "Recovery and Restoration." The feature article, "Riding the Recovery Movement," was based on interviews with me and several ministers from other denominations, also leading recovery ministries in local churches. The article opened with a summary of the remarks made by all the interviewed ministers.

> Somehow the traditional church hasn't relieved all the pain, they say. They may have been headed for heaven, but their journey was still storm-tossed… With God's help, they say, they are finally being honest with themselves, finally recovering from their unhealthy past. And they insist that the deeper problems of an increasingly sick society require the extraordinary measures of recovery groups as vehicles for God's grace.[18]

The article went on to include some of my experiences as an adult child of an alcoholic, and further developed the theme that support groups were meeting needs that were not otherwise addressed by the traditional church. Also included were quotes from me and the other interviewees, highlighting the reasons support groups in churches are effective, how to avoid some of the problems that could occur, and how to deal with the differences between traditional church members and people who show up for the groups.[19]

An accompanying piece, "The Battle Over Biblical Truths," dealt with the question of whether recovery support groups in the church were biblically based. I was quoted as an advocate of the position that support groups were indeed biblical. A Christian psychologist, also quoted, took the opposite position, and was not supportive of recovery groups in the church.[20]

* * *

In the same month that I started teaching seminary classes—the same month the *Leadership* article appeared—I learned that Houston's Second Baptist Church was going to be voting on opening a new campus just minutes away from Kingsland.

Three months earlier, in October of 1991, I had received a confidential heads-up from a deacon who was a member of Second Baptist Church. He wasn't supposed to be telling me what he was sharing: Second Baptist Church was running out of space, planned to acquire a large tract of land about two minutes down the street, and would be building a second campus.

The main campus of Second Baptist Church was located near Houston's inner loop, minutes away from the Houston Country Club, and 16 miles away from Kingsland Baptist Church.

Projections for Houston's growth indicated that the geographical center of the Houston metropolitan area was moving westward toward Katy. Within a few years, population growth in the Katy area was predicted to explode. Second Baptist was looking ahead, making smart plans to avoid the growth plateau that can occur when even the most dynamic church runs out of room for expansion.

Organizationally, Southern Baptists act cooperatively through denominational organizations at the national, state, and regional levels, but each church is autonomous. No denominational hierarchy dictates to a pastor or a congregation, "Don't build a church too close to one of your sister churches."

There was, however, an assumed collegiality among us. Churches would often compete for members and compare statistics, but behind it all was an awareness that ultimately, we were all on the same team. That's why the message I received in October left me feeling like the wind had been knocked out of me.

The normally reliable collegiality was apparently absent in this megachurch's plans to build just down the street.

There was another reason this message caught me off guard. Ed Young, the senior minister of Second Baptist Church, was a role model for me. Five years earlier, I had participated in a church growth conference at Second Baptist, with several hundred people in attendance. At the end of one of the evening sessions, Ed Young invited any minister who was interested to visit with him in his study. I was surprised when only a half-dozen men accepted the invitation to a private meeting with this celebrated preacher. But that wasn't the only thing that surprised me.

Ed Young's office had more square footage than the house I grew up in on

Bonham Street in Odessa. It was two stories high, luxuriously appointed, with a fireplace that would have looked at home in any British manor house. The perimeter of the second level was a library—a narrow walkway flanked by wall-high shelves with what I imagined was surely one of the largest personal collections of Christian books anywhere in the world. But I was impressed with the man himself more than his opulent office.

Even more striking was the serendipitous nature of the event—suddenly finding myself able to spend private time with this remarkable leader. After an hour or so of conversation, several of the others left, leaving three us listening intently to the senior minister of one of our nation's largest congregations sharing his wisdom on how to build a church.

It was almost midnight when we were finally escorted out of his office through a hallway leading to the church's sanctuary. Just before we walked up a short flight of stairs that ended not far from the pulpit in the sanctuary, we passed a small room with a movie star-style makeup chair in the center. Each week, before the charismatic pastor stepped in front of his congregation—and the television cameras—his last stop must have been for a little concealer and a layer of pancake.

Occupying such a lavish office was never part of my vision, but growing a large church was. I was delighted that I had spent this close-up time with Ed Young. And after the conference, I wrote what is now an embarrassingly admiring letter to him that included the following lines:

> Since the conclusion of the church growth conference last week, I have struggled with knowing how to best express to you the impact the conference had on me. I believe I will remember it as long as I live. The most important aspect of the conference for me was your availability and candor. I was deeply impressed with the way you made yourself accessible to us. I want to say thank you for your help. Also, I want you to know that this pastor admires and respects your ministry.

Now, five years later, Second Baptist Church looked like a steamroller. The driver of that steamroller was Ed Young. And I was in his path.

Around this time, members of my church began to periodically pass along comments made to them by members of Ed Young's congregation. There was a common theme that went something like: "Tim Sledge is a liberal. Kingsland Baptist Church doesn't know how to reach people. That's why our church needs to come to your community. We know how to do church growth."

Liberal? As a college student, I had decided not to return to a Baptist college that might be too liberal. I chose Wheaton instead, the bastion of conservative Bible scholarship, a place where students had to pledge to no smoking, no drinking, no gambling, and no card playing.

Liberal? I believed the Bible was the inerrant word of God. I held firm on

Kingsland Baptist's qualifications for deacons: no divorce and no alcohol use. And my position on homosexuality was clear and unwavering.

Doesn't know how to do church growth? Under my leadership, Kingsland's growth rate was more than three times the growth rate of its expanding community. In 1990, *Church Growth Today* had recognized Kingsland Baptist as one of the 540 fastest growing churches out of more than 400,000 churches in North America, putting our growth rate in the top one percent.[21] And, in the same year, Kingsland Baptist Church had been one of 225 churches in the Southern Baptist Convention that baptized more than 100 people. Our annual baptisms placed us at 153rd out of more than 43,000 churches.

The only thing about my ministry that anyone might have labeled as theologically liberal was my work with support groups. That same January in 1992, a national Baptist Press release was titled, "Sledge: If Secular Therapy Method Works, Use It." But the same article also quoted the solidly conservative leader of Southern Baptist discipleship training as agreeing that the church needed to be utilizing small groups and recovery principles to help hurting people.[22]

At the time my ministry was experiencing its greatest impact and doing extraordinary good, I was under attack. This didn't feel like sharing in the work of the Kingdom of God. This felt like a secular playing field where competition was keen, but no referee was officiating.

Second Baptist was boxed in and moving westward. Nothing was going to get in their way. Any justification was acceptable, including maligning a sister church and its pastor if necessary. What made everything worse—one of my role models was setting the tone, leading the charge, and building his domain regardless of the cost.

I wanted to believe that Ed Young was unaware of what some of his congregants were saying. However, he had created the environment that enabled some of his members to disparage our church and demean my ministry. What else might they be capable of?

This wasn't unintentional friendly fire; it was carefully targeted aim from superficially friendly brothers in Christ. I couldn't believe how naïve I was.

The congregation of Second Baptist Church was being asked to approve plans for the new campus by a congregational vote scheduled at a Wednesday night business meeting. A 180-acre plot of land on Interstate 10, the main corridor from downtown Houston to the west side of the metro area, would be purchased if the plan was approved.

I was hearing that one of the associate pastors at Second Baptist was telling people that representatives of their church had talked to our church about their move, and that I supported the move. This couldn't have been further from the truth.

Second Baptist had not widely publicized that such a big decision was on the agenda for a regular Wednesday evening business meeting. More typical handling would have meant holding the vote on a Sunday morning after the congregation had been given multiple opportunities to discuss it. Apparently, adding another campus was a controversial move in the view of some of their members, possibly fearing—incorrectly—that the ultimate plan was to move the church's main campus to the west side of Houston.

Before the Wednesday night business meeting at Second Baptist, I sent a fax to several of their deacons whom I had been told might be receptive to hearing from me. In the fax, I made it clear that contrary to what was being stated by at least one of the ministers at Second Baptist, no official representative of the church had talked with me about their proposed new location. In addition, I indicated that while recognizing the right of any church to do whatever it saw fit to do, I had not expressed support of Second Baptist's plan to build a new campus just down the street from our church.

I sent our director of communications to observe Second Baptist's Wednesday night business meeting. Some 2,500 people showed up. The proceedings didn't go smoothly as multiple members raised concerns about adding a new campus. I was told that one of the deacons to whom I sent my fax, a nationally known business leader, was walking to the podium with a printed copy of my document in his hand, preparing to speak, when someone called for the vote and abruptly ended discussion on the motion.

The vote was taken, and the motion to buy the land and add the new campus passed by 75%. Normally, in a Baptist church, having 25% percent of church members vote against a major decision like this posed a serious problem. As a sign of his dissent, the prominent deacon who was prevented from speaking later left Second Baptist Church.

After the meeting, the front page of the *Houston Chronicle's* Business Section included an article titled "Megachurch Buys Megaparcel" which indicated that Second Baptist would pay $3.3 million for the site and noted that the church had 5,000 members living within seven miles of the new location.[23]   A follow-up article appeared on the front page of the *Houston Chronicle*'s Religion section the next day.

> When the plan for buying the west Houston property was voted on Wednesday, some members said they wanted more time to think and pray about it... Some members are concerned about Second Baptist's debt load. Young said the new plan could keep that debt load, currently $17.9 million, in check.
>
> One member said the church's deacons were not informed of the plan until early in the week and that there was no advance announcement to church members that a vote would be taken. But church officials said they believe Second's members support the project. [One lay leader] said the church's top-

flight staff makes such a plan feasible. "Businesses do this all the time," he said. "Why can't churches?"[24]

[18] Richard Doebler, "Riding the Recovery Movement," *Leadership: A Practical Journal for Church Leaders*, Volume XIII, Number 1 (Winter 1992): 16.

[19] Doebler, "Riding the Recovery Movement," 16-21.

[20]Richard Doebler, "The Battle Over Biblical Truths," *Leadership: A Practical Journal for Church Leaders*, Volume XIII, Number 1 (Winter, 1992): 20-21.

[21] Letter from John N. Vaughn, Editor of *Church Growth Today*.

[22] Terri Lackey, "Sledge: If Secular Therapy Method Works, Use It," *The Baptist Standard*, January 2, 1992, 15.

[23] Cecile Holmes White, Ralph Bivins, Richard Vara, "Megachurch Buys Megaparcel," *Houston Chronicle*, Business Section, (January 17, 1992): 1. ©*Houston Chronicle*.

[24] Cecile Holmes White, "The Bigger the Better: Megachurch Prepares for Growth," *Houston Chronicle*, Religion Section (January 18, 1992): 1. ©*Houston Chronicle*.

28 – Protester Buses

Shortly after the business meeting at Second Baptist Church, I received a surprising call. It was from Avery Willis, the Southern Baptist denominational leader who had written the glowingly positive letter after I had spoken in Nashville in December.

Avery was the program leader for the office that was in the process of publishing my book, *Making Peace with Your Past*. He was calling to let me know that he had been told that I sent *busloads* of Kingsland members to disrupt the business meeting at Second Baptist.

I was stunned. I hardly knew what to say. I had sent our director of communications—one person—to observe, and she had said nothing in the meeting. How could such a blatant lie make its way from Houston, Texas, to our denominational offices in Nashville, Tennessee? I told him the story was untrue. No one from our church had disrupted the business meeting.

Although Avery seemed satisfied with my answer, I was deeply disturbed by the call. Not only did it concern the reputation of the church I was working so hard to build, but publication of the book I had written—a book with the potential of helping tens of thousands of individuals with recovery from childhood wounds—was now being threatened.

Sometime later, I was told that Ed Young had been asked by one of the leaders at the Baptist Sunday School Board, the parent organization of my publisher, whether to proceed with *Making Peace with Your Past*. He was reported to have said, "If it's a good book, publish it."

It wasn't surprising that he was asked the question. At this point in time, he was likely the most powerful man in the Southern Baptist Convention—soon to be elected president. In an instant, he could have pulled the plug on my book—done, over—and it would never have seen the light of day.

I was grateful for the decision to allow publication of my book, and not to punish me for my resistance to his church's move. I was at his mercy.

I couldn't imagine where the story that I sent people to disrupt the business meeting had originated. It was only years later that a friend made it his mission to find out who started the potentially devastating rumor. It took some serious sleuthing, but eventually he found the source—a layman at Second Baptist. When asked why he concocted such a story, he said he did it to help his church.

Blatant lies? Character assassination? Were these permissible if it would help one's church? Was this what passed for being a soldier of the cross? Did the man who made up the story consider this a battle of good versus evil?

All I could see was a dirty, nasty, competitive conflict. This may have been routine in the secular business world, but how could it be justified in the service of God? Weren't we all being led to work together to advance his word? This was a terrible blow.

While the reality of Second Baptist's stance toward my ministry was a mixed bag, the official position was positive, as stated in a letter from a Second Baptist minister responding to a member of Kingsland. The congregant who wrote the letter was a Houston businessman who had made his commitment to Jesus under my ministry. He took it on himself to write to Ed Young expressing concern with their decision to move in down the street. Writing on behalf of Ed Young, the minister communicated his joy over the layman's recent commitment to Jesus and shared a view of how our two churches could work together in Katy:

> Our heart's desire is not to come in and hurt Kingsland Baptist Church in any way... Different churches minister to different needs in different people's lives. Our prayer is to come to the Katy area and touch those that we can touch and for Kingsland Baptist Church to continue to touch the people they are touching and will continue to touch in the years to come.

And he closed with words of support: "...our prayers go with you and your family and Pastor Tim Sledge as you seek to minister to those God has placed upon your hearts and in your lives."

Despite this written expression of support for my ministry, negative comments by Second Baptist members continued long after that decisive Wednesday night vote. At times, I felt my leadership was being placed under a microscope; Second Baptist's impending move brought periodic, unsettling, and disruptive comparisons between Ed Young's ministry and my own.

In April of 1992, I received a letter of complaint from a couple in my church. They were unhappy with my sermons emphasizing recovery and support groups. Their letter began with the affirmation that when they had joined the church five years earlier, my weekly sermons were biblically based. But now, they said, I used scripture to justify whatever subject I selected to talk about on a given Sunday.

They were concerned that the new Christians being reached through our support groups needed to grow spiritually, but they didn't see how that could happen with my current preaching. They warned that we were going to lose many families to Second Baptist Church not because of the megachurch's size, ministries they could provide, or denominational politics, but because Ed Young, unlike me, preached scripturally sound sermons. They ended by saying: "You can deliver sermons of the same caliber because you did in the past. Now is the time for you to get our church back on track."

* * *

About a year after Second Baptist's official decision to purchase the nearby land, Southern Baptist pastors in Houston were collaborating in a citywide outreach effort. In preparation for the event, pastors met to pray for the success of the project. Ed Young was leading the meeting. Following a few introductory remarks, we all got down on our knees for a time of prayer. As we were praying, someone placed his hand on my shoulder. I opened my eyes and looked around. It was Ed Young. He was kneeling beside me.

After the prayer session, as Ed Young was concluding the meeting, he told the ministers they should check out my book. I took the mention and the hand on my shoulder as an olive branch—the closest he could come to saying he was sorry for how things played out. When the meeting ended, I told him I regretted not handling the situation better.

As it turned out, there was plenty of room for both Kingsland Baptist Church and Second Baptist Church to continue our growth in the Katy area. Second Baptist picked the location for their new campus based on available land, not because it was close to our church. And, Second Baptist already had thousands of members living in our community.

Maybe I overreacted. Maybe I should have taken it all in stride. Maybe I shouldn't have made public statements about their decision. On the other hand, the primary issue was not what they did, but how they did it. And there was no excuse for smearing my name in the process.

Four years later, one additional event would remove any doubts I had about what the leaders of this megachurch steamroller were willing to do.

29 – Book Tour

In the spring of 1992, despite the controversy with Second Baptist, Kingsland was continuing its steady growth. Easter worship attendance was 1,947, up from 1,750 the previous year.

In May, the minister of preschool and childhood education search committee had reviewed 94 resumes, interviewed 32 candidates, and narrowed their focus down to Linda as their most qualified prospect. I stepped out of the search process at that point. On the last Sunday of the month, the church had enthusiastically voted her into the permanent position.

Now in my seventh year as pastor, I was working with my staff to develop a leadership vision that would take us right up to the beginning of the 21st century. The plan was called "The Next Seven Years: Preparing for a New Millennium." Looking toward the summer months, we scheduled a July retreat for our lay leaders, at which time we would present our plan to them for discussion, input, and approval. Next, we would discuss the plan with the congregation over a period of several weeks. Finally, the congregation would vote on the plan on two consecutive Sundays in August—in line with the church's constitutional guidelines for decisions of this magnitude.

During this same time, *Making Peace with Your Past* was about to be released, which meant traveling and speaking to promote the book over a 9-week period hitting six national denominational events. The first of these events took place in July at the Glorieta Conference Center, located a few miles from Santa Fe, New Mexico, and one of two national conference facilities operated by the Southern Baptist Convention in 1992. It was that week that I first held *Making Peace with Your Past* in my hands and saw it on the shelves of a bookstore. Those were rewarding moments.

As for my participation at Glorieta, the occasion was Discipleship Training Week. Attendees were denominational leaders, ministers, and lay leaders from churches across the country. That week, I led a class in which I related my personal story of growing up with an alcoholic parent, and then explained how my book could be applied more generally for adult children of dysfunctional families.

To make my point, I highlighted six common characteristics of a dysfunctional family. A dysfunctional family focuses on an emotionally needy family member, limits the expression of emotions, discourages open talk about obvious problems, enables destructive pre-assigned roles in the family, fails to provide appropriate nurture for developing children, and fosters secrets.

Once these characteristics were described, I addressed the life-changing impact that support groups were having at Kingsland Baptist Church, and talked about how to start a support group ministry in a local congregation.

Not only was the response enthusiastic, but as class participants shared their personal stories with me, I was reminded again that many Christians were waiting for someone to give them permission to talk about childhood experiences that left them dealing with persistent emotional pain.

It was a full and fulfilling week, and an excellent way to kick off my next two months of events and activities. I was pleased to see an article from our denomination's Baptist Press that was sent to state Baptist papers across the U.S. reporting on my talks at the New Mexico conference. The press article quoted me as saying, "Jesus wants us to have not only a healthy spiritual life but also a healthy emotional life." The article reported my assertion that a large silent group in the local church was waiting for the help available in a Making Peace Group. While I didn't think everyone needed a support group, I did feel that church members "who don't think they need it should give the rest of us time to get the help we need."[25]

A new phase in my ministerial career was beginning. Because of my book, my name was about to become known across the largest protestant denomination in the United States, the Southern Baptist Convention.

* * *

At the end of my week in New Mexico, I returned to Houston to lead our Next Seven Years weekend retreat in Round Top, Texas, located an hour outside of Katy. With 70 attendees and extensive preparation on the part of our staff, I threw myself into the critical task of carefully describing our vision and securing consensus on our updated mission statement: "To Build God's Kingdom through Support, Study, and Service." Support referred to our recovery and pastoral care ministries, study referred to our educational programs, and service referred to the many ministries we offered.

That weekend we discussed the core values of our church. Many of the values we included were common to Baptist churches, but some—stressing the connection between emotional issues and spiritual maturity, creating an environment of encouragement, planning for a core curriculum in our teaching, and keeping ministry methods sensitive to cultural change—set us apart. We weren't just one more church, and everything we discussed as part of our new plan that weekend grew out of our newly delineated core values.

Some of the changes were nuts and bolts—like a pragmatic restructuring of our schedule. We realized that even our most committed members were facing more competition for their time and attention. So, we would hold a Sunday evening worship service monthly rather than weekly. Church business meetings would be conducted on a quarterly basis rather than monthly. In short, as a congregation we would meet less frequently, but would make each gathering more focused, efficient, and substantive.

And, we decided to think outside the box about when people could worship. What about people who couldn't come on Sunday mornings? We agreed on a plan to eliminate one of our Sunday morning worship services and add a

Saturday evening service in its place.

Other parts of the plan were about a new mindset. We needed a greater focus on reaching unchurched people, and that meant we had to be even more willing to structure everything we did with that goal in mind. If we were going to reach new people for Christ, we needed to train them, and our existing Bible Study program assumed lifelong involvement in the church. To address this need, we instituted a series of progressive classes beginning with Christianity 101.

Another key component: We were discussing, writing down, and zeroing in on a well-thought-out, concise description of our identity and priorities—one that would need to be reinforced in as many ways as possible in the months and years to come.

It was a working retreat, intense, but highly productive. The next step would be presenting our plans to the congregation.

* * *

Just days after Kingsland's leadership retreat, I was able to combine a brief family vacation with my next speaking engagement. Linda, Jonathan, David, and I loaded our bicycles into a large U-Haul hitched to our family van, and headed to Ridgecrest, North Carolina.

Ridgecrest was the other national conference center operated by the Southern Baptist Convention, nestled in the Blue Ridge Mountains just outside Ashville.

Sessions were structured as they had been two weeks earlier in Santa Fe. Again, I found myself in a beautiful setting revealing some of the less than beautiful facts of my childhood. Again, each day, I led a class on *Making Peace with Your Past*. Again, I talked about the life-changing impact that support groups were having at Kingsland Baptist, and how a church could start its own support group ministry.

With the help of five volunteers, I conducted an actual support group meeting in front of the whole class in order to demonstrate the process. The observers quickly grew silent and sat very still. When the support group meeting ended, I looked beyond the small circle where I had been focused and turned my attention to the rest of the class. Many, if not most, had tears in their eyes.

I learned to accept this emotional intensity as a normal part of my life as I continued to travel across the country offering instruction on how to use *Making Peace with Your Past* as the basis for a support group.

Just after leading my last class at Ridgecrest on Friday, we started our vacation in earnest with a drive to Washington, D.C. We settled into our hotel, unloaded our four bicycles from the U-Haul, and had a grand ride along a trail that hugged the Potomac River. We rode across the Arlington Memorial Bridge, past the Lincoln Memorial, and took in some of the most impressive landmarks our nation's capital has to offer—all from our bikes.

The next day—Saturday—I was on the road without my family. I had a plane to catch. It was back to Houston to preach a vision-casting Sunday sermon. The topic was The Next Seven Years.

Back in Katy, church members were invited to stay for a box lunch discussion where they could ask questions about the plan. Later that Sunday, I flew back to Washington, D.C. to rejoin my family.

Over the next few days we visited with our Wheaton College friends, Steve and Valerie Bell, at their cabin on the side of a mountain in the Nantahala National Forest near Ashville, North Carolina.

After four great days with the Bells, on Friday, we made the 14-hour drive back to Texas. On Saturday, I caught up on my sleep. On Sunday, I was back at work, preaching for the two Sunday morning worship services, and that afternoon, leading another question and answer session on The Next Seven Years proposal.

Four days later, I was back in the air, this time headed to California to lead a break-out class for the Steps '92 conference sponsored by the National Association for Christian Recovery in Costa Mesa. And once again, on the following Sunday, I was back in Katy at Kingsland Baptist to preach and to oversee our first vote on The Next Seven Years plan.

On that score, things seemed to be moving in the right direction. Our church newsletter published quotes from some of our lay leaders who had been asked to comment on what they liked about the plan. One member stated that it was a testament to the fact that Kingsland was about reaching people, not just having church. Positive remarks were made about our new study curriculum, and, perhaps the best comment was: "It provides new 'non' traditional changes for those who are not plugged in to any church right now, but still allows us 'old' Baptists our traditional format." That sounded like the sweet spot I was looking for.

The first Sunday morning vote was 90% in favor of the plan.

The whirlwind of activity continued. The next day, I was back on the road, returning to Santa Fe for a 5-day speaking event at the Glorieta Conference Center. This time, I was leading classes during Bible Preaching Week.

I promoted the value of support groups, and throughout the week, taught participants in my class how to use *Making Peace with Your Past* as the basis for a support group. I highlighted a foundational skill: The group leader's role is to model feedback instead of advice-giving. Feedback, I explained, is a non-judgmental sharing of one's own feelings or experiences in response to what another group member shares. I went on to describe how, after meeting three or four times, the 12-week group moved more and more into a shared leadership mode. When a group was functioning properly, as the group leader, I might not have to say much. The group would, to an extent, run itself.

Class participants responded positively, and as was becoming the norm, some of them found themselves opening up to me, clearly relieved to do so. It seemed as if everywhere I spoke, I had similar experiences of committed Christians, including top Baptist leaders, finally freeing themselves from years of undisclosed emotional pain. At long last, they felt permission to be honest about their feelings and talk about what they were going through.

My sense was that addressing the issue of overcoming an emotionally painful childhood was hitting a raw nerve in our denomination. The *once I was lost, but now I am found* concept that had seemed so true and so adequate in the early years of my ministry was hardly sufficient any longer. I was understanding more than ever that helping people heal and change was more complex than that.

At the end of my week at Glorieta, it was time to pack my bags, drive to the airport, and fly home. This was now routine; I thought little about the mechanics of getting to and from the places I was due to speak, to teach, to guide, to listen, and to influence. I was away from my family more than I wanted to be, but I saw it as temporary. How often is one asked to travel to promote a newly-released book—a book that is life-changing for many of its readers.

That Sunday, back in Katy to preach the two morning worship services, we held our second vote on the plan to take us to the next century. Much to my satisfaction, it was fully approved with a 91% positive vote.

After seven entire days without travel—it felt good to share breakfast and dinner with the family, to sleep in my own bed, and to take a jog through my own neighborhood—I was back on the road. Returning to Ridgecrest, North Carolina, I completed another round of *Making Peace with Your Past* sessions. I returned home on the weekend, preached on Sunday, repacked my bags, and gassed up my car. On the last day of August, a Monday, I found myself in Fort Worth for a four-day conference on "Growing Churches through Support Groups" where I was one of the keynote speakers.

As the fall school term began, it was time to embrace Kingsland's new weekend schedule—including the Saturday night worship service.

My summer travel and speaking engagements spanned a period of 60 days and were more hectic and more rewarding than I anticipated. I had spoken at least one time—sometimes two or three—on 35 of those 60 days. I had traveled 10,546 miles and was away from my congregation only two of nine Sundays while traveling. I had spoken at six national Southern Baptist Convention events, met a multitude of Southern Baptist brothers and sisters, and—within the next year or so—sales of my book would reach 40,000.

Making Peace with Your Past was the first book created specifically for a series of Southern Baptist materials designed for support group use. To promote the new series, the Southern Baptist Sunday School Board elected to produce and distribute a video that would enlighten church leaders about the compelling benefits of support groups. In October, a film crew from Nashville came to our church to begin taping for the new video.

The final version of the video was powerful. Beyond opening and closing comments by denominational leader, Avery Willis, the footage consisted entirely of scenes from Kingsland Baptist Church: excerpts from actual support group meetings (members gave their permission), testimonials from individuals transformed by the groups, and me, describing the importance, value, and methodology of our support group ministry.

The video, made available to churches across the Southern Baptist Convention, presented our groups as the model to be emulated. Ironically, while being labeled a liberal by some in the Houston area, my own denomination falling more and more under the control of fundamentalist leaders, embraced my book and our church's model of support group ministries wholeheartedly.

As Christmas season was rolling around, the associate pastor of Houston's First Baptist Church wrote to tell me they had enrolled over 100 people in Making Peace Groups. He shared a letter he received from one of the participants.

> I have just completed the course you taught on *Making Peace with Your Past*. For years I have wondered why I did the things I did, making the same mistakes over and over again, but now I know why. I will never use being from a dysfunctional family as a crutch or an excuse for what I have done in my life. This course gave me an insight into how my original family lifestyle and a truckload of trauma every week gave me the very foundation for conducting myself as I have. I am 62 years old, but I am glad and happy to have all these questions answered after all these years.

Knowing that my book was helping people like this felt extremely good.

Things were going well, but I was getting tired, and was too busy to admit how tired I was, especially to myself. My father and the broom were still with me; there was always more to do, more people to reach, and momentum not to be squandered.

---

[25] Linda Lawson, "Pastor Discovers Need for Dealing with the Past," *Baptist Press: News Service of the Southern Baptist Convention,* 92-112 (July 13, 1992).

30 – Dream Year

The pace of activities at Kingsland—and my commitments—continued to grow as we entered 1993. Traveling, teaching, and speaking took me on repeat performances and new appearances alike. At times, I seemed to bounce from one part of the country to another—addressing audiences, facilitating support group leader training, and discussing emotional healing at regional, state, and national Southern Baptist gatherings.

One week I found myself in Arkansas, and a few weeks later in Hawaii. There were return trips to Ridgecrest in North Carolina and Glorieta in New Mexico. I spoke in Tennessee, in Massachusetts, in Kentucky, and in Texas. I was racking up even more mileage than I had in the previous year, and my words were being heard by ministers, lay leaders, and religious educators. My emerging role—as a spokesman for emotional healing in my denomination—felt meaningful and significant.

Daily life back in Katy, Texas, sometimes had a way of body-slamming me with a dose of alternate reality. In February, I learned that a woman who was a former member of Kingsland, an accountant, had, over a period of years, syphoned off virtually all her employer's retirement funds through forged checks and illegal transfers—to the tune of $2 million. Criminal charges were pending.

I knew her well. She had been a member of the search committee that called me to Kingsland. She and her husband, a deacon, had moved away more than a year earlier, and I had lost touch, but our family had been in their home many times. They had been like grandparents to our two boys.

Her crime was carefully planned and executed over a long period—with her husband's knowledge—before being discovered. How was this possible? This was one more *exception to the rule of faith* I would have to file away—with a headline worthy of the tabloids: "Former Kingsland Baptist Leaders Embezzle Millions." I was grateful I hadn't seen any such headline splashed across the newspapers, but this was tough to wrap my head around.

* * *

David Mains, my pastor from Wheaton days, remained an admired role model and an important connection. He was now the director of The Chapel of the Air Ministries, with its focus: a non-denominational Christian radio program—The Chapel of the Air—broadcast five days a week on stations across the U.S.

Each year, The Chapel of the Air Ministries sponsored a nationwide program for churches called the "50-Day Spiritual Adventure." The adventure kicked off 50 days before Easter with daily radio broadcasts and a program that could be implemented in local churches—both offering a way to focus on spiritual growth in the weeks leading up to Christianity's most important day of the year.

Months before an annual adventure started, pastors could attend a 50-Day Spiritual Adventure Pastor/Church Leader Conference offered at multiple locations across the country. On the agenda for the leader conference: introducing the theme for the coming year and reviewing the leadership notebook, which included sample sermon manuscripts for the seven Sundays leading up to Easter and the final sermon on Easter Sunday.

David Mains asked me to be a member of the leadership team for the 1994 adventure, a role that included helping with brainstorming of sermon topics and related materials. He also asked me to lead Kingsland Baptist Church to conduct a trial run of the 1994 content one year in advance.

In February of 1993, as I began the first sermon of the series, I introduced the theme for the eight-week program: *Daring to Dream Again*.

> How do you know when you're getting old? How do you know when you've started to die? Here's a test. You are getting old when you no longer have dreams, not the kind of dreams you have when you're asleep, but the dreams you dream when you're awake.
>
> You are starting to die when you feel that the exciting parts of your life have already happened.
>
> What are your hopes and dreams? Are you just expecting to get out of bed tomorrow and make it through the day, or do you have a dream? Do you have a dream of being something someday that you are not today? During the next eight weeks, I want to challenge you to be a dreamer.

Over the next seven weeks, the sermon series progressed with weekly topics like "Letting Go of a Painful Past," "Escaping the Comfort Zone," "Removing Relational Roadblocks," and "Rising Above the Me Generation." The final sermon, delivered on Easter, was "Moving Mountains Instead of Molehills." I challenged the audience to be mountain movers—people with purpose, people who change the flavor of whatever they touch, people who bring life to others.

We experienced record-breaking attendance once again at Easter services with 2,084 people present for worship.

* * *

After completing the trial run of the Spiritual Adventure at Kingsland in the spring of 1993, I traveled to Wheaton, Illinois, to record a series of radio interviews for The Chapel of the Air—interviews designed to help promote the 1994 50-Day Spiritual Adventure. I found it hard to take in the scope of this ministry—the previous year's adventure had drawn over half-a-million participants from multiple Christian denominations across the U.S.

The interviews, conducted by my friend, Steve Bell, David's brother-in-law and now an associate at The Chapel of the Air Ministries, focused on chapters from my book, *Making Peace with Your Past*. The Chapel had purchased 10,000 copies of my book to sell to their listeners, using it as a resource for the second weekly topic of the adventure: "Letting Go of a Painful Past."

Steve and I discussed topics like the dynamics of a dysfunctional family, growing up with a shame-based identity, overcoming the fear of waiting for the other shoe to drop, and learning to see perfectionism as an emotional problem rather than a virtue.

Sharing the message of *Making Peace with Your Past* with such a vast listening audience was exciting. And the trial run sermons I wrote and preached were included in the Chapel's leadership notebook for the 50-Day Spiritual Adventure. I was pleased to be, in some small way, a resource for ministers of multiple denominations across the country.

* * *

After finishing the adventure sermon series, I returned to my own planned schedule of topics. I had heard some criticism from *Congregation One* that I was concentrating too heavily on recovery-related subjects. So, for the remainder of the year, I selected—for the most part—topics that were more appealing to them. Some of my sermon titles were: "The Identity and Work of the Holy Spirit," "Forgiveness," "Doing What Jesus Says," "Keeping Faith When God Seems Silent," and "How to Be Spiritually Alert."

* * *

In the spring of 1993, we set aside time in the morning service to hear testimonials from various members of our church. That Sunday, Kingsland members described a happy, helpful, and powerful congregation of believers—a place where members were finding solace, guidance, and fellowship—a real community in Jesus, which brought them joy.

One member shared: "There's a lot of healing and a lot of help in this church that I haven't found anywhere else." Another talked about balance in our approach: "Kingsland doesn't compromise God's word to make people feel more comfortable. However, God's word is not spoken in judgement of people, but in love for them."

One member described our church as an accepting environment: "I think Kingsland is a church where I can open up and be me. I can drop my guard. I can reveal my emotions, and I can be accepted for who I am."

A woman shared that she and her husband drove 45 minutes each week to get to the church because of our support groups. Another testimony was especially candid: "A year ago, I would never have thought about coming to church on a regular Sunday basis. That was a golf day. I had all my answers. I didn't need any guidance. Kingsland opened my eyes."

One of our deacons talked about the excitement of our church: "When I describe Kingsland to other people, I generally describe it in terms of excitement. An excitement about what we are doing, an excitement about how we are doing it, an excitement about who we are reaching."

The embezzling church lady was an *exception to the rule of faith*, and the testimonials we heard that day were the norm—that's how I saw it.

* * *

When December rolled around, Bethlehem Boulevard set a record with 12,433 people attending. As impressive as these attendance numbers were, this wasn't the only Christmas event that impacted our church and community.

Our Christmas Eve Candlelight Service had become a tradition in our congregation, and one that seemed to touch us all, profoundly. It was a family-oriented event—parents were invited to bring small children in their pajamas, which made it easier to get them in bed when everyone went home. And attendees would often arrive with out-of-town relatives who were visiting for the holiday. It wasn't unusual to see three or four generations sitting together.

Candles were distributed as worshippers entered the Encouragement Center, and at the close of the service, the lights dimmed. I lit one candle, then used it to light the candle of a second person, a third, a fourth, and so on, as participants holding a lighted candle turned to those around them, repeating the process. And so it went—this quiet, person-to-person process repeated over and over as a single source of light became a room warmly lit by hundreds of flickering flames. The candles, of course, were a symbol of the light Jesus brought into our world.

That Christmas Eve, to accommodate as many schedules and people as we could, we held three candlelight services. And in each one, each time, as the sanctuary filled with light, I felt completely at home—part of one large, emotionally connected family.

* * *

Our church was growing. My work was steadily continuing to gain recognition. I was making a difference in an amazing congregation and beyond. In so many ways, I was living my dream.

31 – Wind Factor

Despite all the growth, excitement, and publicity our church was experiencing, I sometimes found myself "flying against the wind," dealing with two distinct views of how well I was doing in my work as pastor. One place this became evident was in my annual performance review.

In eight years, the staff of Kingsland Baptist Church had grown from seven staff members to 34, 16 full-time and 18 part-time. This did not include the teaching staff we had added for the weekday preschool Linda had launched shortly after we arrived at Kingsland.

Early in my pastorate, I worked with the church's personnel committee to develop a detailed human resources policy with attention paid to the annual performance review process. Self-assessment was a critical element in the multi-page form each staff member was asked to complete—he or she would evaluate performance against job description objectives and the previous year's goals. The staff member would also self-assess commitment to the job, skill levels, and character traits demonstrated during the past year. In addition, the staff member would write goals for the upcoming year.

The staff member's supervisor used the same criteria to evaluate the subordinate's performance. Following discussion and comparison between the two assessments, a numerical rating between 1 and 100 was assigned, and any pay raise given was based on the result.

I was the only member of the church staff whose performance review was conducted directly by church members—the personnel committee. Given that congregants rotated on and off the committee from year to year, some unevenness in my annual reviews was unavoidable. Nevertheless, the process had been good to me. I had consistently received a performance rating of 90 or more as well as an increase in compensation every year.

In January of 1994, my performance review for the previous year took place as expected. It was customary for the committee to comment on progress I had made on issues raised the previous year, and to share objectives they wanted me to address over the next 12 months. This year was different. The committee commented—in writing—on more areas than usual.

They commented on my preaching: "Your sermons have been excellent. The large majority of the time it is easy to see that your sermons have a strong biblical basis. Be sure this is maintained."

These were positive comments. However, the committee was keeping a close watch, not on my delivery skills, but on content. I could hear the influence of *Congregation One* in the veiled warning, "Be sure this is maintained."

The committee mentioned my outside speaking: "We are proud that you are in demand as a speaker and seminar leader. Please keep us updated as to when you plan to be out of the office or pulpit. The schedule you reviewed with us was satisfactory."

I was a little surprised that time away was on the committee's radar. My speaking engagements were bringing praise to Kingsland. I hadn't exceeded the personnel policy guidelines for days away. Why were they implying that this was a problem?

They asked me to help our associate pastor, Nelson, do a better job in leading our adult Bible Study program. Adult Bible Study attendance had dropped well below worship attendance after Nelson's predecessor had left and had never caught up under the new associate pastor's leadership. Their request made sense.

They encouraged me to stay on track in taking care of my family and myself, saying, "Please do not allow your family and personal health considerations (i.e. vacations, time with boys and Linda, workouts, etc.) to slip down on your priority list."

The committee said I was good on soliciting feedback, but I needed to work on how I received and digested it. They said that sometimes I was too easily offended or defensive. It was a valid criticism.

And they asked me to work on my one-to-one communication skills. They said they did not expect this to ever be my greatest strength but wanted to see some improvement in this area.

The criticism was clear, and something I understood. If someone was talking to me about a serious personal problem, something significant, or something especially interesting, I would readily connect—listening attentively and responding appropriately. In contrast, when I had to tolerate complaints about petty slights or was required to engage at length with a boring person, I could come across as detached. As a Christian, I tried to show—and feel—genuine interest in everyone. But sometimes my impatience or lack of interest was noticeable.

I understood that the committee's criticisms weren't coming out of thin air. However, the fact that the committee had no organized system of gathering feedback from the congregation as a whole rendered their process somewhat unprofessional and uneven. Some of their comments were on target, pointing to areas where I needed to grow, but some of their input was obviously coming from a small group of dissatisfied members.

I felt irritated, but also constrained in any response I might otherwise make, since I had just been scolded for not being better at taking criticism. So, I needed to suck it up and work on improving.

The feedback I was getting from the personnel committee seemed like it was all coming from *Congregation One*. Not one individual on the committee evaluating my performance had ever participated in a support group so it wasn't surprising that the committee was somewhat tone deaf to the kind of feedback I was getting from *Congregation Two*.

I had recently received a Christmas note from a congregant that was a clear reminder of the valuable work we were doing in the area of emotional healing. He wrote that God had led him to Kingsland during the darkest days in his life and that *Making Peace with Your Past* had been a life changer. Regarding my sermons, he noted that it seemed like I wrote them just for him, and added, "They are often just what I need just when I need it, like planks rising out of the water so I can take another step." My communications skills? He wrote: "Your gentle support and encouragement mean so much to me."

And other members of *Congregation Two* seemed happy with my one-to-one interactions. A woman who had participated in a support group I led wrote, "Your kindness and compassion are truly an example of what it means to be Christ-like."

But the encouraging notes weren't limited to members of *Congregation Two*. A young father wrote to thank me for being there "at my daughter's hospital bed in the past, and at the other end of the phone." A mother whose teenage son had gone through a difficult time wrote, "Thanks for being there for our family through our son's ordeal. You have been an inspiring preacher, a wise pastor, and have become a treasured friend."

These messages from church members were consistent with the feedback I received Sunday after Sunday as those who attended worship services shook my hand and spoke to me as they filed out of the Encouragement Center.

Maybe the personnel committee didn't have the full picture, but my relationship with the committee was positive enough. I chose to believe they were acting out of the best interests of the church as they perceived them and attempting to watch out for my family and me as well.

When all was said and done, my 1993 performance rating was over the 90th percentile once again, and I received my eighth annual pay increase at Kingsland.

32 – Mixed Messages

Keeping the concerns of the personnel committee in mind, I paid attention to the amount of time I was away, but continued to travel and speak about emotional healing, support groups, and recovery.

In March of 1994, I made the five-hour drive to Euless, Texas, a city in the heart of the Dallas-Fort Worth metropolitan area, to participate in the three-day Recovery and Spiritual Awakening National Conference.

The event was sponsored by the Baptist Sunday School Board, the parent organization of my publisher, LifeWay. That week, I spoke in one of the conference's main sessions and taught a daily breakout session on *Making Peace with Your Past* and *Moving Beyond Your Past*.

Linking the topic of recovery with spiritual awakening gave an added importance to the work of support groups. While Southern Baptists were still being introduced to the idea of support groups in the church and the notion of Christian recovery, spiritual awakening was a well-known concept that many Southern Baptists hoped and prayed for.

All the important leaders and influencers were present as far as support group ministries in Southern Baptist life were concerned. And, some key figures in the area of spiritual awakening were speaking at the conference. The hope was to create a dynamic mix.

As it turned out, the mix of conference leaders was more than dynamic. In fact, two of the speakers for the week revealed that we did not all agree on how to—or whether to—integrate the tools for emotional healing with the tools for spiritual awakening. And I had personal encounters with both individuals.

During the conference, *Facts and Trends*, a Southern Baptist periodical for leaders, conducted a joint interview with me and another author, Robert McGee. [26] McGee is known for multiple books including *Search for Significance*, which has sold more than two million copies, and according to the late Billy Graham: "should be read by every Christian."

McGee, a keynote speaker that week, was also the founder of Rapha—a national health care organization that provided Christ-centered, in-hospital care for psychiatric and substance abuse issues. McGee's treatment organization and his books had the full support of virtually every fundamentalist leader in our denomination. For the members of this tribe, led mainly by megachurch pastors, Rapha delivered the accepted approach to addiction recovery and related issues.

As leaders at the Baptist Sunday School Board had discussed plans for producing recovery literature for the denomination, one option had been turning the whole project over to Rapha—a plan that was rejected. Instead, a deal was made to republish some of McGee's books under LifeWay's imprint. As a result, the first two books in the Life Support series were *Search for*

Significance and *Making Peace with Your Past*. Thus, McGee and I were being interviewed together.

The interviewer treated McGee and me as equals, which felt a little awkward. And Robert McGee's demeanor during the interview caught my attention. He seemed annoyed or ill at ease about something.

I hadn't met McGee before. But I wondered if he was miffed at doing a joint interview with me, given that he was a superstar innovator in the field of Christian recovery, and the leader of an organization that had already published multiple support group books.

And if that's what he was thinking, I couldn't argue. He was undeniably big league, and I was just a pastor who had written about support groups in his spare time. By any measure, we were not equals when it came to the influence we had in Christian recovery.

Whatever he was feeling that day, one thing was clear—he had no interest in getting acquainted or developing any relationship. Maybe he simply disagreed with my approach. A comparison of *Making Peace with Your Past* and *Search for Significance* certainly revealed differences in how we integrated theology and psychology in the work of emotional healing.

My book cites scriptures and advocates making a commitment to Jesus but employs a methodology that could work for any person—regardless of their spiritual status. The key is a willingness to engage in honest introspection, especially if that personal work is taking place in the context of a properly led support group. I had found that this approach almost always led to a group member's spiritual renewal, and frequently resulted in a commitment to participation in church.

Following the process used in Making Peace Groups, each person's recovery is built upon shared foundational principles, but each person's recovery is also unique. The focus is not on drilling a set of predefined theological beliefs into the individual's head, but rather the emphasis is on learning principles for emotional healing, then figuring out how to apply them in a way that works for oneself.

McGee, with a background as a Christian counselor, has been criticized by some more literal-minded Christians as being too psychological, but his perspective in *Search for Significance* is, in my view, basically one of helping the individual get right with God. His four "answers from God" are theological words: justification, reconciliation, propitiation, and regeneration. And the value of any introspection or group sharing seems to be an adjustment of one's beliefs—becoming able to see yourself as God sees you—which then provides the correct level of self-esteem. McGee's focus is on sin, conversion, and acceptance of one's new identity in Jesus.[27]

Ironically, as a pastor, I was placing more emphasis on the psychological process, one I had seen modeled at The Meadows. McGee, as a counselor and health care provider of treatment, was placing more emphasis on theology—

at least in his cornerstone book.

I wasn't alone in the approach I believed in. Mine was the position held by most of the program personalities that week—but not all.

Yet another of the keynote speakers, Henry Blackaby, was even more focused on the theological side of personal problem solving than McGee. Blackaby was the lead author of *Experiencing God: How to Live the Full Adventure of Knowing and Doing the Will of God*—a book that has sold more than seven million copies and has been translated into 47 languages.

Nine months earlier, Blackaby had spoken at Kingsland Baptist Church where he had come across as a gracious and genuine person. His sermon at Kingsland Baptist had touched our congregation—including me—in a powerful way. I was impressed with him as a person as well. And I wanted my church to experience the kind of spiritual renewal he described.

When Blackaby spoke at the recovery and spiritual awakening conference, I sensed an undercurrent in his message that I hadn't noticed before. He seemed to be saying that the way to deal with any personal problem was to simply get closer to God. He said it didn't take six months of counseling to heal. He said that social workers had nothing to offer. And he insisted that God heals instantly. One of his comments was, "Jesus did not come to teach blind men braille."

Was I misinterpreting his meaning? Wasn't he telling a conference of people committed to support group ministries that what they were doing was ineffective?

Sometime later, my impressions were confirmed. Blackaby wrote the foreword to *The Heart of the Problem*, a scripture-based workbook on personal problem solving by Henry Brandt and Kerry Skinner. In the foreword, Blackaby wrote that God, the Bible, prayer, and faith are the only things to turn to for help. He warned that well-intentioned Christians will share advice that is not from God. The authors of *The Heart of the Problem* convey the same message—help is the domain of God. Seeking to understand behaviors and underlying emotional issues is a fruitless endeavor. It's all about God, you, and your sinful nature.[28]

The authors of *The Heart of the Problem* and Henry Blackaby were on the same page—personal growth comes from experiencing God, period. The sole tools to be used are Bible study, prayer, faith, and obedience. Moreover, support groups and professional counseling are of limited, if any, value. In fact, they might steer you down the wrong path.

I wasn't the only one who noticed that Blackaby's message was running contrary to the view of most of the Life Support writers and staff. We were disappointed in what we were hearing but having seen the fruits of our efforts with support groups, we were not deterred.

Our Southern Baptist version of Christian recovery was gaining momentum. Even though our denomination was supporting and publishing at least three different approaches to emotional healing—views that were contradictory—it felt good to have a voice. *Making Peace with Your Past* was a sales leader in the Life Support series, and my second book, *Moving Beyond Your Past* was about to be released.

LifeWay was moving toward its goal of producing 20 different Life Support workbooks including materials for codependency groups, eating disorder groups, sexual abuse survivor groups, and more.

Those insisting on Blackaby's perspective could minimize or lambaste our approach, but we had witnessed its success—one changed life after another. And most of the individuals who found help in our support group ministries did so after years of unsuccessfully seeking the same relief through Bible study, prayer, faith, and obedience.

---

[26] Chip Alford, "Facing a Hurtful Past" *Facts and Trends*, May 1994, 4.

[27] Robert McGee, *The Search for Significance* (Houston: Rapha Publishing, 1985).

[28] Henry Brandt and Kerry L. Skinner, *The Heart of the Problem* (Rex, Georgia: Kerry L. Skinner, 1993).

33 – Intention Tension

In the remaining months of 1994, I spoke in Missouri, South Carolina, Kentucky, and Florida; and I traveled across Texas, speaking in Amarillo, Austin, Dallas, Lubbock, and Tyler. Not only did I speak in churches, but also on college campuses.

The demand for information on support group ministries continued to grow, but for these events, I was able to organize my travel schedule so that I didn't miss a single Saturday or Sunday preaching responsibility at Kingsland Baptist Church.

I thought that all the members of Kingsland would be proud of their pastor's national audience, but that wasn't the case. Some members of the more traditional *Congregation One* were not on board with my growing sphere of ministry. In addition, some of them were not pleased with my emphasis on emotional health and healing, particularly when that emphasis appeared in my sermons.

In their defense, many of the *Congregation One* members of Kingsland had joined the church precisely because it was a Southern Baptist Church. To them, sermons that intertwined Bible truths with modern concepts of recovery and psychological growth were not part of the deal. The traditional Southern Baptist mindset established the bar for self-acceptance and pride at a point defined more simply—by allegiance to Jesus, and commitment to Bible study, prayer, and righteousness.

Congregation Two displayed a very different response. They welcomed placing emotional self-awareness and growth on a par with spiritual awareness and growth. In fact, this focus was one of the draws to many new members of our church, a reality that didn't seem to matter to some of our long-term members for whom my emphasis was unsettling.

To the guardians of the traditional requirements and practices of Southern Baptist ministry, my priority on emotional self-awareness and growth reset the bar and changed everything. It made them squirm.

I could understand the discomfort. Suddenly, people who felt okay about themselves were challenged to look at personal histories they had avoided for decades. A new definition of wholeness was emerging—one that referenced the Bible but was also enlightened by contemporary psychology.

* * *

In 1993, the day after Henry Blackaby spoke at Kingsland, Ellen, our director of communications, wrote me a letter that gave me pause. She warned that I needed to be careful about placing too much emphasis on recovery, and suggested I look to Henry Blackaby as a model.

She reminded me that when Blackaby spoke at Kingsland, he had preached

119

on John 3:16—for God so loved the world—a simple verse that everybody knew. Yet, God had moved in a powerful way. At the end of the service that day, many leaders of the church, especially men, were weeping, and Ellen's comment was that the powerful response of the people that day was not the result of a recovery-related event. It was instead the result of prayer and the unchangeable power of God's word. Recovery is a wonderful tool, she said, but it is not a replacement for God.

Ellen wrote as a friend, and her final words commended my preaching: "I believe God has gifted and empowered you with the ability to communicate his truths in a mighty way." But her bottom line message was in sync with Blackaby's: God is the answer—just focus on God's simple message—that's where the power is.

In 1994, the first quarter issue of the Southern Baptist periodical, *Growing Churches*, published a lengthy interview with me that spoke to the tension addressed in Ellen's letter. The article shared the story of my adult children of alcoholics sermon series in 1988 and the response it generated, and then addressed a series of questions about how the support group ministry integrated with the more traditional side of the church.

I was asked, "How do you tie in your support group ministry with your larger church program? How do you keep it from seeming like your church consists of two separate congregations?" I talked about weaving recovery concepts into my sermons, and gave some examples, but a more accurate answer to the second question would have been, "I don't know, because we have just that—two congregations."

I was asked: "How do long-term church members by and large regard support group members?" I answered candidly, "The long-term church member may question why so much attention is being focused on people in the support groups."

The interviewer asked, "How do you work to integrate people who have come primarily for the support group ministry to become fully functioning members of the larger congregation?" I answered:

> We try to help church people understand that individuals who have come primarily to have their hurts ministered to need more time before they are asked to do church jobs, such as nursery duty… They may need to be self-focused for a while, and we need to understand that. Their children also may need help knowing how to act in church. One of the most effective ways to integrate them is by ministering to their children…

Another question related to how I helped support group people and non-support group participants understand each other. My short response: "No easy answer to this exists."[29]

Kingsland Baptist Church did indeed have two congregations, and the interview revealed the juggling act I was engaged in as I attempted to be sensitive to the needs of both *Congregation One* and *Congregation Two*.

Ellen's letter and the *Growing Churches* interview addressed a set of critical questions in our congregation, in our denomination, and across the larger world of evangelical Christians: Is God all we need? Are prayer and Bible study all we need? Does psychological self-awareness matter?

It was increasingly evident that we Southern Baptists had something of a multiple personality in this area. LifeWay, the publishing arm of the Southern Baptist Convention, was producing and promoting my books, but LifeWay was also publishing and promoting books by McGee and Blackaby.

McGee certainly valued group work and therapy, but the goal post—as far as I could tell—was simply getting your view of yourself in line with God's view of you. The value of introspective work was ultimately spiritual and theological.

Blackaby's view of healing was even more focused than McGee's on the theological side: Just pray, read and understand the Bible's message better, and get in touch with what God is telling you. And if God isn't enough, the fault lies with you.

Denominational leaders at national and state levels were scheduling events to promote my books, McGee's books, and Henry Blackaby's *Experiencing God*. So, our denomination, not generally known for promoting a plurality of views on topics related to faith and practice, was promoting and selling books that advocated three different approaches to recovery and emotional health. Maybe the leaders at the top weren't paying much attention to these differences, but they were real distinctions.

I respected Robert McGee's success in helping thousands of people through his treatment centers and his writings. I respected the spiritual impact of Henry Blackaby's teaching. But what about the reality that everywhere I went, my message of facing a painful past resonated so strongly? How could I deny the emotional impact—and positive results—of using psychological techniques along with traditional spirituality to deal with healing and recovery?

The people who were touched by what I shared were typically people with decades of prayer, Bible study, and confession of sins under their belts. But they were still suffering, still acting out, still seeking something to ease their pain and improve their lives. They had tried the "God alone will fix it" approach, and it had not worked.

And I was no different. I had found life-changing help at The Meadows, a secular treatment center. But for me, it was never a choice between God and recovery. My message was additive; it was "Turn to God," and also, "Be willing to grow in your understanding of how your past is affecting who you are today so you can make peace with your past and move beyond it." In my view, every person's recovery journey was a little different. And the recovery journey could be a pathway to God. You could get better, and in the process, move closer to God, but you didn't have to start there.

The tension I felt at Kingsland was about more than my emphasis on recovery and emotional healing. Some *Congregation One* members felt I was too intent on reaching unchurched people, and that I wasn't paying enough attention to the long-term members.

How could any follower of Jesus who had read the New Testament think that way? How could we put too much emphasis on reaching unchurched people? Wasn't that essential to our mission as evangelical Christians?

In a sermon in February of 1994, I spoke passionately as I shared my desire to be helping people who are outside the church and alienated from the church find their way back to God. I said, "I am not particularly interested in taking care of people who've known Christ for twenty or thirty or forty years and are still saying, 'Hold my hand and take care of me when I sneeze.'"

Unfortunately, my "sneeze" comment hit a nerve with one of our deacons. He wrote me a letter the next day. He commended the vision I had shared in my sermon and affirmed that we should reach out to the hurting and alienated but wrote that he was troubled by my "relating problems of long-term Christians to a sneeze."

He shared his view that if we were going to be a healing place for hurting people, we needed to show compassion to all segments of our congregation and we could not allow ourselves to decide which pain is worthy and which pain is not. He warned, "Please be cautious in expressing contempt for members of our church. We could dilute the healing theme if everyone is not included."

I responded with a letter of my own. I thanked him for writing to express his feelings and shared my response.

> A deep conviction of my life is that each person's pain matters no matter how insignificant it might seem to someone else. I am deeply sorry that my remarks came across in a way that led you to feel that I regard some people's pain as insignificant. It sounds like I could have done a better job at communicating my position.

> I believe there are people in every church who "sneeze" and want the sneeze to be treated like a mortal wound. The average church is consumed with taking care of itself while a hurting world waits for life-giving words and actions. This was the central struggle Jesus faced with the religious leaders of his day.

> Many organizations in society exist to meet the needs of their own members, but the church is unique in its sacrificial outward focus. As a pastor, I must continue to remind the

church of this important aspect of our identity and of the danger of turning inward.

I wrote that I respected him as a person who cared for others, said I was sorry I had offended him, and made myself available for a visit.

On the following Sunday, I attempted to clarify my position in a sermon titled "How to Measure the Value of a Church." I shared: "The desire of my heart is to be involved in a ministry that is leading people back to God and touching people that are hurting as opposed to focusing just on ourselves." I stressed that we need to take care of one another, that every need in the congregation matters, regardless of how small an issue might seem. Children in our church need us. Teenagers need us. Even if we've been Christians for many years, we still hit bumps in our lives when we need a pat on the back or a hug or a prayer or a word of encouragement. This matters to God, I said, and it should matter to us.

Then I said that every church I had ever served, every church I've ever known anything about, struggles with the issue of whether it will be just one more organization that takes care of its own. Taking care of your own is not unique, I said, then added: "A great church has an outward focus. A great church consists of people who not only know how to take care of themselves, but how to reach out to those who are outside the circle."

Why was it so hard to get some church members to move beyond their own needs? Ironically, the problem was most likely to reveal itself in those who had attended church all their lives.

The tremendous effort required to get a congregation to do what was one of the most important directives from its founder—reaching out and ministering to people outside the church was especially troubling to me.

---

[29] Kay Moore, "Support Group Ministry Fuels Church Growth: An Interview with Tim Sledge," *Growing Churches: Understanding and Applying Strategies for Growth*, January February March 1994, 9.

34 – Balancing Act

Our 1,400-seat sanctuary was packed, mainly with grieving teenagers and their parents, waiting for me to eulogize a beloved middle school teacher. It was an expectant crowd, anxious to hear me speak of this man as a hero, a pillar of the community, a husband and father to whom fate had dealt a tragic blow. But as the officiating pastor for the funeral service, I was aware of a smaller audience in the second row on my left—an adolescent girl who had reported the deceased for sexual abuse—and sitting at her side, her mother.

As if the abuse itself hadn't been despicable enough, in addition to having sex with the girl, the teacher was trying to persuade her to receive Jesus as her savior, to convert her—what Christians call "witnessing."

That wasn't all I was aware of. I now knew that this well-known member of our congregation had not been killed in an accident. He had taken his own life, just before the full weight of accusations—including those from his past— would lower the boom on his world as he knew it.

Despite the dreadful nature of this particular day, as senior pastor of the Kingsland Baptist Church in Houston, Texas, I believed I was exactly where God wanted me to be. We were spreading the gospel, growing by double digits, building innovative ministries, and making a difference in people's lives.

Standing at the center of a tragedy wasn't new to me, and over the years, I had learned that with God's help, I could face whatever was in my path. I was clear on what I needed to do and say: I could not ignore the facts and circumstances surrounding the death of my congregant. Somehow, I had to ease the suffering of those who were mourning, acknowledge the pain of the man's victim, and remain respectful of the truth.

I knew what to say that day, but I could not ignore the dissonance of the reality I faced—a man who was devoted to the teachings of Jesus had been violating a young girl. And this was only the latest addition to a collection of observations I had been accumulating since I began preaching at the age of 16—my collection of *exceptions to the rule of faith*.

* * *

My office window at Kingsland Baptist Church faced northward toward I-10, the major freeway running east and west through Houston. It was late on a Wednesday afternoon in April of 1994. I happened to look up and see helicopters circling over the interstate about a half mile away.

Curious, I decided to take a break to see what was going on. I drove onto the service road near the spot where the choppers were hovering. Police had stopped all inbound traffic. The main west-side entry point to the nation's fourth-largest city was backed up as far as the eye could see.

A body, covered with a sheet, was lying in the middle of the empty expanse of lanes. I parked my car, walked over to the accident scene, and approached a distraught-looking truck driver sitting on the ground beside the shoulder. He told me how the victim had purposely jumped in front of his 18-wheeler, and there was no time to stop. Word among the bystanders: The dead man was a homeless person. He was seen at a nearby intersection just minutes earlier. How tragic, I thought. I offered words of comfort to the truck driver, then returned to my office.

Back at the church, my phone rang. One of our members was missing—a popular teacher and coach. Apparently, his wallet had been found on the body of a homeless man who stepped in front of a truck on I-10. The family suspected that the homeless man had mugged him, and shortly thereafter, wandered onto the expressway where he was killed.

Maybe the missing teacher was lying unconscious somewhere nearby. Since people were beginning to arrive at the church for Wednesday night activities, instead of business as usual, I gathered a group of volunteers and led them to a large vacant lot next to the accident scene. We fanned out across the lot and combed through the weeds, hoping to find the father of three who had not come home.

We searched for 30 minutes or so and found nothing.

Later that evening, I received another call. The body on the freeway had been identified. It was the missing teacher.

Stunned by this news, I immediately went to the teacher's home where a crowd had gathered in the front yard, in neighbors' yards, and on the street. As I was about to enter the house to console the victim's wife, a school official intercepted me.

"There's something I need to tell you before you go in," he said, pulling me aside. He spoke in a hushed tone, glancing around to make sure no one was close enough to hear, and he told me that earlier that afternoon, the teacher had been called to his principal's office. A middle school girl had accused the man of sexually abusing her.

Instantly, the whole chain of events made sense. After meeting with the principal, the teacher drove to the freeway, parked his car, and stepped in front of an 18-wheeler. This wasn't the scenario I expected to process just seconds before walking through the door to speak with his widow.

When I entered the house, it was full of people milling about, speaking in low voices, exchanging looks and words of disbelief, and embracing one another. I was ushered into a room where the dead man's wife was sitting alone. I sat down beside her and encouraged her to talk, not only to find out how she was handling what happened, but to sense how much she really knew.

Still in shock, she was surprisingly composed.

After a few minutes, I told her what I had just learned about her husband. I did my best to be a comforting and supporting presence in those moments, but

I felt that anything I might say or do was insignificant in the face of the family's tragic loss.

The next day, a local counselor contacted me, asking me to meet with someone—a middle school student. I went to the therapist's office, and there, he introduced me to a young girl and her mother. The girl was the teacher's victim. She was 13, maybe 14. I had been called not only to hear her story, but to assure her that this death was not her responsibility.

* * *

Standing at the pulpit, I knew that one of Houston's local TV stations had reported that the dead man was hit by a truck while helping someone change a tire. With only a few exceptions, this was an audience with no knowledge of the truth. Many, maybe most, thought this man was a hero.

I stuck to my well-practiced policy for suicide funerals—this wasn't the first in my three decades of ministry—denying what had happened was not an option. It was vital to acknowledge that something had gone wrong, while still offering solace to grieving friends and family.

I began my message by reading 1 Corinthians 13, the chapter from the New Testament that describes the highest kind of love—a love that is patient and kind, always perseveres, always hopes, and keeps no record of wrongs.

And then I eulogized the deceased, describing him as admired by many, devoted to family and church, and a man who knew how to encourage others. I affirmed his positive influence in the community. I quoted from a letter he had written to one of his players: "Above all, keep things in perspective—work hard and enjoy the game. But always remember there are a lot of things more important—God, family, and friends."

But I also alluded to a darker reality when I said:

> In the last days of his life he was troubled. There was something in his life that was not working out right. Something went wrong on Wednesday afternoon, and we grieve the great loss of that day.
>
> We are troubled because we cannot understand what happened. We are troubled because we cannot change what happened.

I offered a reason for hope for his eternal destiny: "Whatever went wrong in his life, at the deepest level of himself he believed in Jesus Christ."

I stressed that at a time like this, we all needed to look to God for strength. As I continued, I addressed my remarks directly to his widow and their three teenage children.

> Give yourself room to grieve. Grief takes time. Talk about what you feel. Have courage.

You are deeply loved and respected by this community. Each of you is a bright, shining star among us. We love you and support you.

As I think of you, I think of Jacob, the great Old Testament Patriarch. Remember when Jacob wrestled with an angel of God through the night. And when morning came Jacob had a limp. For the rest of his life, that night of wrestling with God was marked by a limp. But even with a limp, Jacob was stronger than he had ever been before.

This event will leave a scar. If you so choose, it can be a scar that is a mark of courage and victory over grief.

I closed with a reading of Psalm 23, "The Lord is my shepherd..." I read its assurance of God's presence: "Even though I walk through the valley of the shadow of death, I will fear no evil, for you are with me." And I read its words of faith and hope: "I will dwell in the house of the Lord forever."

The following week, two women who had attended the service but were not members of my church, wrote to me, raking me over the coals for the content of my message. The first took me to task for implying that suicide was the cause of death. The other woman wrote that she was saddened by the lack of comfort provided by my message and the lack of love in my words. She added, "No guide was given; no hope was provided. I pray for your congregation and for you. So many good things remained unsaid about this man. So many good things remained unsaid about our Lord and Savior. A missed opportunity!"

Given their lack of information, I could see where they were coming from. But the teacher's suicide was a fact, not a possibility. I had also learned, after his death, that a similar accusation had been lodged at the school where he taught in another state, just before the family moved to Texas. So how else could I walk this tightrope knowing what I knew? How else could I honor the audience of two in the second row and relieve their suffering, except by acknowledging the abuser's troubled soul? Hadn't I still offered comfort to family and friends in what I said? Didn't God want us—me—to deal in truth?

Following the funeral, the mother of the abused girl wrote thanking me for supporting her daughter: "Every word you said to her was helpful in bringing her self-esteem back. She said that the main reason she'd asked me to call you was to alert someone who cared to potential difficulties the other girls may have. I know, though, that she also wanted to hear from you that you did not think poorly of her. Thank you so very much for giving my daughter some peace of mind."

A year later, on my tenth anniversary as pastor of Kingsland Baptist, the teacher's widow wrote to thank me for my "patience, concern, and support," and for being there for her family during that terrible time.

Ironically, two months before his death, the deceased had sent me a letter containing the results of a survey on teenage drug and alcohol abuse. He asked me to forward the information to other ministers in the area and wrote, "We are in deep trouble in our suburban, middle-to-upper class neighborhood and we desperately need to address this and other issues."

Yet he never took advantage of options in his own church that might have helped him. While he mentioned to a friend that he was thinking about attending our men's support group, never had he shown up at this or any other meeting in our support group ministry. Never had he asked to speak to me in confidence. Never did he mention or display behavior indicating that he might be suffering from demons of his own. Except, of course, to his victims.

Tragically, those who were convinced that prayer and Bible study alone could cure anything—were wrong. Sometimes, people need psychological help as well.

35 – Triple Threat

In April of 1994, our community was reeling from the death of a much loved teacher and coach. In his funeral service, I had not been able to laud his character to the extent that his admirers desired, and my sermon had drawn some criticism, but I had done what I knew to be right.

In the weeks following his death, there were still many who could not accept what had actually happened—he had taken his own life after being confronted with accusations of sexual abuse by one of his students.

Despite this tragedy, our congregation as a whole was alive, well, and continuing to grow. But we were once again running out of space—for worship, for Bible Study, and for parking. An immediate fix for the worship space issue was discontinuing the poorly attended Saturday evening service and changing our Sunday morning schedule back to two worship services instead of one. Addressing the need for more Bible Study space and parking would require architects and construction companies.

In May, the church voted on two building expansion proposals. The first was a quick, but temporary fix—converting our original worship facility into classroom space and building 100 new parking spaces. This plan was approved by the congregation with a 98% vote.

The second proposal was called "The Family Room Project." This vote authorized hiring an architectural firm to develop initial plans for a major building addition—16,000-square-feet—to include adult and youth Bible Study classes, a large room for youth meetings, a new fellowship hall, a new kitchen, and a new prayer room for our 24/7 prayer ministry. The congregation approved The Family Room Project proposal with a 94% vote.

That summer, keeping my *Congregation One* audience in mind, I preached a worship-oriented sermon series that emphasized the importance of praising God. A senior adult wrote me a note commenting on the series, "I just want you to know how much I have enjoyed your praise services. That first one was probably the most uplifting service I've ever attended." My response: Mission accomplished!

As our revised worship schedule started with the new school year in August, I began preaching a 10-week series: *A Call to Character*. The first sermon in the series was "How to Start Building Your Character." The sermons that followed focused on love, honesty, sexual purity, wholesome speech, anger, envy, patience, humility, and going the extra mile.

The day after the first sermon in the series, I received an encouraging note from another senior adult, and it was about more than the sermon series:

How many lives have you touched in your years as pastor of

Kingsland Baptist Church and how many times do we say thank you? I have been a Christian all my life, but I must tell you that my spiritual life has soared to new heights and still climbing since the day I walked into the welcome center. Our church is a feel-good place. Thank you. The staff that surrounds you is kind, thoughtful and loving. Thank you. Your energy is contagious. Thank you.

Despite the positive feedback, our continuing growth, our building plans, and my sense of optimism about how things were going, we were entering a danger zone. It was the calm before the storm, a quiet period before battle rages, and I was about to be under attack—three attacks that would significantly impact the future of my ministry.

* * *

An international, inter-denominational women's Bible study called Bible Study Fellowship, or BSF for short, had met in Kingsland's building for more than 10 years. Their mission promoted global, in-depth Bible classes in order to produce a passionate commitment to Christ, to the Bible, and to the Church. [30] A key component of the organization's identity was their conservative view of the Bible: "We believe that the 66 books of Holy Scripture as originally given are in their entirety the Word of God verbally inspired and wholly without error in all that they declare, and, therefore, are the supreme and final authority of faith and life."[31]

Many of the women of Kingsland Baptist Church—along with a large group of women not from our church—attended the weekly BSF study, with each week's lesson presented in our sanctuary by a master teacher who, along with BSF teachers around the world, received guidance on the current lesson via a weekly audio tape prepared by BSF's director.

After the large group session, participants organized into small groups to discuss the lesson they had just heard. Some of the ladies who led the small discussion groups were members of Kingsland.

Prior to the fall of 1994, I had never heard one negative comment about BSF. The organization was theologically conservative and espoused the same high view of the Bible held by Kingsland—and by me. But that September, statements by the national BSF leader on the weekly training tape created a firestorm of controversy by raising a nuanced moral question to do with lying.

The BSF leader referenced an Old Testament event from the book of Exodus that took place when the Hebrews were enslaved in Egypt. Concerned that this segment of the population was growing too large, the Egyptian Pharaoh ordered Hebrew midwives to kill any male Hebrew baby as soon as he was born. The Hebrew midwives who lied to Pharaoh to save the lives of the Hebrew boy babies were blessed by God.

On her weekly tape, the national BSF leader applied this biblical event to circumstances such as war or being in some other situation where there is imminent danger of physical violence. An obvious example—those in Nazi Germany who sheltered Jews and lied to protect their lives.

The national BSF leader suggested that lying in such a case would not be a sin, and she took 15 minutes to explain her position, clarifying that the Bible only applies this exception in extreme scenarios. Her point: Sometimes one law of God is superseded by a higher law of God—for example, lying to save a human life.

Some of the BSF participants were upset by her remarks.

Responding to the controversy that was brewing following the lesson, the BSF director wrote a letter to all BSF teachers stressing that one of her goals in the lesson was to challenge class members to think on their own. She reiterated her belief that the Bible contains the answers for all of life's issues, but finding those answers requires "prayer, knowledge of Scripture, wisdom, discernment and just plain hard thinking using the brains which God has given." In closing, she admitted that some of the wording used in the lesson may not have been the best, affirmed that she was not an advocate of lying, and reaffirmed her original position that sometimes one law of God takes precedence over another.

Some of the ladies from Kingsland who attended BSF weren't satisfied with this response and believed BSF was "teaching people to lie." Several women from Kingsland resigned their BSF positions, and some wanted Kingsland to stop hosting their meetings.

After morning worship one Sunday in October, I had a hallway conversation with two of the women who seemed most upset about the continuing controversy. They assumed I would agree with their position, but my stance was the same as that of the BSF director. There could indeed be some rare situations—so rare that they were unlikely to be experienced by most of us—when lying to avert imminent harm to others or oneself would not be sinful.

The two women with whom I was talking were stating their convictions with an attitude of complete certainty. Unfortunately, I slipped into theological debate mode with them—definitely a mistake. At the time, I thought I was just being persuasive. But to them, I was not responding with an appropriate level of consideration and gentleness. The next day, I apologized to both women for being too forceful in my response. Case closed, I thought.

Returning from a speaking engagement a few days later, I learned that Nelson, our associate pastor, was taking a critical position toward BSF, and Ellen, our director of communications, was siding with him—and with the women who thought that BSF was condoning lying.

Ellen went so far as to drop me a note of disapproval, writing: "We don't need any more rationalizations and excuses for explaining away our actions (sins) than we already get from the world. For it to come from a teacher of God's word is sad."

One of the two women wrote me as well, sending a copy of her letter to our deacons. She wrote, "I am deeply disturbed and upset about what I am hearing you say you believe to be the truth concerning the lying issue." She then quoted 17 different Bible verses to prove that lying was never okay.

Not only did this feel like a silly disagreement, but ironically, I was facing a small group spreading lies about lying—specifically, that I was condoning lying. Equally ironic—I was currently preaching a sermon series on character. The third sermon in the series had been "Honesty," and was a direct and forceful call to telling the truth. Nowhere in my sermon had I said anything about exceptions.

Whatever my personal flaws and failures at that point in my life, lying was not one of them. So, what was really going on? Were there some in my congregation looking for evidence—even grossly exaggerated or fabricated—to justify accusations from across town that I was a liberal?

Several families left Kingsland over the BSF controversy. The woman who authored the letter protesting BSF's position moved her membership to Second Baptist Church, and that was one more source of irony. Second Baptist hosted an even larger weekly BSF meeting.

* * *

The roots of the second controversy were three years old, involving the father of one of the boys on my son's football team. I met Stan at a game. As we became acquainted, I learned that he was the number two leader of a large Mormon congregation in the Houston area, but he had grown up in a Southern Baptist church that was anything but typical. His home church had gained notoriety across the Southern Baptist Convention when its pastor experienced a dramatic personal change that resulted in his leading the church to emphasize faith healing, speaking in unknown tongues, and being baptized in, filled with, and guided by the Holy Spirit.

Stan never bought into his church's hyper-spiritual approach. Once on his own in college, he became an atheist, and then a Mormon.

On the sidelines of our sons' football games, he questioned some of the beliefs of the Mormon congregation he was helping to lead, and over time, discussing our beliefs, Stan concluded that he had never made a valid commitment of his life to Jesus—not while growing up as a Baptist nor at any time in the Mormon Church. In my office, he prayed to invite Jesus into his life—this time, for real. I baptized my new friend and convert in the name of the Father, the Son, and the Holy Spirit.

Surprisingly, after being active in our church for about a year, Stan left Kingsland to attend another Baptist church, offering no explanation. A year later, he resurfaced, told me he wasn't happy with the other church, and resumed attending services at Kingsland.

His abrupt departure, short stay at the other church, and quick discontent were warning signs I didn't note at the time but would later see as indicators of unpredictability and antagonism.

Not long after Stan's return to Kingsland, he made a public decision during the invitation at the end of a worship service. He felt called to the ministry. Stan was bright, successful, brimming with enthusiasm, and seemed open to my guidance in forging a new direction for his life. I was convinced he was sincere and following God's lead.

In time, I put him in charge of a team tasked with studying ways we could improve our outreach program. He enlisted volunteers to participate in this effort, met with them for a couple of months, and then presented to me and a staff member at the end of the summer. Although his presentation contained a few good ideas, what stood out was a lack of awareness of—or perhaps an unwillingness to acknowledge—the carefully conceived outreach strategy our church had been successfully implementing and refining for years.

I didn't expect his group to rubber stamp our current course, but I expected him to do his homework.

After hearing Stan's presentation, I knew it wasn't ready for prime time. But there was something else that troubled me. There was an arrogance in his approach, as if none of us knew what we were doing. And, he seemed eager to move into a position of influence—or control.

I had high hopes for Stan and had trusted the sincerity of his prayer of commitment to Jesus. I would ultimately come to understand that this ambitious convert's behavior was about being right, winning, and being in charge. But at the time, it was hard to put my finger on the core issue, and I wasn't ready to give up on him, that is... until I learned that he was criticizing me to the members of his team—and had fabricated a story that our church had a $2 million secret debt. We had no secret debt.

Then I heard that one of his team members was telling people that I did not believe in prayer. I haven't a clue where that came from.

Within a few months, almost all his team members had left the church, but not before spreading their false claims to others—repeating the rumors that apparently originated with Stan.

What had so twisted Stan's thinking—and specifically, his opinion of me? And why would he corrupt the opinions of the people on his team? Had I discouraged him by not immediately and eagerly accepting all his recommendations, or was all this about having been the number two leader in the Mormon congregation instead of number one? Was his real aim to take over somewhere, anywhere? And what did I really know about his previous experiences? Everything I knew about his story—I had learned from him.

Stan eventually stopped attending Kingsland and faded off the scene, though I received reports that he continued bad-mouthing me to people in our congregation.

I had made a significant mistake in judgment—not that making a mistake was a one-time event for me—but when I was present at anyone's embrace of Jesus, I assumed the best. In this case, I turned away from warning signs, expected a positive change, and allowed this man to manipulate me and members of our church.

I came to realize that Stan was an antagonist. In his book, *Antagonists in the Church*, Kenneth Haugk defines antagonists as "individuals who, on the basis of non-substantive evidence, go out of their way to make insatiable demands, usually attacking the person or performance of others. These attacks are selfish in nature, tearing down rather than building up, and are frequently directed against those in a leadership capacity." Haugk writes that antagonists "tend to attract followers. It is the assistance of these followers that accounts in part for the escalation of antagonistic conflict in congregations."[32] Haugk explains that antagonists know how to make their followers feel important, and that part of the attraction to their followers is the fact that truth is often less exciting than half-truths, and bad news is more exciting than good news.[33]

Stan displayed all the signs of an antagonist as defined by Haugk. I had to admit that I could be an easy mark for someone who was convincing in his or her newfound devotion to following the leadership of Jesus.

* * *

As we worked toward funding The Family Room Project, we set up fellowship meetings in the homes of 29 church families over a two-week period in October. We encouraged every member of our church to attend one of the meetings. Each of the home meetings had a lay leader who had been trained to facilitate. The program included watching a video in which I explained why we needed more building space, challenging church members to consider a commitment to regular donations over a three-year period. After the video, the leader led the group in a question and answer session.

These meetings were informational. No one was asked to fill out a pledge card or make a commitment of any kind then and there—only to think and pray about making a giving commitment in the coming weeks.

Of the 29 home fellowships, all but two went smoothly, and in those two, a handful of participants took a hostile approach to the lay person leading the meeting. Their position—that we shouldn't be trying to raise money for building expansion. Also in the air in one instance—Stan's misinformation about a so-called secret $2 million debt.

The church was indeed carrying $2 million in debt at the time, but there was nothing secret about it. Our congregation discussed and voted approval on any debt we acquired. Our debt was within limits recognized by church growth professionals and within our bank's lending guidelines. And, if the church hadn't borrowed money to supplement donations for our earlier building expansions, our physical space could never have kept up with our growth, or to put it another way—our growth would have stopped.

It was part of my job to be aware of member giving records; I knew that one of the individuals kicking up a ruckus in one of the fellowship meetings— a young man—had given almost nothing to our church over a period of years.

He wasn't alone. While there are reasons that some members don't contribute financially—their circumstances simply don't allow it—a surprising number of active church members who could give, actually donate little or nothing. In fact, I have never looked at the giving records of any church I led without being taken aback. For one thing, it is often the quiet, unassuming congregants who have little to give who donate generously, and without a hint of pride or haughtiness. And yet there are people of means who strut about at church but give little or much less than others would assume.

This irony is something you live with as a pastor, and something you work to improve by sharing the Bible's teaching about giving—with the whole congregation—on a regular basis.

As we began The Family Room Project, our records indicated that 38% of our families gave 90% of the contributions we received. Far more than 38% of our members had sufficient means to give and were participating in the activities of our church while contributing little financially. Kingsland wasn't unique in this regard.

Not giving is one thing, but a non-giver trying to dissuade others from giving struck me as unacceptable and hypocritical. It made no sense to argue how "God wouldn't want us to raise this money," if one gave no evidence of ever being willing to give himself. And, since no one knew who gave what, as far as the home fellowship attendees knew, this detractor might well be a sacrificial giver.

I knew how to motivate people to give, and it wasn't by confronting them— privately or publicly—with the knowledge of how much they gave. That was something I would never do.

But I did confront this young man privately because he was urging others not to give. Working to keep my tone measured and my exasperation under control, I asked him how he dared tell other church members not to step out in faith to contribute to our building effort when he didn't have enough faith to give at all.

He was offended by the confrontation, but rather than talking it through with me or quietly letting the matter drop, he told others about my talk with him, and turned his private giving into a public issue.

The next thing I knew, the word among a group of church members was that I was talking publicly about confidential giving records.

When I got wind of this, I was indignant. Not only would I never talk in public about confidential matters, including private giving records, but this jab at my integrity—a third affront over a short period of time—was utterly without merit. I did not share private giving records. I did not think it was acceptable to lie. And I had not somehow led the church to incur a secret $2 million debt.

* * *

Unfortunately, at this point in my ministry, an already disgruntled group, albeit small, apparently believed all three accusations, adding more weight to the stresses I felt in leading the congregation, and sowing seeds of doubt among some of the members.

---

[30] "Our Mission and Values," Bible Study Fellowship, https://www.bsfinternational.org/about/mission-values, 2017.

[31] "Our Statement of Faith," Bible Study Fellowship, https://www.bsfinternational.org/about/statement-of-faith, 2017.

[32] Kenneth C. Haugk, *Antagonists in the Church: How to Identify and Deal with Destructive Conflict* (Minneapolis: Augsburg Publishing House, 1988), 21-22, 38.

[33] Kenneth C. Haugk, *Antagonists in the Church*, 38-39.

36 – Acute Deaconitis

The deacons convened a Sunday afternoon meeting focused on the Bible Study Fellowship controversy about lying. After spending five hours discussing the issue, they ultimately concluded that the BSF group could continue to meet at our church.

I was annoyed at the deacons' involvement in this trumped-up dispute—they were not a governing body according to our church constitution, so this wasn't their decision to make.

A month earlier, Jason, one of the deacons and a senior adult, had written a letter to the chairman of deacons, addressing the body's role at Kingsland. He was concerned that our deacons had no role in governing the business affairs of the church. And one of the reasons he thought moving in that direction would be a good idea was: "If the deacons were permitted to take a direct and meaningful part in managing the church's business, it is my belief that they would gain a higher level of self-esteem." He closed his letter to the deacon chairman with words of support: "I just want to mention that I have been praying for you—that your handling of this somewhat delicate matter, relating to the roles the deacons will be performing in the near and extended future, will be resolved without undue stress on you and without causing discord within the diaconate."

Self-esteem? Your handling of this somewhat delicate matter?

But the deacon who had written the letter was not alone in his views. A regressive, traditionalist tsunami was rolling in, and I had either ignored or discounted the warning signs. Clearly, a sea change was in progress.

In addition, during the same meeting, some of the deacons raised the issue of my confrontation with the man who had tried to dissuade others from giving to The Family Room Project. Apparently, Stan's words and actions had generated some concerns and bad feelings in the group as well.

Not only did the discussion on these issues involve misrepresentations and blatant untruths, I was dealing with my own incredulity at finding myself in this position. However, one subject under discussion—families leaving the church—was a valid and critical concern that needed to be discussed, and one that was arguably within the realm of the deacons' responsibility.

I may not have had full access to my best self for that meeting—or in just about anything I was doing in those days. Although I was only vaguely conscious of it at the time, I was increasingly operating in burnout mode. I had been moving at warp speed for the better part of a decade.

In the previous 36 months, I had written three books on emotional healing and addiction issues along with three corresponding facilitator guides. I had spoken about support groups and recovery to 24 national meetings, 6 statewide meetings, and 12 regional meetings for my denomination. I had traveled to 26 cities in more than a dozen states. My efforts, amplified by my publisher's effective advertising, had been productive. More than 70,000 copies of my books had been sold, and based on the sales of my facilitator guides, as many as 8,000 Making Peace Groups had been conducted across the U.S.

At Kingsland, I could quantify our successes over the same 3-year period. Worship attendance was up by more than 30%, as was budget giving. We had recently paid cash for 4.7 additional acres of property and initiated fundraising for a 16,000-square-foot educational building.

In this same time frame, my personal and family life had been peppered by life events that invariably create stress. Linda's father had died, and shortly thereafter, her mother had a stroke. Adopted as an infant, Linda was dealing with the experience of finding and meeting members of her birth family. As her husband, I was doing my best to be supportive of her through all of this.

Naturally, the teenage suicides, the disclosure of sexual abuse by a congregant who then committed suicide, and the accountant embezzler who was a former member of our church were also profoundly disturbing.

No wonder I was worn down. My life for the preceding three years had been meaningful and exciting, but it had also been demanding and draining.

At a time when I was accomplishing more than ever in my ministry, at a time when I was holding fast to my conservative theological beliefs, at a time when I felt I was working hard to be obedient to God, I had been unaware that a small, largely furtive group of congregants had a very different view of me than the view I had of myself and the view held by the majority of the congregation.

Now, as a direct result of the recent incidents that had led to the Sunday deacons meeting, some of these detractors were questioning my integrity and with it, my effectiveness as a pastor. I felt under attack, discouraged, and emotionally exhausted.

I thought about the deacons—how conservative they were—a reflection of the stringent requirements for deaconship that we enforced at Kingsland. Ironically, our refusal to allow divorced men or men who consumed alcohol to serve as deacons was a more conservative approach than that of Second Baptist Church, whose pastor had been elected president of the Southern Baptist Convention as part of the fundamentalist takeover and imposed neither of these restrictions on their deacons.

I also thought about the fact that in six years of running a highly successful, nationally recognized support group ministry, not one of the deacons in that Sunday meeting had ever participated. Ironically, in the previous year, the Southern Baptist periodical, *The Deacon*, had published an article titled "Road to Recovery"[34] that highlighted Kingsland's support group ministry. I'm not sure any of our deacons had read the article. Kingsland's deacons, now in a pivotal position of influence in our congregation, were largely ignorant of a ministry in their own church that was a model for congregations across the country—a model that could have brought a more balanced mindset to addressing issues like the ones we were facing in the meeting.

Whatever the official role of our deacons and whatever my feelings about their lack of understanding of one of our key ministries, I had to do everything I could to set things right. A positive relationship with the deacons was imperative, and I could not ignore their concerns.

As the Sunday meeting wore on, I asked the deacons to help me deal with the issues that were under discussion. I requested a Pastor's Support and Accountability Group—four deacons who would meet with me on a regular basis to talk about anything that needed to be addressed. The deacons in this new Pastor's Support and Accountability Group (PSAG) would be my trusted confidants and I would be theirs. I would be honest with them about what was going on with me, and I would be accountable to them. As in any support group, I expected this behavior to be reciprocal. I was sure that with more time together and regular communication, this smaller group could help bridge the gap between the deacon body's impressions and the reality of what we were achieving. I hoped this would lead to a broader, more accurate view of the issues our church was facing.

Staying accountable was part of my recovery and emotional healing mindset, and, my request came out of a desire to practice openness, honesty, and transparency in all areas of my life. I also saw it as an effective process that would work as each of us in the new PSAG shared from our personal experiences the way members of other support groups did every week in our church. In addition, I believed we were all invested in a common positive outcome, and that we would be able to address any contentious issue our church might face.

Four deacons were selected for the group: Pat, Stuart, Adam, and Gilbert. Pat was the chairman of deacons. Stuart was the vice chairman of deacons and the chairman of the personnel committee. Adam, an attorney, was someone I had first met nearly 30 years earlier when his brother and I led a summer youth revival together in Houston. Gilbert, also an attorney, was a person I regarded as an even-tempered, fair-minded individual. I had a good feeling about this process, and I was pleased to be working with all these men.

In December, I had my first meeting with the PSAG. It was quickly apparent that Pat, Stuart, Adam, and Gilbert saw their primary role as this: critiquing my leadership. The issues discussed in the Sunday meeting were approached as my failures, period.

It was also apparent that the process taking place in the group would be nothing like what I anticipated, since I would be the only one openly sharing his challenges. This was about my accountability to the larger deacon body, through this smaller group.

The focus on my accountability was driven home by a written communication that listed and described the issues they expected me to work on. The document began by reflecting on my 10 years at Kingsland: "God has accomplished many great things through his people at Kingsland, and he has used you and your talents to provide much of the leadership." The words that followed acknowledged that I had helped individuals in the church to experience spiritual growth. Then, the tone shifted. "At some point in any relationship the participants grow and change. A reassessment of the relationship and the roles of the participants in the relationship needs to occur. The deacons, based upon conversations with many church members, feel that there are several areas of concern that need to be discussed."

Specifically, I was directed to work on the following issues:

- Cease treating church growth as the only significant indicator of success and place greater emphasis on never losing even one church member.
- Do not intimidate anyone in the church.
- Exercise greater care, along with the rest of the ministerial staff, to keep conversations with church members confidential.
- Stop referencing members' giving records for anything other than general study regarding giving patterns.
- Engage in more consensus building when leading the church in its decision-making process.
- Spend less time away on speaking engagements.

The document ended with the following paragraph. "The Bible says that it is not good for a man to be alone. We commit ourselves to be available to alleviate that feeling of aloneness, and we share that commitment with our fellow deacons. As we look to the future, we would like for you to share with the deacons the vision you believe God is giving you now for Kingsland."

The last sentence in their document was a way of demanding proof that I had a vision for leading the church into the future; I needed to verify that God was speaking to me about where the church should be headed. And if I didn't do so, that could be reason to think that I had lost my primary qualification for leading Kingsland—the call of God to lead there.

Reviewing this document in the first meeting, I doubt I could hide the intensity of my feelings. I was shocked. I felt cornered. I was furious. Worse, I felt duped. How could I have been so unwise as to ask that this group be formed?

I felt shamelessly betrayed. The focus of this group was obviously to pressure me to act in a manner that a handful of disgruntled *Congregation One* members wanted.

One of the most disturbing remarks was found in the opening statement of the deacons' document: "Based upon conversations with many church members..." Many church members? What did that mean? What number constituted "many?" I was never able to get a head count of those they had talked to but given the church's continued growth—and virtually every other indicator I could see—the ranks of the disgruntled had to be small.

After taking some time to cool down and thoughtfully consider the positions expressed in the document, I decided to view working with the PSAG as an opportunity for personal growth. I would meet with the group in February to share my written response to their requests.

---

[34] "The Road to Recovery," *The Deacon*, April May June 1993.

37 – Under Scrutiny

As 1995 began, it was hard not to feel that my back was against a wall. I was defending the biblical foundations of my sermons, preparing a response to criticisms from the Pastor's Support and Accountability Group, and getting ready for my annual performance review with the personnel committee. I was making a genuine effort to be accountable while not accepting criticisms I did not believe to be accurate or meaningful.

A small group of people in my church complained that my sermons were not always biblical. Since the Bible—in the theologically conservative view—is the inspired, inerrant word from God, a sermon had to be based on the Bible. Otherwise, it wouldn't ring with the authority of God. From my perspective, in 36 years of ministry I had never preached a sermon that wasn't biblical.

My seminary training had taught me at least four ways to preach a biblical sermon, and I always followed that training. An expository sermon is one in which the main points and the first point under each main point are sourced directly from the biblical text. A textual sermon is one in which the main points come from the biblical text, but the minor points under the main points come from the topic of the sermon or some other source. A homily is a free-form sermon presented as verse-by-verse comments on the biblical text without a structure of main points. A topical sermon addresses a specific topic without reference to a primary sermon text. The topical sermon is based on biblical truths, but the connection to the biblical sources may not be as obvious as in the other sermon types.[35]

Regardless of type, a biblical sermon always had three elements: explaining the original meaning of biblical concepts, discussing how the ancient truths applied to modern life, and illustrating with one or more stories, personal experiences, or current events in a way that would capture the listener's attention and drive home the truth that was being shared.

Virtually none of the laypersons in my congregation knew the four types of biblical sermons nor the three elements of a biblical sermon, and there was no reason they should. But all the members of *Congregation One* were certain they knew a biblical sermon—or an un-biblical one—when they heard it. Unfortunately, their view of what made a sermon biblical was narrower than the guidelines I learned in seminary—my very conservative seminary at that. With the *Congregation One* group, a sermon had to be expository, or better still, a homily, or it wasn't biblical.

When the biblical text was read at the beginning of the sermon and was referred to constantly throughout, this group felt reassured and more relaxed about the content they were hearing. And they enjoyed it when I encouraged listeners to keep their Bibles open throughout the sermon and were happiest when I was holding my open Bible in my hand as I spoke.

Congregation One also liked a considerable amount of explanation of the biblical text. They weren't so high on the application part of a sermon, especially if the application felt threatening in some way that had a new twist to it or was simply something they didn't want to think about. In fact, with this group, the more predictable the content of my sermons, the better. And this sermon-critical group seemed to be most interested in "spiritual" topics like the crucifixion, the resurrection, sin, prayer, and prophecy.

Attempting to do a better job of staying connected with this segment of my congregation, in January of 1995, I began a 4-week sermon series on the second coming of Jesus. My topics were: "Signs of the Return of Christ," "How Many Times Will Jesus Come Back," "The Resurrection of Christians," and "The Punishment of Non-Believers."

This wasn't a game to me. It wasn't political maneuvering or seeking to curry favor among a handful of influential people. As I preached on these topics, I wasn't just acting like I believed what I was saying—I was genuinely sharing my deepest convictions.

Blake, the former chairman of deacons who had resigned from all his positions several years earlier had gradually moved back into an active role in the congregation by this time and wrote me a letter thanking me at the conclusion of the sermon series: "The entire series has been such a blessing to me—especially the past two Sundays. Never have I heard you preach with more conviction and authority as you did on Sunday past. The word we have received through you over these past weeks is clearly authentic, and last Sunday's message rings true at every measure."

Home run for all the *Congregation One* members? Not quite—some members of the congregation were displeased with my exact view on the second coming of Jesus because I didn't hold to the position espoused by an apparent majority of the most conservative evangelicals—premillennialism.

In Christian theology, there are three schools of thought on the second coming of Jesus and the end of history. Not only do they have names that are a mouthful—premillennial, postmillennial, and amillennial—but these schools of thought largely derive from the most complex, conceptually disputed, and final book in the Bible—Revelation.

In my second sermon, "How Many Times Will Jesus Come Back," I explained all three positions, then advocated the amillennial position. The amillennial position holds that when Jesus returns to the earth, history will end, and eternity will begin—there will be no literal 1,000-year reign of Jesus on the earth—a very simple understanding of the second coming of Jesus. I held this position because, in my view, the biblical evidence was greatest for it.

The postmillennial position posits that we are currently in the millennial reign of Jesus on the earth, a view that became hard to sustain with the two world wars at the beginning of the 20th century. I've never met a postmillennialist.

Too complex to explain in detail here, the premillennial position is the one advocated by the late Billy Graham and by writers like the late Tim LaHaye, author of the *Left Behind* series popularized in books and movies. Premillennialism holds that Christians will be snatched up to be with God—the rapture—while everyone else remains on the earth. Bad things will happen on the earth, then Jesus will return again—a second 2nd coming—to begin a 1,000-year rule. At the end of the 1,000-year rule, a great battle will take place in which Jesus will defeat Satan, then eternity will begin. If this seems confusing, you can relax, because it is confusing, even when you've studied it extensively.

I wanted to—tried to—become a premillennialist when I was at Wheaton College. But somehow, the confusing and theologically inconsistent chain of events described therein seemed to short out my brain's circuitry. Regardless of the theological inconsistencies in the position, some in my audience at Kingsland regarded the premillennial position as the only option for true believers of the Bible.

My sermon series garnered criticism from both right and left. The far right didn't like it because it wasn't a premillennial approach. And, on the other end of the spectrum, an anonymous letter from someone who identified himself only as a "concerned white, protestant Christian" took me to task over the fourth sermon before I delivered it. He had seen the title, "The Punishment of Non-Believers," posted on the sign in front of the church and wrote:

> The theme of your next sermon, posted outside the church, which inevitably I read on my way to work—appalls me! Christ is going to "punish" the "non-believers"???
>
> It is obvious and publicly stated that Christ, in your view, is coming to punish those who do not believe—Jews, Hindus, Muslims, Atheists and probably Roman Catholics, Presbyterians, Episcopalians, and others as well—in summary, all but premillennialist, backward, legalistic, Southern Baptists like yourself and your right-wing, culturally-deficient and psychologically-needy congregation. Heeeew haaaaw to that, partner.
>
> Christ is love! But it is easier to control the congregation with threats, is it not, doctor? In summary, the billboard is offensive to Christians and non-Christians alike. Take it off now! Your flock will be there on Sunday, anyway. Spare the rest of us.

I was glad for his reminder that Christ is love.

Despite these criticisms, my sermons on the second coming did connect with most of my audience—in both *Congregation One* and *Congregation Two*.

Not quite the home run I hoped for, but it was close.

* * *

Bible-based sermons on the second coming or not, my day of reckoning with the PSAG was near. On February 2, 1995, I had my next meeting with them. I arrived with a carefully prepared 7-page document in response to their list of things I needed to work on. I attempted to take responsibility for areas where criticism seemed valid. On other points, I used my written responses to challenge and clarify issues they had raised and to communicate what I needed from them as a group. Pat, Stuart, Adam, and Gilbert knew me well enough not to be surprised that I brought challenges back to them.

- *Church Growth as the Only Significant Indicator of Success*: I wrote that I never felt and did not feel that church growth was the only measure of a pastor's ministry. I committed to being more sensitive to how the church family as a whole was getting along.
- *Do Not Intimidate Anyone in the Church*: I acknowledged that I sometimes responded with too much intensity and committed to being extra careful about communicating with a listening and caring attitude.
- *Maintain Confidentiality*: I asserted that I never violated confidentiality in conversations clearly defined as personal. In fact, I regarded my ability to maintain confidentiality as a strength. However, I committed to going the extra mile in being sensitive to this issue.
- *Limit References to Giving Records*: I affirmed that I always maintained the confidentiality of giving records, and this was not an issue that I needed to work on. However, if I saw someone who I knew did not give to the church trying to influence other church members to withhold financial support, I would still confront that individual privately. I conceded that while I had strong ethical grounds for confronting the man who disrupted the home fellowship meeting, in retrospect, he may have simply needed a listening ear and some loving acceptance.
- *More Consensus Building*: I committed to working harder on consensus building. I told the group it was important for them to understand that as the church grew, more people were likely to disagree with any decision that was made.
- *Spend Less Time Away*: I clarified that during the almost 10 years I had served at Kingsland, I had never used more time away than that allotted in the guidelines established by the church's personnel policy. However, I recognized that the church was now in a period when I needed to be away less frequently.

I realized I needed to be more patient with people whose needs were neither urgent nor intense. It was important that everyone in the church feel I cared about them and their needs. And given the current situation, I did need to spend fewer days out of town. This was useful feedback, I told myself. At the same time, I couldn't help feeling that some of the recommendations I was getting were pushing me in the wrong direction.

For more than a decade, I had been reading every book I could find and attending every conference I could get to on how to grow a church and how to best lead a large church. Competent researchers and consultants had created an accepted body of knowledge on growth and management principles for large churches.

What the accountability group was emphasizing was quite literally impossible—to be accessible to anyone who wanted my attention, to spend one-to-one time with every leader, to secure 100% agreement on all issues, to avoid confronting someone who was impeding the growth of the church because of their personal issues, and to focus on every disgruntled member.

Moreover, these directives ran counter to recognized principles for leading a growing church, especially as the church exceeded a certain size threshold—a threshold we had already passed. One church leadership article that appeared the following year echoed my understanding of the inevitable departure of some church members: "Some folks need to leave. The people who resist all change will stand in the way of what God might be doing. Some are never going to be happy unless they are in power."[36]

Our church was experiencing growing pains, and the solution proposed by the deacon group was diametrically opposed to prevailing church growth wisdom—and common sense. They expected me to act like I was leading a small church. In my written responses to the group, I attempted to spell out these issues and reminded the group that the biblical guideline for resolving differences between two people is for the offended person to attempt to talk to the offender one-to-one—as in talk directly to me if you have a problem with me—and to involve other people only if I am not responsive. And I noted that the deacons had a responsibility to guard the pastor against frivolous complaints and criticism by those seeking divisiveness, not reconciliation.

After discussions, both the PSAG members and I felt we were making progress. In the months that followed, I began to trust the group more, and gradually moved to a place of openly sharing with them whenever we met.

* * *

The same month that I met with the PSAG, I had my annual performance review with the personnel committee, chaired by Stuart, one of the members of the PSAG. And my performance rating of 86 out of a possible 100—the lowest rating I had ever received—but it still placed me in the "Commendable" category, one level *above* "Exceeds Requirements." I received my ninth annual pay raise since coming to Kingsland, but the performance review was also a warning sign—a flashing caution light.

As usual, as part of the process, I shared my professional goals for the upcoming year. I also talked about what I needed: more professional staff and a sabbatical, for which I qualified under personnel policy guidelines. The committee's response to my two requests was noncommittal. I'm not sure they even responded at all.

My interactions with both the PSAG and the personnel committee seemed surreal; the universe I inhabited daily was filled with consistent, ongoing positive feedback from the caring Christian people in my church.

At least 90% of the congregation had no idea of the scrutiny I was under. Sunday by Sunday, they saw a dynamic congregation participating in uplifting worship and being moved by an inspirational sermon. On a regular basis, I received notes of gratitude and encouragement from congregants—like this one from a senior adult: "I shall never forget that you were there for me when I sorely needed help, and I will always be thankful and grateful for that. Thank you for being a loving and caring pastor." A twenty-something woman who, along with her mom, had participated in our support group ministry wrote: "You gave new meaning to my mom's life, my life, and my mom's and my relationship. Thank you for being a "real" person I will always look up to. I thank God most of all for the love and endurance he has given you."

Another attendee who drove almost an hour to participate in our services each week wrote:

> I want to let you know what a difference you've made in my life through your insight, direction, and understanding of God. Your sermons are unlike any I've ever heard before. They go to the depths of my soul and touch a part of me that seemed to have long ago grown cold. I faithfully attended church for 20 years with a sense of emptiness, loneliness, confusion, and distance from God. My husband and I now drive almost an hour, one-way, to hear God's message through you, and take in our hearts a new feeling of hope and joy.

Despite the wide range of positive feedback that contradicted what I was hearing from the PSAG and the personnel committee, I did my best to be responsive to their requests. There was no question that some members were unhappy with my leadership.

---

[35] H.C. Brown, Jesse J. Northcut, H. Gordon Clinard, *Steps to the Sermon* (Nashville: B&H Publishing Group, 1963), 134-136.

[36] Donald Bubna, "Is It Time to Leave?", *Leadership: A Practical Journal for Church Leaders* (Winter, 1996): 51-52.

38 – Turning Point

W hen Christians are at odds with one another, an intervention from God—the healing, reconciling, unifying God—is in order. In April of 1995, the Palm Sunday sermon was not delivered as planned. Instead, we experienced what Christians call an outpouring of God's spirit—a revival moment.

True revival can come only when God pours out his Holy Spirit on his people like rain falling on a parched land. It touches people individually in a way that affects a congregation collectively. It always involves a powerful sense of conviction, confession of sin, a rediscovery of spiritual passion, and a healing of differences among believers.

There had been at least two and possibly three major revivals in U.S. history—Great Awakenings, they were called—the first dating back to 1730. These were extraordinary periods—monumental movements when revival broke out, swept across the land like a holy fire, and sustained itself for years before burning out. Christian leaders perpetually hope for another Great Awakening that will spread across the United States.

Three weeks before our Palm Sunday service, a worship service at Wheaton College had turned into all all-night meeting of confession and prayer that lasted four days. Similar events were occurring on other campuses and in churches. At Southwestern Baptist Theological Seminary, a white student who stood and confessed the sin of racism was immediately embraced by two African-American students as the assembled audience applauded and wept.[37]

During our first morning service that Palm Sunday, I talked about the revival that was breaking out across the country, and then I shared personal words, pressing myself into a vulnerable zone in the same way that I often pushed myself at recovery-related speaking engagements. I expressed a deep and sincere desire for more of God's work and presence in my life and in the life of the church.

Once finished, I asked if anyone in the audience wished to speak. One by one, people stood and shared. Some testified to the life-changing ways God was at work in their lives. Some confessed their sins. Many who spoke wept. The Spirit of God was present and at work!

The sharing came first from one part of the room then jumped to another— a man on the fifth row, then a woman from near the back of the main floor, then someone from the balcony. Men and women were being filled with the passion to connect more deeply with God.

We had no second worship service that day; the first worship service just spilled over into the time slot for the next as those arriving for the second hour found themselves walking into a revival meeting in progress.

Afterwards, congregants shared their comments about what we had experienced. One member described a uniqueness in what had occurred: "I have grown up in church, and I have seen a lot of revivals, but I have never seen anything like I saw yesterday. I sensed a real moving of God's Spirit. I don't know how I could explain it to someone who was not there."

Another member wrote: "When a church is an emotionally safe place, the healing work of God can be seen. Sunday, I saw confession, I saw witness to God's healing power. I praise God I was there."

After the controversies addressed by the deacons in their October meeting, the "lying" controversy and other issues, we had lost a number of members—some to Second Baptist—and our attendance stumbled.

One woman went home after the worship service, and wrote a letter letting me know that her feelings toward me had changed that morning: "I've been very hurt by my very best friends leaving Kingsland, and I've had very bad feelings toward you. Today, I can truly call you pastor because I know you care about me and each one of your sheep."

The spirit of revival that rippled through multiple American locations that year, though significant, did not attain the status of a Great Awakening. However, in our congregation, the Palm Sunday service and the response that followed gave me hope that we were moving closer to the unity we needed to forge ahead. And, it gave our membership a renewed sense that God was at work among us.

One week later, Easter services were not only inspiring, but our attendance of 2,175 was our highest ever!

---

[37] "At Evangelical Colleges, A Revival of Repentance," *The New York Times*, April 30, 1995, http://www.nytimes.com/1995/04/30/us/at-evangelical-colleges-a-revival-of-repentance.html, and "Wheaton College Revival, 1995," Billy Graham Center Archives, http://www2.wheaton.edu/bgc/archives/revive.html.

39 – Fast Lane

In May of 1995, my sons, 19 and 15, were growing up fast, and regardless of what might be of concern to me in the congregation, I wanted my father-son relationships cemented by positive moments Jonathan and David would never forget. That month, I took both boys to the Indy 500, a racing event I knew we all would love. Getting tickets wasn't easy. You didn't reserve seats—you applied for them, at least a year in advance—and you could be turned down because alumni attendees took precedence.

We were delighted when our hard-to-get tickets came in the mail, and excited to find our place in the stands along with tens of thousands of others at what was the nation's largest spectator sports event. The roar of the engines was deafening—old-timers brought ear plugs—and watching the cars speed through their 200 laps around the 2.5-mile track was a unique thrill.

After the race, we swung through Chicago to visit the Museum of Science and Industry. It was a terrific few days, but what mattered most—the lasting memories we were making as father and sons.

Back home, on the heels of our Palm Sunday renewal and our exciting Easter services, we were ready to move beyond the issues that had bogged us down. The timing was perfect as a new opportunity was opening for the men in our church. In June of 1995, a citywide Promise Keepers conference would convene in Houston's Astrodome.

Founded in 1990, Promise Keepers is a Christian men's ministry based on the premise that men can best help other men grow spiritually. The goal is changed lives. The desired transformation includes ethical and sexual purity, a strong commitment to marriage and family, racial equality, obedience to Jesus's command to reach out to unbelievers, and honoring—as well as praying for—one's pastor.[38]

The Houston Promise Keepers conference was a perfect follow-up to our recent season of renewal. A part of the Promise Keeper plan was the organization of accountability groups where men could open up, share, and become accountable to other men. And, these male-only groups offered a way to mainstream some of the principles we were implementing in our support group ministry. In fact, a few months earlier, a full-page ad for *Making Peace with Your Past* and *Moving Beyond Your Past* had appeared in the national Promise Keepers magazine.

Unlike our existing support groups, Promise Keeper groups didn't require an admission of personal brokenness or unresolved pain from the past. The only requirement was to be a "regular guy" who hoped to become a better Christian man. This made participating an easier decision.

That weekend, 180 men from Kingsland Baptist Church attended the conference. There, speakers offered a series of uplifting and unifying messages.

Following the conference, we organized a Men's Ministry Coordinating Council at Kingsland, and began training leaders for new accountability groups that would use the Promise Keeper model as a guide.

In keeping with that model, one of the key aspects of this ministry was prayer, and specifically, laymen being supportive rather than critical of their ministers. Each day in July, a Men's Ministry Prayer Team member and his family were praying specifically for me and for the church staff.

In August, our Men's Ministries Coordinating Council sent out a mailing to all the adult men in our congregation. It was an invitation to participate in one of 26 men's accountability groups that would meet for a period of seven weeks focusing on prayer, support, and personal accountability

At the same time as the men's accountability groups were taking place, we were starting a new round of support group ministries. Our support group options included: Making Peace Groups, separate eating issue groups for men and women, grief support groups, a co-dependency recovery group, a stop-smoking group, a counselor-led therapy group for victims of sexual abuse, and separate talk-about-any-issue groups—one for women and one for men.

In addition to our ongoing recovery ministry and our new men's accountability groups, I was also training leaders for six Home Bible Study Groups, another new ministry we were piloting as an alternative to Sunday morning Bible Study. Our plan was to launch the first six groups, learn from them, then add more.

Despite all the good work taking place at the church, I still harbored concerns. For months, I had been meeting with my personal therapist and sharing my worries about where things were heading with Kingsland. Her well-intentioned response was that I was overly concerned. She advised me to relax and trust that things would work out.

There were good reasons to follow her counsel. With a new sense of spiritual unity and new ministries flourishing, it was logical to trust that we had moved past the dissension that previously plagued us. And I was thrilled that we were providing an expanding set of opportunities for people to sit with a small group of peers, to honestly express their feelings in a safe environment, and to engage in healthy introspection that would lead to new levels of fulfilment, personal growth, and hopefully—congregational harmony. I chose to embrace hopefulness.

When my 10th anniversary at Kingsland rolled around that August, I had even more reason to feel reassured by countless notes of praise, appreciation, and congratulations. These heartfelt expressions touched Linda and me deeply, painting a portrait of a congregation that was more than just satisfied with its leadership. We were making a difference. Lives were being changed by the ministries we had nurtured. And we were moved that so many in our church were grateful for our contributions.

I was heartened as I read notes from our more traditional *Congregation One* members. One wrote: "Thank you for your reverence, sincerity, and deep devotion to biblical truth. You… speak to me in a way I need to hear." Another congregant shared: "Thank you for challenging me to a deeper level of faith and service than I have ever known." And there were these encouraging words: "You've touched my heart, opened my mind, and really taught me how to focus on the Lord."

Congregation Two was alive and well, with other messages reflecting the impact of our support group ministries, noting their success in achieving emotional healing. I was delighted by a note that linked recovery to a new connection with God and included the words: "I want to thank you from the deepest place in my heart for your vulnerability, role modeling, and leadership. You have been a huge part of bringing God into my life." I felt I was making a difference when I read: "Thanks to your guidance my husband and I were able to save our marriage. Thank you for letting me feel comfortable with the fact that I didn't have to get better overnight."

One of my main objectives was helping people make dramatic positive changes in their lives, and this note helped me to feel I was on track:

> Two years ago, I was in trouble. I had built walls and was isolating. I didn't trust very many people…. Two years after beginning recovery, I have broken the shopaholic compulsion. I no longer feel relationships are threats or risks I can't afford… I can honestly say that you were the model for much of this and I want to thank you. In you, I saw another person who had been deeply hurt, but could use that to help others as well as himself. I saw how hard you worked at learning and growing and giving. I don't know how much you are aware of the impact you have on the lives you come in contact with.

Not every person or response fit neatly into *Congregation One* or *Congregation Two*. Some of the messages expressed gratitude both in traditional spiritual terms as well as in the language of recovery and support groups—notes like this one: "Your sermons have inspired, taught, and comforted us. Because of your commitment to recovery, my life changed. The healing I received in my *Making Peace with Your Past* group emptied me of a lifetime of shame and pain." And this one: "Our family has never been to such a powerful church. Just after a few Sundays we had learned more than a lifetime of attending other churches. The Life Support classes saved and changed my life."

Many of the words our membership shared focused on appreciation to both Linda and me for who we were One kind individual wrote: "God has been evident in your lives by your openness, love, and honesty"

When it came to priorities, sensibilities, and expectations of what a church should be, it was clear enough that we had two congregations in one church. Yet now, members of both groups seemed not just happy, but genuinely grateful for what was transpiring in our community, and openly appreciative of their pastor and his partner in ministry.

The flood of appreciative words on my anniversary meant the world to me, especially after the scrutiny of the PSAG and the deacons. And, these encouraging messages were in sync with the tenor of the face-to-face feedback I received from congregants every single week. Surely my critics were an atypical minority.

These expressions of gratitude were a reality check: "No, I'm not losing my mind. Yes, we are reaching people and changing lives for the better. No, we are not veering away from our biblical foundations. And yes, our church is heading in the right direction, honoring God, and regaining the momentum of innovation, ministry, and growth that has become our standard."

We were back in the fast lane.

---

[38] "About Promise Keepers," http://promisekeepers.org/about/about-promise-keepers.

40 – Problem Solving

In the fall of 1995, I was encouraged by the success of our new ministries and by the outpouring of gratitude and support on my 10th anniversary, but I knew there were still murmurs of discontent in the congregation—concerns that had been voiced by the deacons and the PSAG.

I was marching ahead with a problem-solving leadership approach, one that was positive, forward-thinking, and aggressive: providing training for a new group of deacons, spearheading a fundraising effort to increase our budget giving, and initiating a congregational self-study to be led by an outside consultant.

In September, I led our annual deacon ministry training. We met at the church on a Saturday morning. Training was especially important this year since 13 of the 23 men were newly elected, and 7 of the 13 had never served as deacons before.

During the training, I reviewed roles, task assignments, upcoming calendar items, and talked about specific ways the deacons could help strengthen our fellowship in the coming year.

As I led the deacon training event, I was feeling energized, operating with the hope that we were on the road to resolving our prior conflicts and were moving ahead together. On the surface, at least, training went well. If an observer had been a fly on the wall that morning, they would never have guessed the controversies we had so recently navigated.

Our budget giving had fallen behind the required target levels. As part of an effort to increase the congregation's commitment to sacrificial living and giving, I preached a sermon series titled *Season for Sacrifice*.

In the Christian world, sacrificial giving means giving "until it hurts" or better still, giving beyond that point. But the emphasis on sacrifice wasn't just about financial giving. It concerned the whole of our Christian living. In each of the three sermons, I challenged the congregation in specific ways to live with an "extra mile" attitude, seeking daily opportunities to reach out and exercise their Christian faith—beyond their usual comfort zone.

The goal of the October 1st offering was to catch up on our budget needs. The church gave $73,443 that day—almost three times the normal weekly offering. Because of that Sunday's offering, by the end of the month, our operating budget had gone from $50,000 in the red to $16,000 in the black—another reason to feel like we were moving beyond our period of disunity.

Wanting to show the deacons that I was all in for consensus building (and not just interested in having things my way), I sought out our denominational leader in Houston and secured him as an outside consultant to lead a congregational self-study. He would provide objective feedback on how to get our congregation on the same page, incorporating the needs of all members, including the dissatisfied few.

After securing the support of the Great Commission Task Force and the diaconate, I asked our nominating committee to put together a group of 20 Kingsland members, who along with our church staff, would work with our consultant. The congregation approved the members recommended by the nominating committee, and the study was scheduled to begin in January. We would spend roughly three months examining our direction, communication patterns, growth trends, decision-making, and leadership needs.

Once the study task force was organized, I provided them a 247-page manual that included every piece of information I could round up that might conceivably be helpful. I had complete faith in our associational director's trustworthiness and competence, and my hope was that the study committee would help all our members feel they had a say in shaping our future direction—even those few with grievances.

41 – Galveston Gang

As far as I was concerned, things were definitely looking up. But I couldn't deny the extra stress generated by the disunity our congregation had experienced. Like anyone else, I needed an outlet. But as a minister, I had few venues where I could discuss the very particular stresses that I faced.

I was delighted when one of the leaders of our local Baptist association organized a ministers' support group. Six Baptist ministers, all close to the same age, showed up for a two-day retreat at my friend's Galveston beach house. It was a comfortable setting that would be conducive to openness, sharing, and true fellowship. There would be no phones ringing, no traffic noise, and only the sound of the waves and the soft touch of the Gulf breeze.

Aptly, one of the guys dubbed the group, "The Galveston Gang," and the name stuck, as all six of us embarked on what became an extremely meaningful experience. We were creating a safe place in which we could talk about anything—most importantly, the unique challenges of life as a minister—and truly empathize.

In our first small group discussions, as the resident small group guru, I modeled some basic support group principles that we used in our groups at Kingsland. My minister friends were quick studies; they immediately adopted the sharing style I modeled, and in no time, we were operating in a leaderless mode with no one in particular driving the discussion, yet with everyone ensuring that each person was heard and validated.

We conferred on a variety of stresses we felt in our vocational roles, but we also had one other thing in common. All six of us had teenage children, and we had much to discuss on the special stresses and challenges our ministries created for our children. This was a hot button—like any parents, we lived our responsibilities and our failings intensely—and it was obvious that none of us had a place as appropriate as this new group to deal with this complicated aspect of our lives.

Early in life, I had noticed that the child of a minister tended to be one extreme or the other—either a compliant high-achiever or a hell-raising antithesis of everything the preacher parent stood for. By the time I was in my twenties, I had met both types, and I couldn't understand why this pattern was so consistent.

In the church, pastors' children have a special name—preacher's kids or PKs—and even the secular world takes notice. There were no songs about the "Son of a Business Man" or the "Son of a Doctor Man," but there was a popular song titled "Son of a Preacher Man."[39]

As I attempted over the years to understand this perplexing phenomenon, I developed a simple theory: If a minister's child rebelled, it was because the

156

parents were too strict and made the child feel he or she had to do everything right. The antidote, I thought, was finding the middle ground—parenting that is neither too permissive nor exceptionally strict.

Linda and I were married eight years before we became parents, so we had plenty of time to think and talk about how we would raise our children. And we were always on the alert for any adult we met who had grown up in a minister's home, so we could pick their brains and better understand the unique struggles that came with this special role in life.

By the time our first son arrived, almost all the parenting principles we agreed upon applied to any contemporary family. We would give our kids unconditional love, share as much laughter and fun together as possible, and create an open environment for discussion. We would enforce consequences for broken rules, but with no shame for what are natural human feelings, frailties, and foibles. We would be honest about our own shortcomings, and we would be quick to forgive.

However standard these principles were, another only applied when there was a parent in the ministry: We would teach and uphold values for their own sake, not to make the church or one's ministry look good.

Linda and I worked hard to implement these parenting principles, and generally, they worked well. But, my thinking failed to take several things into account—things I could only understand by experiencing them in my own family. As an example, I learned that for preacher's kids, the pressure to fit someone else's mold could come from outside one's parents, even from outside one's church.

Case in point: My younger son was attending a large public elementary school, but given my role, our family was highly visible in the community. When the teacher asked the class to draw a picture—whatever they chose— my son drew a gun. His teacher's response: "What would your father think?" What did I think? Here's what: "That's what I would have drawn when I was his age." It was as if his teacher made it her responsibility to stamp a "preacher's kid" label smack in the middle of my son's forehead.

Peers were another issue, with special challenges for the child of a minister, as classmates and friends could apply formidable pressure on the child who refused to participate in some forbidden behavior. The inevitable taunts could be hurtful and effective in influencing choices—taunts like "What's the matter? Can't do it because Daddy's a preacher?"

On the other hand, being the child of the pastor of a large, successful church had its perks, like being a highly visible, favored member of a giant extended family; enjoying a healthy exposure to a wide variety of interesting people; and gaining extensive practice at developing better-than-average people skills.

There were also subtle negatives. The preacher's weekly family schedule was out of sync with the rest of the world—weekends would never be normal. Even if the minister's day off was Saturday, it was hard to escape the mental

157

preparation (even if only subconscious) for the following day, the most important—and stressful—day of the week.

By the time our elder son hit middle school, I understood that Linda and I had been extremely naïve about how my vocation—regardless of our approach to parenting—created a challenging world for our children. And, it was increasingly clear to me that the way each minister's child responds to the special circumstances of his or her upbringing is influenced by a myriad of factors: personality type, intelligence, athletic ability, social skills, gender, specific friends, and personal choices.

In some ways, these choices where just like those faced by every adolescent, but in other ways they were uniquely tied to being forced into a role not chosen for oneself, and virtually impossible to live up to. Compliant high-achievers seemed to handle the situation best, but for other personality types, the pressure could become an open invitation to quiet rebellion. For still others, it was the impetus to act out, to be the daredevil, even to be the pacesetter for rebellious behavior.

Some rebellion in adolescence is required in order to begin the process of establishing a separate identity. But what does "normal" adolescent rebellion look like for a preacher's kid? How can you rebel in a measured way, especially when everyone—even people who don't go to your church—are monitoring your actions and enforcing an unrealistic standard? Factors like these can easily push rebellion to the edge.

Another challenge: If the child of a minister does do something wrong, handling the issue can get very complicated. The child may simultaneously want to rebel and yet not want to hurt the parent's vocational work. And, a preacher's kid in secret rebellion may find adults who become allies, supporting misbehavior out of some desire to enable the PK's "normalcy" in rebelling, while also helping the child to shield the parent from awareness of the forbidden behavior.

The Galveston Gang's discussion on how to help and support our children was a meaningful one for all of us—we all had opinions and experiences to share. It was good to be able to talk about something so personal.

And this was a subject that touched a nerve with me. Our sons had two minister parents since both Linda and I worked for the church.

Our children were bright, independent, and like their parents, whatever they did, they did it wholeheartedly. That included adolescent rebellion, which in their case meant they were subject to a large, interested, and overly involved audience. As an adult, my younger son clarified the experience when he said, "The mistakes I made would have been mistakes for anyone, but for me as a preacher's kid, they had more consequences."

---

[39] John Hurley and Ronnie Watkins, "Son of a Preacher Man," 1967.

42 – Too Vulnerable

On the last day of October in 1995, I met with Pat, Stuart, Adam, and Gilbert. In the preceding months, I had become more comfortable with trusting these men and with believing that maybe they really did have my best interests in mind. That day, I was still in the Galveston Gang mode of complete transparency, which in this case was not in my best interest.

I brought a lot of emotional baggage to the October PSAG meeting. Our family was facing a challenging year, and we were seeing a family counselor. Our sons were going through trying times. I was worried that they were being negatively influenced by peers, predispositions from our family tree, and subjected to worldly distractions beyond the faith and values Linda and I taught and practiced.

I also felt burdened—beaten down, really—by the controversies of the previous 18 months. I was encouraged by much that had happened in the current year, and I was trying to feel hopeful—I *was* hopeful—but I was still dogged by a feeling that all was not well.

It was also clear to anyone who was close to me that I was emotionally and physically exhausted, the result of so many years of rapid church growth, traumatic events in the lives of church members, schedule changes, staff searches, fundraising, writing, speaking, and traveling.

Despite these concerns and stresses, I had a sense that my writing and support group training were having a significant positive impact in the lives of thousands of people across the U.S., so much so that sometimes I wondered if that was what I should be doing full-time.

As I met with Pat, Stuart, Adam, and Gilbert that day, I was raw, unguarded, and completely vulnerable. I poured my heart out. I spoke of my concerns and frustrations, of my worries as a parent, of my incredible fatigue. With all the usual boundaries down, I wondered aloud if I should cease being a pastor and focus my ministry on writing and support group ministries.

I broke down in front of these four men whom I now allowed myself to believe were there to help me, to hear me, to be my support system. And, in my support group world, that was exactly the right thing to do if it was what you felt. You express your doubts and your human frailties in a safe space, surrounded by acceptance and support—behavior that is regarded as normal, healthy and cathartic by the group—a cleansing moment. You walk away feeling renewed and uplifted.

But my show of emotion—a sort of meltdown—was not taking place in a support group environment. Not one of the four men I was talking to had participated in any of our church's recovery groups, and they had no experience or understanding of the dynamics of such an environment, much less my comfort with this sort of openness.

When you share at this level in a genuine support group, you're not consciously thinking about how the group is responding moment-by-moment. Instead, your focus is on what you are feeling—on getting what is gummed up inside you out so you can see it and deal with it.

Why couldn't these four men see what was in front of them? Why couldn't they recognize that I was a dedicated, high-output leader in burnout mode who just needed some time off—time to recharge, regroup, and regain my usual perspective?

Without the context of any therapeutic or sharing framework, this kind of vulnerability was foreign to these men. And my outpouring of anxiety, frustration, and uncertainty was a mistake—a *terrible* mistake.

I wouldn't realize it until later, but it occurred to me that either my emotional disclosures that day made them worry about my stability as a leader, or they saw my exhaustion, discouragement, and emotional pain as signs that it was the perfect time to take me down. If the latter was true, I had forgotten one of the most important rules for personal boundaries: *When you're with sharks, don't bleed.*

43 – Law Office

The day had come for another meeting with Pat, Stuart, Adam, and Gilbert. It was Monday, November 20, 1995. Thanksgiving was only three days away. For Linda and me, Thanksgiving was not only a family time with our two sons—a time to enjoy roast turkey, green bean casserole, and cornbread dressing—it was also a time when our high school friend, Gail, joined us with her husband and their daughter—our goddaughter. We would share a great meal and the wonderful warmth of a holiday with friends. The day after Thanksgiving, construction of Bethlehem Boulevard would begin as usual, requiring weeks to complete.

On this Monday before Thanksgiving, I wasn't thinking of Turkey Day nor Bethlehem Boulevard. My guard was up as I prepared for the PSAG meeting. Was I just being paranoid?

I knew the feeling of waiting for the other shoe to drop—I had known it since my childhood—and I sensed something afoot in the very location of the meeting. We were convening in Gilbert's fourth-floor law office—a location 45 minutes from Katy, and ironically, across the street from the main campus of Second Baptist Church. Meeting offsite meant that no church members would be around to overhear what was said or note the look on my face as I left the meeting.

As I took my chair in the law firm's conference room, something was in the air—the proverbial tension you could cut with a knife. What occurred next is largely a blur. I do remember—clearly—that Pat, Stuart, Adam, and Gilbert each told me that it was time for me to resign. Was this really happening?

They assured me they had prayed about their decision. In fact, they said they had "bathed it in prayer," a Christian expression designed to communicate, "We've prayed about this so much, no one should dare question it. This decision is from God."

As I try to piece together how I felt, all I can come up with is numbness. And somehow, the fact that Second Baptist Church was visible through the large office window added to the pain I couldn't feel.

Leave the church I loved? How could I leave these congregants I cared about; these people with whom I had shared joys and tragedies; these friends who welcomed me into their homes and who joined Linda and me in ours; this community where I had spent 10 years building something deeply spiritual and pragmatically useful; this place where I bared my soul so we might all heal our emotional wounds.

How could I leave these good, kind, caring Christians who had joined in these efforts and in God's work? They were my family. This was my home. This couldn't be happening.

"Why?" I asked.

161

"There's been a loss of confidence in your leadership."
"Who? Who are the individuals who have lost confidence in me?"
"We're not at liberty to answer that."
"How many people feel this way?"
"We're not at liberty to answer that."

How do you explain what betrayal feels like? How do you find sufficient words to convey the physical and emotional pain? How could I make sense of what was taking place?

Despite the assurances that they had fervently prayed about the decision, somehow, I wasn't hearing the same message from God they claimed to be receiving. Although at times they tried to make it sound that way, the tone of the meeting was not one of friends giving helpful advice. It was one of a confrontational group telling me what I had to do.

Worse—they wanted me, as part of my resignation, to act like it was my idea—no, God's idea. They wanted me to tell the congregation that God was leading me elsewhere.

I don't know how long the meeting lasted. When I walked through the door at home, Linda could see I was visibly shaken. I was more than shaken. I was stunned. And devastated.

Before leaving the meeting, I had agreed I would resign—I was so tired and discouraged, it seemed the only possible response. But after thinking about it for several days, I changed my mind. If my critics were a group of significant size, they would not be afraid to share a head count. This had all the marks of a small, cowardly group attempting to exercise disproportionate power in the life of the church.

I spoke to Stuart, the personnel committee chairman, and told him I was not leaving. I also made it clear that I wouldn't meet with the PSAG anymore. I no longer trusted them. I asked him to deal with any issues of job performance through the personnel committee's annual performance review, set for the following month.

Was I throwing down the gauntlet or was my refusal a pushback that would save the day? I couldn't begin to guess, but I knew this was not the way to leave the church I had served for more than a decade.

And would God really let my ministry at Kingsland end like this? What had I done that was worthy of such an ignoble termination?

As the shock began to lessen, I switched into survival mode. I began evaluating my options. I was planning my "defense" to this apparent assault. In fact, it wasn't so easy to fire a pastor at Kingsland. The requirements were spelled out in the church's constitution: A special business meeting had to be announced one week in advance, and during the pre-announced meeting, at least 75% of the members present had to vote to terminate the pastor.

I told Stuart that if things were as bad as he and Pat, Adam, and Gilbert had indicated, he was free to ask the church to vote to fire me. He laughed, then said, "There's no way I can get 75% of the church to agree to fire you." "That's my point," I said. "So back off."

Based on their unwillingness to give me names or a head count of those who wanted me out, the immediate admission of the inability to get close to 75% of the congregation to vote to fire me, and other relevant observations, I estimated the size of the group represented by Pat, Stuart, Adam, and Gilbert to be somewhere around 10% of the congregation—at most.

Implying that if I stood my ground, the battlefield could get bloody, Stuart warned me that I should leave while I could, asserting that most people were attending for reasons other than my leadership. Then he told me that Kingsland should be growing faster than it was, and that I was hindering the growth of the church. As for those claims, I was beside myself. They were clearly excuses. These four men had told me nine months earlier that I should stop making church growth the measure of all things—and now, suddenly they were concerned that we weren't growing fast enough.

Our worship attendance had started to drop slightly, just around the time of the controversies over BSF and the other issues. Our average weekly worship attendance for the last 12 months was 1,006 compared to 1,016 the previous year. But it's normal for a growing church to hit attendance plateaus, and they aren't necessarily permanent. Our worship attendance had plateaued five years earlier when the minister of education and the minister of music resigned within three months of one another, but the plateau had lasted only a year and was followed by three years of steady growth with a worship attendance increase of 30%.

Signs of early recovery from our current worship attendance plateau were only a month away from my November meeting with the PSAG. By the end of December, for the first time in eight months, our average monthly worship attendance was higher than the same month the previous year, and we had experienced a net gain in membership of 20 active families in the preceding 12 months.

Stating that most people were attending the church for reasons other than my leadership, and that I was hindering the church's growth was a remarkable reversal of opinion by Stuart. He had written me a letter of encouragement expressing a very different view only 18 months earlier.

At the time, the president of Southwestern Baptist Theological Seminary, Dr. Russell Dilday, had just been fired by the fundamentalists who were now in control of many, if not most, of the power structures of the Southern Baptist Convention. I spoke about the event in my Sunday sermon, just a few days after the firing. I described Dilday as a man of deep conviction, a man of dignity and kindness, and an effective leader. But he had become the victim of "friendly fire," and I found that very discouraging.

I'm saddened by what has happened this week. It's not right.

It is an embarrassment to the church, and I have to confess to you that sometimes as I start thinking about things like this I get really discouraged and I start to think, "Is it worth it? Do I really want to pour my life into an institution that shoots its own people when they don't play the game just right?"

I went on to say that even though what happened was discouraging, Jesus had taught us to not be deterred by disappointing behavior on the part of other believers. So, even when discouraged, we should not give up on working together for the cause of Christ. Two days after my comments in the sermon, Stuart sent me a supportive note.

I just wanted to drop you a note to tell you how your recent series of sermons have impacted me. I have always viewed your sermons with a great deal of appreciation and, in fact, your ability to preach God's word is one of the major reasons [my wife] and I had for joining Kingsland. However, during the past few months I have been particularly moved not only because of what you had to say, but also because of the conviction and sensitivity you displayed. I have no doubt that the Holy Spirit routinely inspires you when you preach, but lately he has been noticeably present.

Last Sunday it was obvious to me that the "friendly fire" which transpired at our seminary really bothered you. How unfortunate it is to have committed people of God hurting one another while the real enemy is slowly but surely destroying our moral, ethical and spiritual fiber… I have to believe it breaks our Father's heart when he sees his saints argue among themselves and put their personal agenda ahead of his.

Tim, let me encourage you to remain committed to the ministry you were called to. You have very special talents which God has blessed you with and your service to him has positively affected countless people, of which I am one. You are certainly entitled to question why men act the way they do and you are perfectly right in feeling let down when Christians do things that are not Christ-like. However, we are called to "press on" and rely on Jesus Christ for strength and direction.

You have an extremely difficult job that most of us can't even comprehend. I also know that everyone feels they are entitled to tell you how you should do your job which I'm sure causes you to question sometimes whether it's all worth it… I just want you to know that you are needed and that there are many people like me who are thankful for people like you.

Now, this same man was telling me I needed to leave, and if I didn't, I would be fired. Just three months earlier, like so many others, he participated in a video celebrating my 10 years at Kingsland. And he had ended his positive comments with "Hope it's another 25 years." Thanksgiving came and went. And the day after, it was time for Bethlehem Boulevard preparations, and overseeing 1,000 volunteers.

I have a clear memory of working outside on the set of Bethlehem Boulevard and trying to hide my feelings of profound sadness and anxiety. I didn't want the people happily working around me to know that I wasn't sure how much longer I would be their pastor.

And I wondered: How did a church with an average Sunday morning attendance of 1,006—a church that has supposedly lost confidence in its pastor—get 1,000 volunteers to show up for a holiday project?

44 – Downward Spiral

As I was preaching a four-part sermon series titled *How to Make Good Decisions* in January of 1996, a small group of leaders in my church were moving forward with plans to force me out.

I was aware that the members of my Pastor's Support and Accountability Group wanted me to resign, but I knew a 75% vote by the congregation was required to fire me. Out of the more than 1,000 people who were likely to show up on a given Sunday, I might have been able to identify 50 individuals who would possibly support an effort to oust me.

I hoped I had called the bluff of the PSAG. I was wary, but still believed I could weather the storm from a small, chronically dissatisfied group. However, I had no idea how quickly a series of sickening, hurtful, and destructive events was about to unfold.

Monday, January 8th

I normally had one or more meetings with the personnel committee in January to discuss annual performance reviews for all staff. I called the personnel committee chairman to schedule the next meeting, and his response was that he didn't know when the next meeting would be, but he would get back to me.

Wednesday, January 10th

I learned of a scheduled personnel committee meeting—unknown to me— from someone outside the committee. I called Stuart to verify the meeting time and was told they were doing some work on procedural matters and I wouldn't need to attend. Stuart said we would begin performance review meetings on Tuesday of the following week.

Monday, January 15th

I received a call from a pastor friend who lived on the other side of Houston, about 50 miles away. He told me he heard that the deacons at Kingsland had met the previous day to discuss my ministry. I sat in stunned silence for a few seconds, then explained to my friend that I knew nothing about the meeting.

I immediately called Pat, the chairman of deacons. I told him what I heard and asked him the purpose of the meeting I had missed. He acknowledged that it had taken place but told me the agenda was a private matter. Apparently, the meeting and its agenda had not been so private that a deacon who attended couldn't discuss it with someone in a church on the other side of Houston.

I reminded Pat that our church constitution stated that as pastor, I was an *ex officio* member of all committees and groups in the church. I asked him how he could refuse to disclose the agenda of the meeting to me when I was a member of the deacon body. His response: He wasn't in a place where he could talk; he would get back to me.

Resolved to get to the bottom of things, I called several deacons to ask them what happened at the meeting. Each one said that they had been asked not to discuss it. Two deacons referred me back to Pat, who had already refused to tell me anything. Another referred me to the personnel committee chairman, Stuart, who had also refused to tell me anything.

I was stunned and deeply disappointed but determined to confront whatever was going on.

Tuesday, January 16th

I received a message from Stuart indicating that the personnel committee would not be doing performance reviews as planned. Unclear about the meaning of his message, I called him and asked what the agenda would be. He said the meeting would address leadership issues. I asked him the time and location of the meeting. He gave me the information, then added, "Tim, you should not come to this meeting."

"Why?" I asked, in a measured tone. "Because it is about you," he replied. I took a deep breath, remained calm, and asked if I had also been the topic of the meeting the preceding week. Stuart said yes. I asked him why he previously told me that meeting was about background and procedural matters. His reply: "That's not what I said it was about."

As requested, I did not attend the Tuesday night meeting.

Wednesday, January 17th

Stuart called in the morning to say that the personnel committee wanted to meet with me that afternoon. As I was preparing to leave for the personnel committee meeting, Pat called to tell me that the deacons had met on Sunday, and that 14 of the 18 deacons present had affirmed a no confidence motion on my leadership. The other four had abstained.

Four of the 22 currently active deacons hadn't been present, but a select group of inactive deacons—ordained deacons not currently elected to an active 3-year term—had been present, though they hadn't voted. I had to assume, however, that they had participated in the discussion. The vote, Stuart said, was based on a loss of confidence in my leadership.

I had been anticipating some trouble with the personnel committee, but the knowledge that so many deacons had supported the no confidence vote was unexpected. I was shaken by the sudden awareness that a coup was in progress. It was one of those times when the fight or flight response worked for me, and I wasn't fleeing. As I drove directly to the personnel committee meeting, I focused on what I would say and how I would handle the situation. I would not let them walk over me.

We met at the home of one of the personnel committee members. After entering the two-story foyer of his exceptionally large house, climbing the sweeping staircase, and joining the others in the second-floor family room, I was sickened when the committee member whose home we were in began to speak. In a distinctly sanctimonious tone I had never heard from him, he announced that the committee had earnestly prayed about their decision to ask for my departure. In Christian parlance, that meant, "Don't question this decision. We've discussed it with God, and he has told us what to do."

Stuart explained once more that asking me to resign was based on a loss of confidence in my leadership. There were no issues of immorality or ethics involved—common reasons to oust a minister—but there was, he said, a strong feeling that our church needed a change in leadership.

I asked how many members of the congregation had been consulted, but Stuart refused to answer.

I was asked to begin an immediate leave of absence, which would result in my not being present in the pulpit again until I had offered my resignation. I was then told that I should explain to the congregation that I felt that God was leading me to resign. There was to be no reference to pressure from the personnel committee or the deacons.

If I followed their instructions and agreed to the terms of a legal document that was being developed, I would receive 10 months of severance pay. One of the non-negotiable provisions that would be included in the document: I was forbidden to pastor a church within a 20-mile radius of Kingsland Baptist Church for the next five years.

I almost laughed. In metro Houston, 20 miles could easily mean a 45-minute drive one way. So great was the loss of confidence in my leadership by the deacons and the personnel committee that they feared a significant exodus of Kingsland members who would be willing to drive 45 minutes to participate in a church I led. And the committee was concerned that this danger could persist for up to five years! What would the boundaries have looked like if they still had confidence in my leadership skills?

This was a tipoff as to their numbers. If the count of dissatisfied members was a great as they said, they wouldn't be putting limits on where I could serve when I left.

Naturally, if I was out, Linda was out, too. As the minister of preschool and children, they would expect her resignation, and they indicated her severance pay would be for a mere two months.

I was pressed for a decision, right then, before leaving. I refused.

I told them I couldn't make such a major decision on the spur of the moment. I would get back to them in two days, on Friday. I added that I would be consulting my attorney, though I didn't mention that I currently had no attorney—the reason—up to this point, two different members of the PSAG, both attorneys, had addressed legal issues for me.

The personnel committee's response: If I didn't accept the offer, I could be fired—and would receive no severance.

Inwardly, I was bruised, broken, and disoriented. Outwardly, I was strong, steely, and seemingly impervious to these indignities. I would not pretend that God told me to leave the church, and I needed two more days to decide what I was going to do.

Maybe I should have anticipated what was happening. Instead, I felt utterly blindsided. But as one who is not easily intimidated, I wanted to fight back. And I was convinced there couldn't be many people who wanted me to leave. After all, if what the deacons and the personnel committee were saying was true, how could I be getting so much positive feedback from so many congregants every week?

Given that the church constitution required a vote of at least 75% to fire a pastor, did these individuals now believe they could achieve that figure? I could not see how that was even close to being possible.

Yet here I was, sitting in this beautiful family room. It seemed an odd location for such a cold, calculating maneuver, and it surprised me that one of the committee members—a fifty-something woman who held an HR position in a large company—was buying into the committee's actions.

Her support for the committee chairman made me wonder what she had been told, especially since no specific charges were being made, none were being discussed, and I had no way of knowing what information had been given to the committee members and deacons. If someone like her supported firing me, someone I had always considered kind and reasonable, were there others I didn't suspect? Could the numbers be larger than I imagined?

I felt as if I had been put on trial with no explicit accusations, no Miranda rights, no institutional due process, and certainly no chance to defend myself.

I was running names and faces through my head, trying to tally up those who didn't care for my style. Even now, all these years later, I cannot come up with a comprehensive list of those who opposed me. A few names were obvious—they were spokespersons for the group. But the others? For the most part, that shadowy minority hid their identities well.

Faced with the immediate, painful realization that I had lost the support of most of the deacons and the personnel committee, I began to consider my alternatives. Should I fight and decline to resign? Should I utilize an attorney to hammer out the best possible severance package?

When I got home, Linda and I discussed our options. I talked to several Kingsland lay leaders not associated with the diaconate or the personnel committee. Their reactions were consistent: shock and disbelief.

I also heard that the few other church members who had caught wind of what was happening found it so incredible that their response was to ask, "Is there some moral issue?" The assumption was that the only conceivable reason for dismissing me would be an extreme breach of ethics or a moral transgression.

Despite my brave, even defiant face, I was struggling. I found myself confused as I tried to figure out the true extent of the congregation's loss of confidence in me. How could I be asked to resign after accomplishing so much for so long?

I couldn't hide my disappointment when I learned that staff members Nelson and Ellen had known about the deacons' meeting and never told me about it. In fact, letters announcing the meeting had been sent from Nelson's office. This bit of information was especially demoralizing.

After a brief conversation with an attorney and reflecting on the previous 18 months, I decided that refusing to resign wasn't just an uphill battle; it was a losing one. I was exhausted anyway, and the spectacle I saw unfolding left a bad taste in my mouth. Now, I wanted out. Linda could see the writing on the wall, too. It was like a switch had flipped; we were ready to leave.

I decided to work with the personnel committee toward a quick resignation, believing that to be the best course of action. They seemed willing to help me leave with a financial package that would make a good transition possible. They seemed to show some concern about my future ministry and my family. Though I didn't agree with how the committee was handling the situation, I chose to believe they were working to do what they thought was best for the church.

Friday, January 19th

I had been asked to meet with representatives of the personnel committee on Saturday morning. Vacillating, I thought briefly about bypassing them and taking the issue directly to the church on Sunday. In fact, I drafted a letter to the congregation in which I took a stand against those who opposed me and asked for the congregation's support. Then I put the draft away. Instead, I stuck with my decision to work with the committee to make a clean break, which meant attending the Saturday meeting. On Friday morning, I sent a fax to Stuart indicating that I would work with the committee toward a resignation agreement.

Saturday, January 20th

The Saturday meeting included Gilbert, who was acting as the church's attorney, members of the personnel committee, my newly enlisted attorney— not a Kingsland member—and me. If they were going to force me to leave, they would have to work all day Saturday to make it happen. The meeting started at 8:30 a.m. and lasted until 5:00 p.m.

The committee had requested that my resignation be finalized so I could announce it the next day, but as it turns out, they didn't have the authority to offer me a severance package without approval from the finance committee and a vote by the congregation. Ignoring this roadblock, they still wanted me to sign a resignation document with only their *promise* that they would then ask the church to approve the severance package they had offered.

My attorney's response was "no way." He told the committee in no uncertain terms that without church approval, any offer they made was meaningless. And without a guaranteed severance package, they could forget about my signing the resignation document as currently written.

We finished the day with a different document—five pages long—stating that:

- No immorality or ethical impropriety on the part of Linda or me was alleged or inferred.
- I would receive my regular pay package for 10 months.
- Linda would receive her regular pay package for two months.
- Linda and I agreed not to attend Kingsland Baptist Church—ever.
- Linda and I would waive any conflict of interest claims against the two attorneys who were members of the PSAG and had done legal work for us.
- I would not pastor a church within 15 miles of Kingsland Baptist for a period of *two* years.

Exhausted, we left the meeting in agreement that there would be a Sunday morning announcement of a business meeting for the following Wednesday. The purpose of the Wednesday meeting was to approve a severance package that would result in my resignation as well as Linda's. I had agreed to the wording that would be used for the announcement.

Sunday, January 21st

At the request of the personnel committee, Linda and I didn't attend church that Sunday. The following announcement was read at the end of both morning worship services:

> After prayerful consideration and discussion, the deacon body and the personnel committee have recommended that Dr. Sledge resign as pastor of Kingsland Baptist Church. After prayerful consideration, Dr. and Mrs. Sledge believe that it is in the best interest of the church and in their best interest for them to tender their resignations subject to the church's ratification of the separation packages which have been developed by the personnel committee and by Dr. Sledge and approved by the finance committee. Dr. and Mrs. Sledge agree to the proposed separation packages and, along with the personnel committee, ask the church to approve them.
>
> It should be expressly understood that no immorality or ethical impropriety on the part of either Dr. or Mrs. Sledge is alleged and none should be suggested or inferred.

There will be a called business meeting this Wednesday night at 7:30 p.m. in the Encouragement Center for the purpose of voting on a motion to approve the separation packages and to accept the proposed resignations of Dr. and Mrs. Sledge subject thereto.

During the worship service, a little girl filled out a prayer request form for me with every box completed. It was written in the handwriting of someone who was still working on her penmanship. Under relationship, she had circled "friend." She wrote, "Why does he have to resign? I like him. He never did anything wrong, and he never stutters during a sermon. Please don't let them make him resign." Her father was the member of the personnel committee who had hosted the meeting in which I was asked to resign. Her father was part of the "them" she was trying to stop.

Monday, January 22nd

The next day, the wife of one of our inactive deacons wrote to Linda and me.

> I was totally unaware of any existing conflict in the church. So, you can imagine the shock and the pain I do feel for you. I have been praying for both of you and for your family and I'm not sure at this point of what's going to happen next; but nonetheless I felt like writing you. I can only imagine the confusion you must be feeling, and I know that your pain and disappointment are beyond my grasping.

> What you've done with your lives in our church, for our church is not in vain. You've reached rocky hearts. You've loved unlovable people. You've shown kindness to starving souls. You've guided searching creatures toward the Creator. There's no way that I can count the times that the Lord has reached me through your sermons, Tim.

> And Linda, your love for the children has been overwhelming. Your kindness and smiles and the many encouraging cards that my children had received has been heart-warming. I know that you've shown many children an example of how to be a Christian.

> Linda and Tim, I love you both and no matter what the outcome of this mess is, I know that the Lord will guide your steps whether you go or stay. He'll lead you and show you the way you should go. I'll continue to pray for you dear friends. You're so much loved, but seldom told.

Tuesday, January 23rd

I walked into the foyer where volunteers were folding copies of the week's newsletter in preparation for mailing. Part of the agreement with the personnel committee was that the announcement that had been made on Sunday would be printed in the newsletter the following week. I picked up one of the newsletters and read the title over the announcement. It read, "Dr. and Mrs. Sledge Resign Positions." That wording was not part of our agreement. Our resignation was contingent on the congregation approving the severance packages. I instructed Ellen to stop the mailing, destroy the copies of the newsletter, and print new copies with the appropriate title, "Dr. and Mrs. Sledge to Resign Positions Subject to Separation Package Vote." Reluctantly, she did as I instructed.

Wednesday, January 24th

Six hundred people, almost all adults, gathered for the Wednesday night church business meeting that was called to vote on my resignation.

Linda, Jonathan, and David sat with me on the right front row of the Encouragement Center. What was about to happen wasn't going to feel very encouraging to anyone involved.

Oddly, one other person joined me on the front row that night—a multimillionaire owner of a national business. He was a self-proclaimed skeptic of religion, now retired in his forties. Though not a member of the church, he had begun to attend services on a regular basis. He liked my sermons and he liked me. That night, he cried, and his wife later told me she couldn't remember the last time she had seen him shed a tear.

As my family and I sat shoulder to shoulder, we positioned ourselves with as much pride and courage as we could muster, and we could feel all eyes on us as if a spotlight was focused on us. I felt solidarity with my wife and kids—so strong, stoic, and steadfast—all of us so together in that moment. I was proud of how we supported each other that night.

And yet it was impossible not to feel echoes of my oldest foe—shame—when circumstances conspired to suggest that I had done something wrong. Why else was any of this happening?

I felt so terrible that my family was subjected to this spotlight. But for years we had been living in a fish bowl. In a way, this evening was no different, though adding to the emotional complexity of the moment—most of the people in the room were there because they loved us.

The personnel committee had told me that there had been a loss of confidence in my leadership. My Pastor's Support and Accountability Group had indicated that a significant number of people were unhappy with my leadership. Following my practice through years of ministry, I had asked for names and numbers of my critics. "We are not at liberty to share that," was always the reply.

A part of me never believed that large numbers wanted me out. Another part of me assumed that I had misread the congregation to such an extent that I was totally out of touch, in which case a larger group than I suspected must have opposed my leadership. In either case, I had taken my eye off the ball. What hadn't I seen? What hadn't I done? Why was this group determined to see me gone?

Baptist business meetings operate under *Robert's Rules of Order*, and I was, by default, the normal chairperson of any business meeting. For the sake of fairness, I needed to turn the chair over to someone else since the primary item of business concerned me.

Earlier, I had requested that our local denominational leader for the Houston metropolitan area be allowed to chair the meeting as an outside objective party. However, the personnel committee had rejected this request, unwilling to trust the man because they knew he was my friend. So, I chose Blake, the deacon who had years earlier wanted to be considered for a staff position and had resigned from all his positions when I said no. I had to assume he was one of the group who wanted me out, but I trusted him to moderate fairly.

A motion to approve the document from the preceding Saturday was put to the congregation.

> Resolved that Dr. and Mrs. Sledge's resignations be accepted as Pastor and Preschool and Children's Minister respectively, and that the separation packages proposed by the personnel committee and approved by the finance committee, and agreed to by Dr. and Mrs. Sledge, be approved without amendment. Should the church fail to approve the separation package without amendment, it is understood that Dr. and Mrs. Sledge will remain in their present positions.

I had agreed to resign as I had been asked, only if the church adopted the agreement with no changes, and the committee had agreed to pay me for 10 months only if the agreement was adopted exactly as written.

Part of the arrangement the committee made with me was that the agreement would be read, the motion would be made, then, with no arguments from me or the committee, I would make a brief statement asking the church to support the proposal. Following that, the church would vote. My attorney and I had understood the agreement to mean that Stuart would present the motion from the personnel committee, I would speak in favor of it, and then whatever guidelines were dictated by parliamentary procedure would be followed to allow the congregation to discuss and vote on the motion.

Apparently, the deacons and the personnel committee had already received some negative feedback from church members since the Sunday announcement. Most of the congregation was in a state of disbelief. "Why is this happening? Tell us, what has Tim done?"

I was shocked when I heard Stuart deliver a 15-minute discourse explaining the actions of the committee. Worse, some of the information he offered was very misleading.

Once Stuart finished, Pat spoke on behalf of the deacons. By the time they were done, I felt somewhat vindicated; unintentionally, they had helped my cause. The clear reaction as I scanned the audience was skepticism. The unspoken question I saw written on faces in the audience was, "Okay, so why do you want Tim to leave?"

After the unexpected "speeches," my attorney announced that though I hadn't planned to do so, because of the presentations that had just been made, I would address the issues at hand.

I stood and gave my side of the story—speaking for about 10 minutes. I poured out my heart. I wept. I explained that I thought what was happening was unfair, but that I felt the church should support the proposal, because our church was divided, and I could no longer lead the church in a unified way.

When I finished, as I looked out at the audience, 70%—maybe more—stood and gave me a standing ovation. That was when it struck me, hard. I had been duped. Most of the congregation was happy with my leadership. Yet a small group had pulled off something remarkable—my ouster—and it was only possible because I was burned out.

After the meeting, many who hadn't stood and applauded came up to me and reassured me that they supported what I said, but simply didn't feel that applause was appropriate in that setting. I was comforted by their words and dismayed. With what I had just witnessed, there was no way the 75% majority that was needed to fire me existed—the opposite was true, more than 75% supported me. But it was too late to go back now. If I abandoned the agreement we had reached, even with a vote of confidence, I would be in the untenable position of leading without the support of the personnel committee and at least half of the deacons.

The floor was opened for discussion. Nineteen people were recognized by the moderator and spoke one-by-one.

Only one person spoke against me—the senior adult widow of one of our deacons who had died only a month earlier. As I was sitting with her husband the day before he died, barely able to speak, one of the last things he said to me was "I support you, pastor." That night, the deacon's widow stood up and said, "I am in favor of this motion, and I believe my deceased husband would support it if he were here tonight." The reason for her ill-will toward me was mystifying—just one more puzzle for me to deal with when it came to those I must have offended or not served in the ways they believed I should.

All the remaining speakers that night gave strong support of my ministry, some of them sharing personal testimonials about how I had helped them. Also ironic—one of the individuals who spoke in support of me was the man I had confronted after he took issue with our fundraising campaign during a home fellowship meeting. Any animosity he felt at the time had clearly been dispelled.

One of my sharpest and most painful memories from that night was the sight of Rodney, who was our minister of music, along with my other staff members, Ellen, and Nelson, sitting together near the back of the room. They were absolutely silent. They were individuals I counted on, people I considered friends as well as colleagues, individuals whom I had helped and with whom I had worked toward our congregation's goals.

I had fought for Rodney to be sure he had health insurance that would cover his wife's chronic illness. Ellen had started as a volunteer, and I had gone to bat for her with the personnel committee year after year, pushing first for paid staff status, then for one pay raise after another until her pay package was in line with our male ministerial staff members. Finally, as I looked at the third member of the silent trio, Nelson, I saw the man with whom I had sat on a bench by the Pacific Ocean as I confided that the one thing I truly needed from him was his loyalty.

To my surprise, during the meeting, someone stood and proposed that all the deacons and all the members of the personnel committee submit their resignations and that a vote be taken as soon as possible to replace them. Another person seconded this motion. Other members of the audience reacted with sounds of support as the motion was made and seconded. It sounded like the rumblings of a mob about to erupt.

I couldn't help but feel somewhat vindicated. At the same time, I knew this wasn't the way. It wasn't the right thing for the congregation.

I stood and asked that the motion to remove the deacons and the personnel committee be withdrawn. I explained that the church needed another pastor to lead in the healing of the differences that existed in our church. I explained that Linda and I had neither the emotional nor physical strength to continue in the present contentious climate. I encouraged those who were there to support me to approve the severance package, so we could leave.

The person who seconded the motion that the deacons and the personnel committee resign withdrew his second, but then another person replaced his second of the motion with a new second. Since the motion to oust the personnel committee and deacons was still on the floor as a result of the new second to the motion, I stood again, forced to repeat my request that the congregation vote against the motion for the resignation of the deacons and personnel committee. The congregation followed my request, and the motion on the floor was defeated.

I had made my position clear. I wanted the congregation to approve the separation package. I wanted it over. And that's what happened next—the motion to approve the separation package was approved with a near unanimous vote.

Another motion was made and passed to take up a love offering for us. That motion was made by the wife who had joined her husband in writing me four years earlier, warning me that I needed to preach fewer recovery sermons and more bible-based sermons to keep from losing families to Second Baptist. Her husband was one of the 18 people who had spoken on my behalf that evening. The motion to take up a love offering passed.

Next, a motion was made to provide Linda and me with a letter of recommendation. The motion passed.

Linda and I signed the separation agreement after the meeting was adjourned, and our resignations became official the next day.

It all felt unfair, especially for Linda. No one had ever found fault of any kind with her or her work. The ending of this extraordinary chapter in our lives felt brutally cold-hearted, particularly in that we were allowed no official farewell. Although we had served the church for 10 ½ years, the only chance we had to say our goodbyes was that night, after the meeting, as people filed by to encourage us. And, there were few children or teenagers present, so there were no goodbyes with them. We would never see many of these people again. We would grieve the loss of this "family" for years.

Our denominational leader for Houston was in attendance that night. When the proceedings were finally over, he made a point of saying to me, "You have two congregations here." He was right. His comment made more real something I already knew. He was highlighting the difficulty I had been facing for years.

I told him and others, "I am never going to be a pastor again." No one believed me. They knew that being a pastor was all I had ever dreamed of doing. It was my life, my life story, my life's blood. "In six months or a year," they said, "you'll be ready to do it again." They were wrong.

Friday, January 26th

Linda wrote a final letter to the volunteer children's workers in the church.

> It is with great sadness that I write my final letter to you. You are so faithful to the children you teach, to Kingsland and to the Kingdom of God. I thank God for you and your loving support of our ministry. I regret that I don't have the opportunity to say goodbye to the children. Will you do that for me? Tell them that Pastor Tim and I love them and are so proud of how they are growing up in Jesus.

Saturday, January 27th

Sometime after the Wednesday night meeting, I don't remember when, I had begun packing up a decade of work and memories—sermon notes, personal letters from congregants, hundreds of books, some photographs, and a few mementos given by friends. I finished moving out of my office on Saturday, January 27th.

Wednesday, February 7th

Two weeks after my resignation, the associate pastor wrote the following article for the church newsletter, *The Encourager*.

> What is going on at Kingsland? I don't know if you have been asked this question yet, but I have. For a great number of people this question is about what is happening right now at Kingsland, and what is going to happen in the days ahead. Sometimes this question is about what happened on Wednesday night, January 24, when our church accepted the separation package proposed by Dr. Tim Sledge and the personnel committee.
>
> First, and most importantly, we are absolutely trusting in God. I believe that I speak for the entire staff in saying that we feel God's leadership right now in a very real and personal sense for ourselves and our church... We believe that God is with us and has in store for us great days of victorious achievement in and for his Kingdom.
>
> However, we do not want to ignore the past or make it an off-limits topic. Our desire is to meet with and talk with anyone who has questions. If you or anyone you know would like to have a lay leader and/or minister contact you, please call the church office. Your request will be treated confidentially.

The message from the associate pastor was, "Don't worry folks. Everything's fine because we feel God's leadership." Even after I left, my adversaries would not publicly provide specific reasons to justify forcing me out. The associate pastor was essentially saying, "We don't want to make it an off-limits topic, we're just not willing to talk about it publicly."

Had they stated any of their reasons, they knew they would have been shut down. Instead, they said nothing, and in the process made it appear that there was some horrible hidden circumstance that could only be discussed confidentially. This was what many had assumed in the absence of concrete reasons for my firing, even though two weeks earlier, the church newsletter had made it clear that no ethical or moral issues were involved.

Over the next two decades I would hear rumors circulating around Houston about my departure—usually one of three scenarios—two of which were patently false, and one that contained at least a grain of truth. One suggested there were fishy financial dealings—"He must have done something wrong with money." Another accused me of sexual misconduct—"He was fired because he had an affair." And the third, the only one with any truth to it, was this: "They asked him to leave because he had too many of those groups with problem people."

Years after I left Kingsland, I discovered that after my resignation, when people across the country called the church to get in touch with me—people who had been helped by my books and who wanted to reach me—the standard reply given was: "We're not allowed to give out that information." I had to wonder what was accomplished by refusing to share my phone number with people who were trying to contact me.

45 – Shocked Members

As with any large church, Kingsland Baptist had many faithful members who regularly attended Sunday morning worship services, but stayed away from the business side of the church. Some of these members, upon hearing the Sunday announcement that my separation package was going to be discussed the following Wednesday evening, assumed my leaving was a *fait accompli* and consequently, wrote me letters on Monday expressing their feelings. This was prior to the business meeting that would seal my fate.

One man wrote:

> Thank you for your ministry to my family and myself for nearly a decade. We have not shared with you as frequently as we should have the numerous times that your messages helped us during times of sorrow, special need and triumph. God has richly blessed you with an understanding of his word and the ability to present it in a meaningful way to his people. God used you and your family for grand works at Kingsland Baptist and I am most certain that he will continue to guide you in his service.

Another congregant wrote on behalf of herself and her husband.

> It was indeed a sad day Sunday! I just want both of you to know how my husband and I feel about this turn of events. We love both of you and appreciate your service to us. We are leaving Kingsland and will be looking for a church without all the hatred and turmoil. I don't know any of the background, but after going through a similar situation at our last church, I don't care to do it again. We go to church to worship and serve God and it is almost impossible when fellow Christians are behaving like this. Our prayers and wishes for God's blessings (and our tears) go with you.

Following the Wednesday night meeting, reactions intensified. A woman in a key leadership position ran out of the Wednesday night meeting in tears and was so discouraged she didn't get out of bed the next morning. With sadness and anger, she proclaimed: "This has changed my life."

In the words of another church member who put her feelings into writing:

> My heart is really aching. I am still in shock over the events of last week. I am so saddened by your leaving. You must know from last evening what an outpouring of support is

behind you. God must have greater things for you in mind—otherwise this calamity would not have transpired. I shall follow closely what your future brings—if you lead a church in the Houston area I would like to join!

In the weeks that followed, a stream of cards, letters, and phone calls poured in expressing shock, grief, and kind words intended to console.

One woman's lengthy, handwritten letter began by expressing how unsettled she was at what had just occurred. "I wanted to let you know how upset and troubled I am by your resignation," she wrote. "I cried out of pain and anger as the announcement was made Sunday." She shared her disappointment with the direction the church was taking. "In a place where I feel there should be unconditional love and acceptance, there's gossiping and self-centered people who feel things must be run their way, the old 'turn off' way." She particularly wanted me to understand the impact our church and my ministry on her life.

> I wanted you to know that you have been an important influence in my life and put me back on track to a Christian life. Before coming to Kingsland, I was going through a spiritual death, even though I kept going to church I was feeling nothing. You're a special person with a definite gift for speaking and helping those around you. This isn't something that comes out of a textbook. It's a gift you have and use well. If you decide to start a new church, I'll be your first member.

Her letter touched me deeply.

There were more notes that reminded me of the support of the people I had served—words that I still treasure. From one of the inactive deacon's wives—both she and her husband were supportive of Linda and me—we received this:

> My heart has been heavy since the moment I heard about this devastating situation that led to the end of your ministry at Kingsland. I would like to thank you both for the wonderful way you served the Lord during your 10 years at Kingsland Baptist Church. My life has certainly been blessed.

> You touched numerous lives in so many different ways. You are both already missed. My husband and I are keenly aware of what you are feeling right now. If there is anything we can do for you, please don't hesitate to ask.

In another letter, the wife of one our active deacons touched on a number of issues, including her awareness of obstacles I had been facing.

My purpose in writing this to you is to let you know that we care for you and are praying for you, as we have been for many months now. My husband and I cannot understand what has happened here, but one thing we do know is that God in his goodness has a plan for both of you and his plan will be accomplished despite those who try to stand in his way.

She shared the discouragement she and her husband had felt at times and indicated they had grown frustrated with Kingsland members who had refused to help in its work. She added, "We often felt that there were those among us who were critical without being helpful." She continued:

So many times, I have been hurting or in need of encouragement and it seemed that your words were just for me. Just two weeks ago, I had had a particularly stressful week. I had spent much of the week in tears and started not to come to church. I had chastised myself for falling apart and feeling weak. In your sermon, you taught about the seasons in our lives: a time to laugh, a time to cry.

You said that we should savor all the seasons, even the "winter," the difficult times, and through this we grow and experience the fullness of the emotions that God gave to us. That lesson was for me. I went away feeling uplifted and ready to face the week. This is just one example. I have been blessed again and again by your teaching.

She also expressed feelings we were hearing time and time again about feeling helpless in not being able to protect me from what happened.

I'm sorry if somehow, we failed you. My husband and I really believed that if we stayed out of the negative rumblings that went on, that we could move on and everything would be all right. We made every effort to support your vision of outreach here at Kingsland. We always put a stop to any negative comments that came our way. As a result, there are those in the church who do not acknowledge us when we pass. There is something wrong with that. I can only imagine how tough the last few months have been as you tried to deal with this and continue to lead the ministry God had called you to.

Yet another congregant focused on the impact of my ministry on her and on her marriage.

I truly hurt for you and I am deeply saddened with what has happened. Even though we are grieving, we are so thankful

God put you in our lives. I know that I would not be where I am today and my husband and I, as a couple, would not be where we are today. We are just two out of thousands. Through your preaching, teaching, books, and most of all your love, we learned there is hope and we were shown that through Jesus there is forgiveness and healing. Thank you for being you and being a vessel that God is using to help emotionally damaged and hurting people like us. We want you to know that we miss you very much. We love you dearly.

As church members continued to share appreciation for my ministry, they were generous in expressing their gratitude. And many addressed their words to Linda and me, reminding both of us what a difference we had made in their lives. One note was especially touching:

Tim, we saw the love of God shine through you. We know because of God's love that you have helped so many people come through hard times and come to know Christ. Linda, you have shown us through your actions what a godly woman, wife and mother should be like. We love you both and can't tell you how much we grieve to see you leave.

To this day, rereading even a small selection of these heartfelt comments reminds me of the wonderful people whose lives we touched and whose lives touched us.

In the months following my resignation, when we were out and about in the community, we routinely encountered church members who would stop, offer a hug or take our hands, speak to us, and often—break into tears. These frequent meetings were intensely emotional for them, as they were for us, as we all continued to process the shock and grief over our departure.

46 – Shocked Me

My ministry at Kingsland was over, but I still had an unrelated commitment for a speaking event. Six days after my resignation, I headed out of town to lead a regional retreat for a group of Disciples of Christ (Christian Church) ministers on the topic, "Making Peace with Your Past." The event was held at a retreat center near Denton, Texas, north of the Dallas-Fort Worth area.

I should have been glad to take leave of Houston for a few days, but the reality was—I felt like a zombie, just going through the motions.

My audience surely expected a presentation from a confident and focused speaker, but standing in front of the room, all I could think was, "What on earth am I doing here? I'm in no condition to be doing this."

I managed the situation the only way I could—with an honest check-in with the group—in other words, an explanation of what had just transpired in my vocational life. Since my talks at the retreat were all about emotional health and healing, I chose to model what an emotionally healthy person does—honestly addressing the feelings I was struggling to process rather than trying to pretend everything was okay.

Once I had finished my emotional check-in, I felt a small measure of relief. But now I had to shift beyond my personal pain. I was, after all, supposed to be there for them. My job was to deliver a quality presentation focused on their needs, and that's what I did.

When I completed my talk, one-by-one, the ministers in attendance expressed sympathy and encouragement. As it turns out, I was in the best place I could possibly be at the time. I was surrounded by empathetic and spiritual men and women who understood my world, and instinctively offered words of consolation.

After the session, I went straight to my room for the evening. It was a bitter cold North Texas night, and the room was chilly. The furnishings were typical retreat center fixtures—functional and nondescript.

I felt depleted. I felt terribly alone. Despite the momentary distraction of speaking to the other ministers and the kindness of their supportive words, my sense of comfort was short-lived. I was skillful with the tools for making peace with my past, but I was having trouble making peace with my present. Metaphorically speaking, the room where I was to sleep that night was where I found myself in general—gloomy, isolated, and disconnected.

Unable to sleep for long, I woke at 3:15 a.m. and journaled.

> There is no telephone in the room, no television, and only two Gideon Bibles to read. I am writing to fight the fear and loneliness I feel. This is the first time I have been truly alone

since resigning almost a week ago. I am feeling a tightness in my throat. Is it fear? I am shaky. My chest is pounding. Typing these words into my laptop is the only way I have to keep my mind focused.

Four hours later, waking up from a nightmare, I journaled again.

I had a lengthy dream. I showed up at the church in old clothes and suddenly found I was being quizzed by a lady whom I had never met. Somehow, she had become the spokesperson for the personnel committee. They were waiting in an adjacent room.

My friend Gail, an attorney, appeared. She was representing me before the committee. Gail had a new sport coat for me to wear. She sent me to another room where I could change. While I was undressing—thinking I was alone—I realized that the shutters had been opened on a large window looking into the room where the personnel committee was. I had no clothes on. I could not see the committee members in the room, but I knew they were there.

The events of the last two weeks have become like some spirit that hovers behind my neck. They descend upon me without warning, beckoning me to defend myself once more.

I know that I am a strong person. I will survive. I will emerge stronger. I just hope I don't have many more nights like last night. If I do, I will remember that I battled the loneliness and fear of the night and survived. I will do it again if I must.

I do not hear God speaking to me in the way some seem to. As I have become more honest with myself, it seems that there is a lot of game-playing with the idea of God's leadership. I have come to fear those who claim, without the blink of an eye, that God is telling them what to do.

I have decided to stop living under the thumb of people who use the authority of God to live in ways that even unspiritual, secular people would recognize as dishonest.

Three days after that cold, desolate January night at the retreat, I was back home, and I journaled after waking from another unsettling dream.

I had been accused of some crime. I was a few minutes late to the courtroom. It was a large room seating about 2,000 people. I was led by a policeman to a lone chair that was at least 100 feet from the judge and jury. I saw that many of the people there were looking at me and talking about me.

Not long after I sat down, the chair became a gondola like the ones military pilots sit in to test their reaction to G-forces. Suddenly I was spinning around the courtroom, zipping by the judge, jury, and everyone at a dizzying speed.

I tried to be strong, and at first, I was. Then I started to be sick. The next thing I knew the chair had landed outside, far away from the courtroom. I started making my way back to the courtroom with the chair when I was met by the policeman. He was very angry with me for leaving the courtroom. I tried to explain that I had been hurled away from the room and couldn't help it. He was still angry.

When I got back into the courtroom, one of my accusers, a stranger who was obviously a liar and a low-life, was on the witness stand. I looked to the other side of the room and saw a special section of high-backed pews. The backs of the pews were so high that one could hardly see the heads of the people in them, but I could see some of the deacons from my church, sitting there, watching me.

About this time, I was aware that no matter what I said, or what anyone else said, I was going to jail. Nothing I could do would stop it.

I woke up struggling with the fear of being locked up, relieved at the realization that I had been dreaming, grateful that I was not going to prison, but also aware that I am living in a prison of sorts. I am not able to escape the pain of what has happened.

And, I had still another disconcerting dream. This time, I was walking around in a massive church complex on a Sunday morning. I was surrounded by crowds of people. I tried to talk with them, but they couldn't see me. They couldn't hear me. I was a ghost to them. This dream as well as the one in which the personnel committee was watching me from an adjacent hotel room—as I had to withstand their scrutiny in an utterly vulnerable state—recurred at random intervals for several years.

My ouster from Kingsland was like a divorce—and a grueling, contentious, embittered divorce at that—a divorce I never believed would happen, cutting me off from the people I loved and cutting me off from my spiritual family.

Despite my grief and shame at being forced out, I also felt an enormous sense of relief. My work had weighed on me constantly. Someone was always unhappy with me. No matter what I did or how much, there was always more to be done.

While I felt lightened in some ways, I was also wondering "Who am I? Where do I fit in?" Since the age of 16, my identity had been built around God and ministry—my goal of becoming a successful minister, and then living that life, devoting myself to that life, and inhabiting it as fully and faithfully as I possibly could.

So now what?

I had served on the board of a local hospital since 1988, attending at least 50 meetings and witnessing the hospital change owners twice. Our board meetings were attended by the hospital's administrator, several physicians who sat on the board, and other representatives from the community. After my resignation from Kingsland, I called the hospital administrator and conveyed my new status. I explained that I understood I had been serving to facilitate contact with the community, and since I was no longer Kingsland's pastor, I wouldn't have the same ability to perform that task.

I was hoping the administrator would say, "Don't be silly. You've helped us so much through the years. We need you to stay on the board." But he didn't say anything of the kind. Instead, at the next board meeting, I was given a plaque as a show of gratitude for eight years of service. The board wished me well and said goodbye.

Shortly after my departure, Kingsland called an interim pastor. In Baptist life, an interim pastor preaches on Sundays until the church finds a new pastor. He may also engage in some aspects of leadership and direction-giving, primarily to help the congregation see itself more clearly as it moves to the next stage of congregational life and seeks a new leader.

The individual called as interim pastor was a seminary professor at Southwestern Baptist Theological Seminary, the school I attended. After he had been preaching at Kingsland for several months, I began to receive reports that he was talking to the congregation in his Sunday morning sermons about my forced termination.

One church member informed me that the interim pastor said something to the effect that "everything about the way Tim's exit was handled was wrong." I'm not sure how often the subject came up—in the pulpit or elsewhere—but my impression was that he discussed it several times.

I was still living just minutes away from the church. When I heard that the interim pastor was taking a stand against the way my departure had been handled, I thought he might call or ask me to join him for coffee. He never did.

In those early days after I resigned from my pastorate, despite a profound sense of loss and isolation, I knew I was fortunate to have my family around me. But Linda, Jonathan, and David were also grieving, each dealing in their own way with the pain and disorientation of our new status.

My younger son, David, was deeply affected, though I didn't fully understand how profoundly until many years later. He was only five when we arrived in Katy from Arizona, and he was 15 when our lives—his life—which had always revolved in large measure around our church home, was suddenly cast into the no man's land that followed my ouster. More than 20 years later, he wrote about what leaving Kingsland was like for him.

> Being the child of two pastors meant that I spent multiple mornings, afternoons, and evenings running wild around the church. Some of my best friends to this day, I met at Kingsland. I obviously have some really great memories at the church and I experienced quite a few monumental milestones in my life while growing up there.

> During those 10 years at Kingsland I brought many of my friends from school and sports to church with me. At least 18 of those friends eventually committed their lives to Jesus and were baptized at Kingsland.

> My life revolved around Kingsland in every aspect. When my dad and our family left the church, it was very clear to me that a significant number of the long-term and senior members felt extreme anger, resentment, and negativity toward my father. The sad part is that being 15 years old meant that anything aimed at my father was felt by our whole family. They did not consider that all that anger and hostility were felt by me directly.

> The people who I spent my whole life looking up to suddenly turned their backs on my entire family. The people that were the actual definition of Christianity, love, acceptance, support and so many other foundation blocks of what the church and faith are built upon, suddenly no longer projected any of those things to me anymore. The church had been my home almost more than the house we lived in, and it felt like I was thrown out.

> People who were my Sunday school teachers, families we had spent numerous holidays and special events with, suddenly— overnight—would no longer make eye contact with me much less wave or say hello.

> I remember sitting with my family the last night when the congregation came to vote on my dad's resignation. I remember how tense and uncomfortable the mood was that night. One of my specific memories—clear as day to me— sitting on that front pew on the right side of the sanctuary facing the pulpit and looking over at the opposite side and

making eye contact with one of the deacons and his wife. When I looked over at them, the look that they both gave me back—directly looking in my eyes—was what I can only describe as disgust, anger, and hate.

This deacon's wife was one of the first people I remember meeting when we came to the church. I had countless memories of such happy times spent at their home and with their family. Up to that point, this woman was literally my reference for Christianity, kindness, and love. Sadly, more than 20 years later, the looks she and her husband gave me that night now define my concept of disgust and spite.

So many in the community that had been foundation blocks of Christianity for me were no longer that in any way. I am aware that most, not all, but most of those people likely never intended to be mean to me specifically, but it took years for me to understand that.

I was always a wild, curious and mischievous kid. I became very rebellious and made a lot of poor choices. As off track as I may have gotten in my life, I was always someone who genuinely cared for others.

When all the people that represent the church in your life suddenly no longer represent the things you were so absolutely sure that they did, you are forced to question all your beliefs. I progressively questioned my beliefs and everything I had been taught about Christianity. Eventually I lost my faith altogether.

I held onto a lot of anger and feelings of betrayal for many years. Thankfully I met my wife who helped bring back some of the faith I had lost. Having kids brought me back into the church willingly for the first time, and I eventually came to a place where God is a part of my life again.

David articulated the situation perfectly. Our foundations were rocked. We felt betrayed. We felt cast out. We were no longer welcome in a community we had helped to build. The very people who represented Christian values now seemed to be acting in direct conflict with the beliefs they espoused.

Reeling from the loss of my pastoral ministry, I wasn't as sensitive as I should have been to how the rapid unraveling of my position at Kingsland was impacting my sons. If it was hard for me to absorb the way our world had been turned upside down, what must it have been like for David and Jonathan?

Despite the difficulty of this period for all four of us, our family received significant support from other ministers, friends, and from some of the members of Kingsland Baptist Church. We knew we were loved, and that many still believed in us.

I continued to work with my therapist of six years. She was a tremendous source of insight and strength. The Galveston Gang was another powerful connection. After our initial retreat, the group continued to get together regularly. Our meetings were characterized by openness, honesty, and compassion. Just like my family, my "gang" was a bright spot in some very dark days.

To show our appreciation and keep some kind of connection in place, Linda and I drafted a short boilerplate note that we sent out to select church members and friends.

> We are deeply hurt by the events that happened with our church, but we believe that God is very much at work in our lives leading us to new areas of creative ministry. Please keep praying for us as we seek God's healing and direction.

An article I had written several months earlier appeared in the February edition of *Home Life* magazine—weeks after I left Kingsland. The title was "Bridge Over Troubled Waters." It was an article about forgiveness in which I wrote:

> Forgiveness is giving up my right to revenge and bitterness...
> As the hurt goes deeper, the giving of forgiveness becomes more difficult... Forgiving is one issue. Rebuilding trust is another. Rebuilding trust may take longer than giving the gift of forgiveness.[40]

In those early days, it seemed too soon to consider forgiveness. And I was certain of one thing—trusting myself to a congregation of Christians as the primary source for my spiritual sustenance and the sole source of my family's income—was something I would never do again.

---

[40] Tim Sledge, "Bridge Over Troubled Waters," *Home Life: A Magazine for Today's Christian Family*, LifeWay Press, Nashville, February 1996, 42-44.

47 – Debriefing Myself

I had been thrown off a fast-moving train. I was dazed. I was banged up. Even today, I cannot say I fully understand what happened. The Wednesday night standing ovation was too brief to readily identify those who remained seated, much less figure out who among them were my actual adversaries, and what their specific complaints were. As many times as I play it through my head, I will always have some doubt as to the validity of any conclusions I draw about my termination.

I've heard explanations by analysts of commercial airline crashes where the experts say, "It wasn't just one thing; it was multiple things going wrong, all at the same time." The end of my ministry at Kingsland Baptist Church wasn't driven by just one thing; rather, it was the result of multiple, almost synchronized issues, coming into play at the worst possible times.

As I attempt to reassess the circumstances leading up to my termination, and to do so with the perspective that comes from looking back decades later, I have tried to be honest with myself, to be willing to take responsibility for my mistakes, and to be open to seeing things differently than I saw them when they occurred.

* * *

There's no question that I contributed to what happened. While people who worked with me in support groups commended my kindness and sensitivity, in other areas of ministry, my rough edges sometimes hurt and offended, causing some of the church's leaders to see me as less than "easy" to deal with.

I could be unyielding if someone was blocking a plan to grow the church and I knew it was simply out of their resistance to change. I could be impatient with people who insisted on being catered to, with no reason for any such special handling. I could be stubborn about moving in the direction I felt we needed to go. I could bristle at criticism, though I would consider it after, and often subsequently make changes. And apparently, I could be intimidating—though that was never my intention.

My intensity as a pastor was proportionate to the seriousness with which I took my commitment to Jesus, the teachings of the Bible, and my call to ministry. There's no doubt that my zeal and intensity created some of my rough edges, but rough edges aren't normally a career-killer for the leader of a large church. Megachurch pastors, especially behind the scenes, are generally tough as nails and good at getting what they want.

In fact, when I was at Kingsland, church growth experts were expressly recommending that as a church moved to the 1,000-person mark in weekly attendance, more of the major decisions should be made by paid staff, not volunteer committees—a change that Kingsland Baptist resisted. One could easily argue that I should have been more authoritarian—not less—if we were to move the church toward megachurch status.

My rough edges contributed to the events that took place in my last few years at Kingsland. However, in my view, they were one factor, not the whole reason for the ending of my pastorate.

* * *

In 2002, an insightful article addressing forced termination of ministers was published. It was written by Charles Chandler, Executive Director of Ministering to Ministers Foundation, an organization focused on helping clergy deal with forced termination. Chandler wrote that forced ministerial terminations were often the result of the church not growing or the church growing too much.

> ...when too many new members come into the church, the homeostasis or status quo is interrupted. Change is threatening. Power structures are affected. Church patriarchs and matriarchs may assume their power is diminishing. Power cliques recognize that with so many new members, their block vote could lose its vantage point. Not only do they not know everyone, everyone does not know them nor recognize their power. Sometimes social strata become more diverse and church members grumble "Things are just not the same at church anymore." Since the pastor was the catalyst that brought the new members in, or at least mobilized some of the church members to get involved in outreach and evangelism, the new pastor is the threat. He or she must go in order to save the church and the homeostasis.[41]

With a mixture of appreciation and sadness, I recognized my own forced termination in Chandler's words.

When I was called to be pastor of Kingsland Baptist Church, I believed I had come to just the right place at just the right time. And, Kingsland Baptist had indeed proved to be the perfect place for my ministry to bloom. In the end, however, dramatic changes related to our numerical growth created pressure on the status quo that contributed to my demise as pastor.

* * *

Another factor in what happened was theological dissonance. In the summer of 1992, when *Making Peace with Your Past* was released, the president of our Baptist Sunday School Board said that churches needed to become hospitals for broken people—not country clubs for the well. He believed that broken and hurting people would beat our doors down if we would welcome them into our churches in their broken state.[42] And my book

192

was one of the tools that would be used to make that welcome known.

My own denomination, the Southern Baptist Convention, became the largest promoter of my books and my message. However, they were simultaneously publishing and promoting others like Henry Blackaby whose message was the antithesis of mine.

I said: "God, self-awareness, and personal reflection."

Blackaby said: "All you need is God, the Bible, and prayer."

I said: "Talk to selected safe people and grow."

Blackaby said: "All you need is God, the Bible, and prayer."

Our two contrasting views—both supported by my denomination—reflected a dissonance that resonated down to the congregational level at Kingsland Baptist Church.

I was calling for an end to denial among Christians in emotional pain—believers who had been taught to act like everything was okay when it was anything but. I wasn't dismissing the importance of God; on the contrary. But I wasn't presuming that psychological intervention and methods weren't vital to mental and spiritual health.

Many in my congregation saw my teachings on emotional wholeness as biblical, truthful, healing, and fostering greater closeness to God; on the other hand, Pat, the chairman of deacons who helped force me out, was a disciple of Henry Blackaby, and heard God telling him I needed to go.

The pastor of one of the nation's largest churches, Second Baptist in Houston, gave the go-ahead for publishing my book—even recommended it—but members of that same pastor's church told my congregation I didn't know how to reach a community for Jesus.

It was a little bit crazy, really. My approach was simultaneously being promoted and questioned by varied elements within my congregation, my denomination, and in my larger evangelical Christian world.

* * *

A 1991 article in *Parade* titled "Ministers Under Stress" placed my burnout in the context of the culture-wide strain on ministers. One example was William Self, a well-known Southern Baptist pastor.

> Members of Atlanta's prestigious Wieuca Road Baptist Church were shocked last year when their long-time pastor, Dr. William L. Self, then 58, announced that he was resigning because the stress of the job had become too much for him. "Unless I quit now," he told them, "my obituary will read, 'Bill Self today sank like a rock—beat up, burned out, angry and depressed, no good to himself, no good to the people he loved.'"

> "I did not have a crisis of faith, but of emotion and energy,"

he says. "It's almost impossible for leaders of a congregation to accept that their pastor needs pastoring… I was unraveling, collapsing inside and coming to realize that if the church was not going to take care of me, I'd have to start taking care of myself."[43]

Parade reported that after maternity benefits, the largest portion of the $642 million paid to pastors in medical claims during 1989 was for stress-related illness.[44]

A Los Angeles Episcopalian minister who had suffered burnout said, "I allowed my life to become a work binge of giving, giving, giving… Over time, I moved from being physically tired to emotionally exhausted and finally wiped out."[45] Another Episcopalian minister said that it was a six-week sabbatical that turned him around and allowed him to continue in ministry after burning out.[46]

The article, written five years before my burnout and subsequent resignation, was eerily prophetic.

* * *

Years earlier in seminary, I had interviewed John Claypool, my pastor in Fort Worth, for a doctoral class paper on "Integrity in Church Staff Relationships." In the interview, Claypool said:

> My concept of loyalty is not that a staff member must never have any critical assessments of what I am doing or never express this. My concept of loyalty would be that we are in this together and that we are trying to help each other grow and do ministry. And, therefore, my criticisms of another person's performance will always be to them, with the aim of trying to help them do better. And I will not go and criticize them to somebody else who could hurt them.
>
> I would not like it if I found out that a staff member was giving critical assessments of me or divulging things about me when they had not talked to me first. In other words, I would feel that this meant they had some other agenda besides our trying to do the best work we could.[47]

Claypool's comments on staff integrity pointed to one of the issues at play in my forced termination.

Before we brought him to Kingsland, Nelson, our associate pastor, was serving as minister of education, music, and family ministries in a small church in California. Having served as a minister of music at another Houston church before attending seminary, he appeared on our radar through someone at Kingsland who had known him at the Houston church.

In seminary, he had obtained both a Master of Divinity degree—the one pastors usually get—and an M.A. in Christian education. So, academically, he seemed well qualified since we needed him to work in two major areas: pastoral care and our Christian education program, focusing on our adult Bible Study program.

When I interviewed him in California, our most crucial conversation took place on an outdoor bench overlooking the Pacific. I explained that his attention to building close personal relationships, providing comfort, and counseling individuals would enable me to focus increasingly on leading the whole congregation, which was an essential transition as the church grew. I made it clear that the nature of his extensive one-to-one involvement with individuals, coupled with my increasing emphasis on leading the whole congregation, would give him potential power to undermine me.

Looking him directly in the eye, I pressed home the most important thing I would need from him if he joined my staff—loyalty.

His references were laudatory, but in reviewing them later, one thing caught my attention: Though he was degreed in Christian education, all his references stressed his likability and his interpersonal skills, but no one commented on his effectiveness as a Christian educator nor his leadership ability. And the conditional nature of one recommendation in particular stood out years later, courtesy of the word "if." "If you are considering him for pastoral care work, he would be wonderful."

Kingsland's worship and Bible Study attendance had plateaued when Rick Gregory—the individual the associate pastor replaced—moved on. Worship attendance—which reflected the drawing power of my sermons and our music ministry—rebounded within a year, and over the next three years rose by 209. During the same period, average weekly Bible Study attendance increased by only 30. Where was the weak spot in our Bible Study program? During that three-year period, our adult Bible Study enrollment—the responsibility of the associate pastor—dropped by 175 people while enrollment for children and youth increased by 401.

As it turned out, the associate pastor was high on people skills, but low on organizational skills. We needed both. As I talked to him about his job performance in the course of annual reviews, I challenged him to do better in his work with our adult Bible Study program, and, in one instance, the personnel committee challenged me to motivate him in this area.

I had other concerns. The associate pastor was in charge of working with our nominating committee, the group responsible for recommending key lay leadership positions. Early on I noticed some odd choices on his part for some of our most important roles. He explained that he had picked some of these people not based on their skillsets but based on how having such a position might build their self-esteem. Shades of the New Jersey church treasurer pick!

I set the associate pastor on a different course. I explained that this wasn't how you build a growing church. Leadership positions are not assigned as tools for building self-esteem. Competency matters.

What I viewed as constructive criticism apparently did not sit well with him. After my fateful meeting with the personnel committee a week before my resignation, a church member I considered a friend approached me. She was well acquainted with Nelson. He had counseled her through a difficult divorce. With some urgency, she pulled me aside and said she wanted to talk to me about him. Her voice was low and her expression, concerned. "Tim, he doesn't support you," she said.

Then she related a conversation they had in which my leadership came up and Nelson volunteered the following: "Imagine a school principal with five teachers. One of the five teachers tells the principal he doesn't like the way the principal did something." Then, the associate pastor made a finger gun with his hand, extended his arm, and pretended to fire a shot at the complaining teacher. After that disturbing illustration, he explained how terrible it was to go into my office to chat with me.

I couldn't say I was shocked, but I was surprised. Maybe he had issues with authority figures. Maybe he was especially sensitive to my rough edges. I welcomed and respected honest feedback, and I thought he understood that. I knew I could push my staff hard when we were working aggressively to achieve our goals, but had I been as harsh as Nelson seemed to think, he would have been under review for termination—for lack of leadership in our adult Christian education program.

Had we given him too much to do? Wasn't it normal to focus on the parts of a job you like best? He excelled at one-to-one interactions, and was praised for that, and his job description could have been two separate positions. But why the animosity toward me?

In our Next Seven Years plan, adopted several years earlier, we had made one concession to our "traditionalists" by reinstating a more conventional Wednesday night prayer service that I had assigned Nelson to lead. In so doing, unwittingly, I had likely connected him with a ready-made cadre of disgruntled antagonists.

As I thought about this new information—that Nelson actively participated in undermining me—I had to look at my own responsibility in bringing him to Kingsland. I made the final call before he came to visit the congregation. I had veto power but didn't use it. I trusted him. I supported calling a minister whose greatest skill was getting other people to like him, though he, in the end, decided he didn't like me.

The letters for the secret deacons' meeting to discuss my dismissal had gone out from Nelson's office. For no discernible reason on my part—no ethical lapse nor failed promise—Nelson had failed to give me the single most important thing he had pledged—his loyalty.

If I mention to someone acquainted with Nelson that I once worked with him, the response is always the same: "What a wonderful man!" One former staff member described him as, "the kindest man I've ever known."

I don't question those assessments—people remember how we make them feel. I just know that he took advantage of power that I gave him. And he used it against me.

The staff betrayal didn't stop with him. One of my other staff members, Ellen, was—personality-wise—the opposite of Nelson. Though she had started as a volunteer, I valued her opinion and could always count on her to tell me what she really thought. She was a tireless worker who excelled at every task, continuously acquired new skills, and truly helped get our church on the map through its printed media, advertising campaigns, and a host of other actions not specifically in her job description. In other words, she consistently outperformed the stated requirement of her job.

I respected and trusted Ellen implicitly, and it was a healthy professional relationship. In the final months of my tenure at Kingsland, she, on more than one occasion would say to me, "Tim, there are some people in the church who are unhappy with you."

Years of experience had taught me one response to a comment like hers: "How many and who are they?" Her answer: "I'm not at liberty to tell you." Her answer evoked another learned and long-practiced response from me: "Then I'm going to have to ignore what you just said."

Later, as I reviewed all that led up to my resignation, it struck me that Ellen was the one who wrote the letter lauding Henry Blackaby's "Jesus is all we need" sermon at Kingsland and downplaying the importance of the recovery ministry. Ellen was among those who were most vocal during the BSF lying controversy. She and Nelson took a stand against BSF, and in so doing, against me.

I didn't speak to Ellen for two years after leaving Kingsland. Painful images and memories don't fade easily. I could still see Ellen, Nelson, and Rodney sitting near the back of the Encouragement Center on that terrible Wednesday evening.

Over time, my feelings softened. Perhaps Ellen felt torn between her role working for me and being the wife of one of our deacons. Perhaps she did what she truly believed was best for the church. I offered forgiveness. We resumed our friendship and were able to exchange birthday greetings and talk once or twice a year.

But years later, I heard that just before the Wednesday night meeting during which I tendered my resignation, Ellen told another church member, "If Wednesday night doesn't work, *Plan B* is ready."

* * *

Six months before I was asked to leave, 13 new deacons had been added to the active group out of a total of 23 men. This was an unusually high number of changes for a group of 23. Seven of the 13 had never served as deacons before and were in their first six months of service when they were required to vote on removing me.

In addition to the 13 new active deacons, Pat, the chairman of deacons, had asked five in the diaconate who had already served the maximum uninterrupted term (three years) to continue an extra year—something contrary to the guidelines of the church's constitution.

Those five appeared to have been chosen based on how easy it would be to sway them toward ousting me. They included: Gilbert, one of the members of the PSAG; Jason, the deacon who had written the letter advocating more authority for deacons to increase their self-esteem; a man who had been oppositional toward me for years; and a man who was easily influenced and likely to follow whatever the group decided to do.

Three additional deacons who had been loyal and supportive of me for years were apparently not asked to serve an extra year—this, despite their being in the same situation as the five deacons who were pressed into additional service. The deck was being stacked against me, and somehow, in my burned-out state, I failed to notice.

And, whether by accident or intention, other members of the diaconate may have had an ax to grind. The secretary of the diaconate was Merrill, whose wife I had removed from phone duty 10 years earlier. Also serving was Elliot, our minister of music search committee chairman, who had fielded calls from a disgruntled former minister of music, and with whom I once had a confrontation in one of the meetings of the committee. And the vice chairman of the diaconate was Stuart, the chairman of the personnel committee and a member of the PSAG.

One of the founding members of Kingsland Baptist Church (who had moved away) was now a national leader in Southern Baptist life. He felt that the roots of the conflict we were experiencing had been present in the church from its beginning. In a letter to me he wrote:

> As a founding member of Kingsland Baptist Church 19 years ago, I am struck by the way the same issues that hounded the formation of the church then were key factors in your dismissal now. The dichotomy you described in your memo was present at the birth of the church. I had hoped your support-group ministry would have bridged this gap—though
>
> I must confess that all along I could not imagine how some of your deacons that I know personally could have changed so radically. Obviously, the gap continues.

* * *

My recovery journey was another factor in ending my pastorate. My 1988 visit to the Arizona treatment facility, The Meadows, was a life-changing event. It was truly the beginning of my own walk in recovery. Directly or indirectly, I credit my experience at The Meadows for setting me on the path to a deeper understanding of myself and others, and for making me aware of the time, care, and openness required for emotional healing.

Those five days in Arizona empowered my adult children of alcoholics sermon series, led me to organize support groups in my church, and inspired me to write *Making Peace with Your Past* and *Moving Beyond Your Past*. Those five days led to a national audience for my work on the topics of support groups and recovery. Those five days altered the way I relate to others— occasionally to my detriment—willingly sharing a painful past for the benefit of meaningful connections and as something of a work-in-progress model of the healing process.

The emphasis on emotional healing that I initially discovered at The Meadows attracted a new audience that contributed to the growth of my church and, eventually, created a congregation within the existing congregation at Kingsland Baptist.

The principles I learned at The Meadows dovetailed with my seminary education in pastoral care to create a synergetic subtext for my ministry. I began to call people not only to repent of their sins, but also to understand how past events had made them who they were. Some people loved this. Others did not.

Psychiatrist Dwight Carlson, in a *Christianity Today* article titled "Exposing the Myth that Christians Should Not Have Emotional Problems," described Christians as the only army that shoots its wounded. He cited three wholly counterproductive rules that are practiced by many Christians in relation to emotional problems.

- We don't have emotional problems. If any emotional difficulties appear to arise, simply deny having them.
- If we fail to achieve this first idea and can't ignore a problem, strive to keep it from family members and never breathe a word of it outside the family.
- If both of the first two steps fail, still don't seek professional help.[48]

Carlson noted that not only do many Christians practice these rules for themselves, they also seek to enforce these rules on others: "I have also found that many not only deny their problems but are intolerant of those with emotional difficulties. Many judge that others' emotional problems are the direct result of personal sin. This is a harmful view."[49]

I was attracting people who wanted to be open and honest about their emotional pain. At the same time, I was offending some in my church because I was violating the prohibition on not admitting to that very pain, which the unspoken rules of our church taught us to deny.

Over time, I felt more at home with the openness, honesty, and attitudes of the support group community within my church. No doubt, long-term traditional members picked up on this. I still cared about everyone and felt close to those in both of my "two" congregations, but the atmosphere around the support group members felt so much more breathable.

Did this create a wedge between me and some congregants? Yes, albeit unintentionally.

* * *

I've learned from taking personality inventories that I can fit the profile of a counselor or an executive. Support group ministry participants in my congregation saw the counselor. Church leaders saw the executive.

If I had always walked in the counselor role, I wouldn't have ruffled so many feathers, but my church wouldn't have grown as it did.

Had I always walked in the executive mode, I would have taken no prisoners (and would have never been taken down), but I also wouldn't have been a compassionate force for emotional healing.

Like everyone, I'm more complex than what is captured by any label. Nonetheless, I acknowledge that these two sides of my personality were both an advantage and a disadvantage; my norm was a hybrid mix of the honest acceptance characteristic of recovery, the hardened resolve of a decisive change agent, and occasionally, the self-serving behavior of an adult child of an alcoholic. Some people saw all three sides of me. Some individuals saw only one.

Participating in recovery made me stronger, but from time to time it led me to being more transparent than was healthy, and possibly, appropriate for the situation. I made a mistake in asking for a Pastor's Support and Accountability Group. And then I made things worse by making myself vulnerable to a group that had no idea how to handle what I was sharing.

Compounding my difficulties, I was burned out. My judgment was impaired. I trusted the wrong people at the worst possible time—confessing my weariness and discouragement. I was easy prey, and my adversaries saw it. They launched their attack when they knew I was vulnerable.

Maybe it was time for me to go, but I should have had the opportunity to come to that conclusion myself. Had loving and sensitive discussions occurred, I might have chosen to resign out of a sense that God was leading me in another direction—and my departure could have taken place with a sense of support from the leaders of the church that was so much at the center of my life.

* * *

In the 12 months prior to my resignation, 5,490 different people had attended some event at the church. In my 10 ½ year tenure, I led the church to grow four times as rapidly as the exploding community in which it was located.

Four building programs had been completed. We had become a leader in evangelism and a national model for recovery ministries.

How could I achieve so much and still be forced out? Were my rough edges really so terrible? Was serving hurting people really so exclusionary to more traditional church members? What had I missed?

I was wrestling with questions about the effectiveness of Christian commitment, Bible study, and prayer—when not accompanied by a healthy sense of psychological self-awareness. I was wondering why Bible Study classes didn't seem to change people for the better as much as support groups did. What I was going through was complicated. Though I was profoundly disappointed as I pieced together the duplicitous actions that led to my termination, and I believed that such behavior should never be condoned—maybe it was the fatigue talking to me—but some part of me wanted out of my role as pastor.

If I wanted to give the Pastor's Support and Accountability Group a pass, I would say they saw that I wanted to try something else—full-time writing, for example—before I could see it for myself. But I remain stymied by their failure to provide me with any other path forward, for example, through some protected time away like a sabbatical, which would have allowed me a period to renew, regroup, and decide—unclouded by the threat of expulsion.

---

[41] Charles Chandler, "To Grow or Not to Grow," The *Servant*, Volume 7, Issue 1 (January 2002): 3-4.

[42] "Baptist News in Brief: Jimmy Draper," *The Baptist Standard*, July 1, 1992, 4.

[43] Hank Whittemore, "Ministers Under Stress," *Parade*, April 14, 1991, 4.

[44] Whittemore, 4.

[45] Whittemore, 4.

[46] Whittemore, 4-5.

[47] John R. Claypool, Interview by Tim Sledge, Broadway Baptist Church, Fort Worth, Texas, February 27, 1975.

[48] Dwight L. Carlson, "Exposing the Myth that Christians Should Not Have Emotional Problems," *Christianity Today*, February 9, 1998, 29.

[49] Carlson, 29.

48 – Predictable Pattern

O
n Saturday, January 13, 1994, 11 days before my Wednesday night resignation, the *Houston Chronicle* ran a story on the front page of the Religion section titled "More Clergy Forced Out, Survey Says." The newspaper article was reporting on a survey of pastors that had been done by *Leadership*, a quarterly journal for pastors in conjunction with the evangelical monthly *Christianity Today*.

> Squabbles that end in the ouster of ministers are a recurrent and very painful part of church life; congregations are often bitterly divided, with a loss of membership.

> The survey reported that such dismissals leave pastors and their families wounded spiritually and psychologically, as well as financially, because they frequently must move to find a new position, with children switching schools and spouses changing jobs. Perhaps one of 10 drop out of the ministry entirely after such an episode, the study indicated.

> The survey showed that many pastors, even those who never left a church involuntarily, work in fear of dismissal. About one-third of the respondents said they believed that it was either somewhat likely or very likely that the major areas of tension in their congregations could lead to an ouster.

Noting that Southern Baptist congregations were believed to have a forced termination rate three times higher than other denominations, the *Houston Chronicle* article indicated that "conflicting visions for the church" was the number one cause for forced terminations.

> Outreach versus taking care of the people already there, that is a very major conflict of vision for the church. A new pastor says here is a five-year vision plan for outreach, and people in the church say "vision-shmision, I don't even feel my needs are being taken care of now."[50]

The Winter 1996 issue of *Leadership*, one of the sponsors of the survey, included an article titled "Forced Out," recounting one pastor's personal experience that was remarkably similar to my own.

> The phone rang, and Pastor Andy's ministry at First Presbyterian began its predestined end.

> The call was from the presbytery, the denominational board that oversees congregations and pastors within its jurisdiction.

Andy was told that for several months a small faction of disgruntled members at his church had been airing their unhappiness in each other's homes. When their frustrations hardened, they bypassed Andy and the session (the church board) and went straight to the presbytery.

Their charges? Andy hadn't visited church members enough. And the visits he made were "unsatisfactory." Andy also hadn't given enough personal attention to a mentally disabled confirmand. And he had "made too many changes without going through the session."

After its call to Andy, the presbytery alerted the committee on ministry (the sub-committee that oversees pastors), which quickly brought the two sides together in a series of meetings. But the denomination wielded as much power as a United Nations peacekeeper in Bosnia, and the meetings degenerated into carping and became more personal. Says Andy's wife, Peggy: "One family complained that because I attended a Bible study on Monday evenings, Andy was forced to take care of our kids. Thus, he couldn't be a minister to them when he had to be home babysitting."

At one of the last meetings, a supporter of Andy, fed up with the ambiguous charges, demanded, "I would like to know exactly what the charge is against Pastor Andy." "He's changed," blurted the chief antagonist, "and we would like to go back to the way things were."

Summer interrupted the proceedings, but as soon as vacations ended, the faction asked the session to convene a special congregational meeting. They demanded Andy's future at the church be put to a vote. Divided, the session reluctantly agreed. Just days before the meeting, several members of the session colluded and made Andy an offer:

"If you resign before the meeting, we'll make sure your needs are met until you find another church." Andy declined.

The Sunday of the vote, Andy preached to a congregation of unfamiliar faces. The faction had rustled up inactive members or members who had silently left the church during Andy's tenure. Many of Andy's supporters were new to the church and hadn't yet become members and, consequently, couldn't vote.

After the message, Andy closed in prayer and then in the ensuing vote lost his job. He was number five—the fifth pastor in a row from that church to be terminated or forced to resign.

"I thought I could break the cycle," says Andy, but the cycle broke him.

Andy's story is shocking, yet surprisingly common. A church with a history of abusing its pastors; an impotent denominational hierarchy; a small, but potent faction—these elements of his firing could fit the stories of many pastors who've been forced out. The names and places change, but the storyline remains the same; it transcends denominations and regions of the country.[51]

In the following years, I would come to better understand a pattern in the forced termination of ministers. In May of 2000, Linda and I attended "Healthy Transitions: A Wellness Retreat for Ministers and Spouses." Held in Rockville, Virginia, the retreat was sponsored by the Ministering to Ministers Foundation.

The mission statement of Ministering to Ministers is "to serve as advocates for clergy and their families in all faith groups who are experiencing personal or professional crisis due to deteriorating employment congregation-clergy relationships."

The retreat was a powerful learning and healing experience for both Linda and me. Several months after returning home, I was asked to serve on the board of the Ministering to Ministers Foundation and was pleased to accept.

In October of 2000, Charles Chandler, executive director of Ministering to Ministers, wrote an article in which he shared that a psychiatrist working with his group had observed three common traits in the stories of ministers who had been forced out.

First, each minister had been "blindsided." A group of two or three persons, usually self-appointed, approached the minister without warning and said he/she should resign because of loss of effectiveness. They convinced the minister that the whole church shared their feeling. The "group" presented themselves as merely "messengers" and insisted there was nothing personal about the request. The messengers told the minister they loved him/her and really hated to deliver the resignation request.

Second, while the minister was in a state of shock after being "blindsided," the "group" dumped guilt on the minister. They said the resignation and related conversation must be kept very quiet. If word got out, it could split the church. And, the minister would not want to be known as one who caused a split church! Any negative effect from the minister's leaving was dumped directly on him/her as though a minister could just slip away and never be missed.

Third, while the minister was still in no condition to decide of any kind, the group pressed for a decision. In most cases, a few weeks or a few months of severance was offered—provided the resignation was given immediately and the entire conversation kept quiet. The "messengers" added, "We have to know what you plan to do, because if you refuse to resign or if you talk to other church members, we will take away the severance and call a church business meeting to fire you. Then you will get nothing." Again, the minister was told there was nothing personal about the request. They had to do what was best for the church. No reasons were given for the forced termination except that the church needed new, more effective leadership.[52]

Chandler continued:

The self-appointed "messengers" often horde the inside information, because only 20 percent of the forced-out ministers said the real reason for their leaving was made known to the entire congregation.

I am convinced the statement telling the minister to remain quiet or risk losing severance money translates, "We do not have the votes to remove the minister via a church vote." Ministers often remain quiet because they are afraid to take a chance on having nothing with which to house and feed their families… They often fall victim to the "group's" argument that remaining quiet is taking the "high road."[53]

In January of 2002, the same newsletter included an article titled, "It Can Happen to You," by Archibald Wallace III in which he wrote that more than 200 American pastors were being forced out every week. Wallace featured a short description of how it happens:

For a few, the process involves a formal proceeding. For most the process involves a "gang" of three who appear without warning and suggest the pastor should leave immediately for the "good" of the church. Don't think. Don't ask why. Don't resist. Just go. By the time the gang of three arrives there is little chance of reversing the process. Ministering to Ministers has fought hundreds of these cases. In most a common thread has emerged. That thread is how unaware most of the pastors were that a precipitous action was coming.[54]

I could relate.

---

[50] Peter Steinfels, "More Clergy Forced Out, Survey Says," *Houston Chronicle*, Section E, (January 13, 1996): 1E, 2E. ©Houston Chronicle.

[51] David L. Goetz, "Forced Out," *Leadership: A Practical Journal for Church Leaders* (Winter, 1996): 40-42.

[52] Charles Chandler, "Is There a Rulebook on Forced Terminations?", *The Servant*, Volume 5, Issue 4 (October 2000).

[53] Chandler.

[54] Archibald Wallace III, "It Can Happen to You," *The Servant*, Volume 7, Issue 1 (January 2002): 1.

49 – Left Behind

Following my termination, many were shocked, upset, and disheartened by my forced termination. Some members left the church. For most congregants, however, leaving Kingsland meant leaving a network of long-established friendships, separating from a favorite Bible study class and teacher, and possibly withdrawing from a youth or children's program that was helping one of their kids.

Furthermore, few alternatives were available in the area as far as growing, dynamic churches were concerned. And, when it came to our recovery ministries, no other church in town was offering anything comparable—the recovery people still had each other, and they had nowhere else to go.

Kingsland Baptist Church regrouped and moved ahead, making mid-course corrections which gave the small faction that had forced my resignation what they wanted—a more theologically conservative, more traditional, and less innovative church. The church called an all-out fundamentalist as their next pastor. The 24-Hour Prayer Ministry continued, but Bethlehem Boulevard and the Home Bible Studies died. The support group ministry held on for a while, then faded away. While the church continued to grow, it grew at a significantly slower rate.

Oh, and there was one more item of note.

Nine months after my resignation from Kingsland, the interim pastor sent a letter to church members. The heading read "Welcoming a Sister Church: Defining and Refining Our Vision." Second Baptist Church of Houston had reached out to Kingsland, and preliminary meetings had taken place.

Representatives of Second Baptist had met with two Kingsland groups, the Great Commission Task Force, which had been the official leadership group for the church, and the Kingsland deacons, now restored, at least in practice, to their traditional role as an authoritative board.

Second Baptist's intent, as explained in the letter, was the discussion of a possible merger of the two congregations. The interim pastor wrote that Second Baptist had posed a "very sensitive" question for consideration by the members of Kingsland Baptist Church: "In light of our established ministry at Kingsland and current staff needs, and given the near-term plans of Second to build in this vicinity, could there be a benefit, could it be God's will, for us to join our resources and abilities as one body, merging or marrying our two churches into one?"

The interim pastor challenged the Kingsland congregation to take the time to evaluate its own identity, mission, and vision before deciding about the offer being made by Second Baptist.

Second Baptist, a megachurch with 10 times as many members as Kingsland, wanted to talk about "marrying" the two churches. "Gobbling up" would have been a better phrase to describe the possible union.

Prior to reading the letter from Second Baptist, I could have convinced myself that I had been paranoid about the megachurch's acquisition of a new campus down the street. Now, I wasn't so sure. The offer to merge struck me as stunning. I had never imagined such a bold move.

Eventually, Kingsland said no to the merger. Yet what sticks with me today is the fact that Kingsland's deacons had entertained the idea and had not stopped it from presentation to the entire congregation. I had to ask myself how long the possibility was under consideration, and if the thought of being part of a megachurch had pre-dated my termination. If I were a conspiracy theorist, I definitely had food for thought.

Today, with a membership of more than 64,000,[55] Second Baptist Church is one of the largest churches in the Southern Baptist Convention, and in Houston is exceeded only by Joel Osteen's church.

In 2004, the Forest Cove Baptist Church on the north side of Houston did merge with the megachurch. In 2006, additional Second Baptist campuses were established in Pearland on the south side of Houston, and at a location in northwest Houston. More recently, Second Baptist established a second satellite campus in another part of Katy.

Under the leadership of Ed Young, the church has grown from an average weekend attendance of around 500 in 1978 to over 23,610 in 2014.[56] The whispering members of Second Baptist had been right about one thing: I didn't know how to grow a church like Ed Young.

* * *

Having said no to Second Baptist's offer to merge, Kingsland called a new senior minister about a year after my resignation. In the printed flier sent to introduce Kingsland's members to the prospective pastor, he was described as "a literal interpreter of the Scripture. He believes for instance, in a literal Eden, in a literal Adam and Eve, and in the literal Noah who survived the universal flood of old." As conservative as I was, even I conceded that Adam and Eve might not have been two actual individuals, and that the earth could be much older than the 6,000-year estimate promoted by biblical literalists.

More indicative of his theological stance, the new pastor had been elected to serve on the board of trustees of the Southern Baptist Foreign Mission Board in 1995. This was a clear indicator that he was aligned with the fundamentalist group that was tightening its grip on the Southern Baptist Convention as they made sure that only the theologically pure were being placed on any such boards.

His ultra-conservative approach was further evident in a significant change he made in the annual U-Turn weekend for senior high students. Since its inception, the event had been co-ed as multiple groups of a dozen or so senior high boys and girls stayed with church families for a weekend focused on spiritual growth. The new pastor directed that the weekends would no longer be co-ed. To my knowledge, no problem with the mixed arrangement had ever occurred, but I guess it was like the West Texas ban on mixed swimming during my teenage years. Baptists could never be too vigilant about inadvertently contributing to some lapse of morality, especially among the youth.

Unfortunately, a lapse in vigilance did occur. It was five years later. This same pastor, the one who believed in a literal Adam and Eve, resigned after admitting a literal sexual affair with a woman he was counseling.

* * *

In the months following my departure, Kingsland's leaders reassured support group ministry participants that they were not unwanted stepchildren. But in the words of one of the lay leaders of the recovery groups, "The support group ministry came to a screeching halt. There just wasn't much support from the church staff." Groups using my books and other books in the Southern Baptist Life Support series were replaced with a new program called "Celebrate Recovery."

Celebrate Recovery originated at Saddleback Community Church, led by Senior Pastor Rick Warren. Today, Saddleback Community Church has more than a dozen locations in Southern California as well as four international locations. Rick Warren's book, *The Purpose Driven Life*, has sold more than 30 million copies.

In 2001, I attended a one-day Celebrate Recovery leader training conference in Austin, Texas. That day, I learned that Celebrate Recovery is an evangelical Christian version of the Alcoholics Anonymous 12-Step Program—one that identifies Jesus as the one and only true higher power. Celebrate Recovery focuses on eight recovery principles found in the teaching of Jesus: conviction, conversion, surrender, confession, restitution, prayer, quiet time, witnessing, and helping one another.

For those who wanted the comfort and familiarity of a process completely rooted in Christianity, Celebrate Recovery provided it. For those unsettled by co-ed sharing of confidences, Celebrate Recovery met their needs as groups were always restricted by gender. For those who wanted no feedback or commentary from other participants, again, Celebrate Recovery fit the bill.

In my view, the effort to make sure Celebrate Recovery's approach was purely biblical, completely spiritual, and not secular in any way had resulted in a program that was easier to duplicate, but less powerful in bringing about meaningful change.

Celebrate Recovery's insistence on no co-ed support groups was based on the belief that sharing is deeper in same gender groups. This is true in some respects, but we had seen powerful results in co-ed groups that could not have been obtained in a same gender group.

Celebrate Recovery's prohibition on allowing group members to offer one another feedback—following traditional 12-Step programs—eliminated a potentially valuable process that creates connection and enhances healing. Our group leaders modeled a form of feedback that was not advice-giving but enabled group members to provide mutual help and support as the group meetings progressed.

In comparison to Making Peace Groups, Celebrate Recovery was light on psychology, light on introspective self-awareness, and heavy on finding every answer in a Bible verse. One participant at Kingsland called it a "watered down version of a traditional 12-Step group."

I first met Rick Warren 30 years earlier in New York. He was scheduled as the featured speaker for a denominational event in New York City. For some unknown reason, only a half-dozen of us showed up to hear him, yet his response to the low turnout was to take it in stride. He had come all the way from California to New York, and his audience consisted of six people. So, instead of continuing in a formal format, we all went to lunch and talked.

Warren came across as a humble person—friendly, calm, and plainspoken. His convictions were clear and definitive; he truly believed in the simple, practical principles he was using in leading his church. I was impressed.

Attending the Austin Celebrate Recovery conference decades later, I was surprised to hear that one of the guidelines for starting a Celebrate Recovery ministry in a church was not to use any other Christian recovery materials—only Celebrate Recovery materials should be used.

The conference leader that day was the co-founder and national leader of the Celebrate Recovery ministry. I introduced myself to him during one of the breaks. He knew who I was, and he spoke favorably of *Making Peace with Your Past*. He showed no embarrassment or discomfort with the fact that I had been sitting in his audience moments earlier when he had directed those present not to use anyone else's books—and that included my books—in their church recovery ministries.

I asked why he was taking this position. I can't remember the exact reason he gave in response, but I can describe the attitude that fueled his answer: "We have the truth. We have God's way to do it. You don't need to use anyone else's resources. They may mislead you." It seemed to me he might just as well have said "It's nothing personal. Just business." After all, Celebrate Recovery was developing their brand, establishing customer loyalty, and preventing vulnerability to competitive products.

Kingsland Baptist Church began using Celebrate Recovery materials—and only those materials—for their support group ministries.

Celebrate Recovery continued for about five years at Kingsland, then it too passed away, and with it, the last remnant of recovery-oriented, support group ministries. Just a decade earlier the nation's largest protestant denomination had sent cameras to Kingsland Baptist to film support groups in action and testimonials from individuals whose lives had been changed. The purpose of the video: to provide a model for other churches to see and emulate. Now, that model was dead.

There was a positive note, however. The same leader who reported the "screeching halt" of the Making Peace-style groups eventually moved to another church in the Katy area. There he launched what became the largest support group ministry on the far west side of Houston, including a Saturday night recovery service. And he did this while completing a seminary degree. His ministry continues to grow.

* * *

The fourth pastor of Kingsland Baptist Church was a young man who had been the associate minister of youth and later the prayer ministry coordinator while I was pastor at Kingsland. He and his wife were likable, kind, and completely sincere—admirable people by any standard. He returned to become the senior pastor of Kingsland Baptist Church in 2003.

In November of 2011, someone told me that I should go online to listen to his sermon from the preceding week because he had mentioned me. That got my attention. I had received no contact from him in the almost nine years he had been the pastor of Kingsland.

Listening to the online recording of his sermon, I heard something more significant than the mention of my name. I heard a pastor who was disheartened and burdened enough that it was bleeding over into his sermon for all to see and hear.

He was emotional as he talked about when he and his wife had first come to Kingsland, broken and dispirited. They sat on the back row, Sunday after Sunday, and heard me preach a message of grace and encouragement. He talked about how much my sermons had helped them as they were recovering from a bad experience in the last church they had served.

Returning to the present, the pastor said Satan was at work in Kingsland's congregation. He talked about how the congregation needed to have a spirit of mercy and unity, and how important it was to work together in harmony. Listening between the lines, I heard a pastor who was facing conflict in his congregation. I wondered if the conflict involved some of the same individuals who had generated problems during my tenure. Then again, maybe it had been just one discouraging week that came bubbling up in a Sunday sermon.

When a large church is involved, it can take 9-18 months for a senior pastor to make a move to a new pastorate. One year after this pastor preached the sermon I had been asked to listen to, a news story carried the report of his call to be the senior minister of a church in his home state on the East Coast. The reporter quoted him as saying, "I heard the Lord and he started to speak to us very clearly through the scriptures that we were supposed to go home."

I could not help but think back to the original request made by the personnel committee in 1996. I was to say that God was leading me somewhere else—something I refused to do. After I was asked to leave, I learned that Kingsland's first pastor had also been asked to leave and had done so quietly—"under the Lord's leadership." But maybe this time—in 2012—God had actually spoken to the pastor and was leading him to return home.

Regardless of how or why he left, the young pastor's years at the church had been productive in many ways. Under his leadership, Kingsland started three mission churches in the West Houston area and a ministry that assists families in adopting children. Worship attendance increased by more than 70% in the 10 years he served as senior minister.

* * *

In 1996, Stuart, Kingsland's personnel committee chairman, told me that when I left, the church would go right on without me. It was one of the things he said to minimize the significance of my decade of pastoral leadership. When he made the statement, I disagreed. But in the years that followed, I began to wonder if Stuart had been right.

As the years passed, and I moved forward with my life, I became less aware of what was happening at Kingsland Baptist Church, but I couldn't help but notice that the church continued to add new buildings, which was a sign of growth. Over time, I was humbled by how little impact my leaving seemed to have had. I wondered at times how much difference I really made.

While writing this book, I decided to take a closer look at the growth of my former church during the 20 years following my termination. With time and distance, I hoped to be able to establish some objective measure of what I did—or did not—accomplish. As part of my inquiry, I made a trip to the office of the Union Baptist Association—Houston's Southern Baptist denominational office—where I spent a morning reviewing two decades of statistics. I was surprised by what I found when comparing growth statistics for my 10-year tenure (from 1985-1995) to the first and second 10-year periods after I left. I used the growth rate of the Katy Independent School System as a reference point for the growth of the community.

During my 10 years of leadership from 1985 to 1995, worship attendance grew at a rate of 271%—four times the growth rate of the Katy community.

In the two 10-year periods following my departure, the rate of growth for worship attendance was 74% and 43%, in both cases, lower than the community's growth rate. Or, to put it another way, if for the first 20 years after I left Kingsland Baptist Church, growth rates had been the same as under my leadership—in 2015 the church would have had an average weekly attendance of 15,278 instead of 2,770.

For Baptists, the ratio of baptisms to the number of church members is one way of measuring the effectiveness of a church's evangelistic efforts. A lower ratio indicates that it takes fewer members to win one convert. In the 20 years after I left Kingsland, the ratio almost doubled—meaning—less effective evangelistic efforts.

Would the church's growth numbers be better today if, in 1996, I could have taken a short sabbatical and returned with renewed vigor and vision? Maybe. Maybe not. But one fact is clear—Stuart told me that under my leadership, the church was not growing fast enough and that I was the problem.

Just for the record—*Stuart was incorrect.* But the real significance of these numbers is not about my leadership. It's about another dramatic *exception to the rule of faith.* In the church, tribalism—placing priority on established, long-term members, maintaining the existing base of power, and doing things the way they've always been done—are likely to take precedence over the call of the church's founder to make outreach to hurting people the top priority.

Having made my point, I should note that Kingsland's Sunday morning attendance is more than double what it was when I left. The church's size and growth are more than noteworthy—it is one of Southern Baptist's largest churches. In 2014, based on average weekly worship attendance, Kingsland Baptist Church was the 142nd largest church in the Southern Baptist Convention[57]—an impressive number out of 46,499 churches.[58]

The church's fifth pastor arrived in May of 2014. He is a graduate of Jerry Falwell's Liberty Baptist Theological Seminary. He has led the Kingsland congregation to acquire a second campus and is challenging them to dream a bigger dream.

Kingsland Baptist Church is vibrant, dynamic, and alive—offering a myriad of ministries and a comprehensive emphasis on missions—and worshipping three times each Sunday morning in the Encouragement Center we opened in the fall of 1989.

---

[55] Allan Turner, "Churches Reach Out to Suburbs for Growth," *Houston Chronicle Online*, April 5, 2016, http://www.houstonchronicle.com/news/houston-texas/houston/article/Churches-reach-out-to-suburbs-for-growth-5379696.php.

[56] Thom S. Rainer, "Largest Churches in the Southern Baptist Convention: Data Represents 2014 Average Worship Attendance," Thom S. Rainer: *Growing Healthy Churches Website*, http://thomrainer.com/sbc500/.

[57] Thom S. Rainer, "Largest Churches in the Southern Baptist Convention: Data Represents 2014 Average Worship Attendance," *Thom S. Rainer: Growing Healthy Churches Website*, http://thomrainer.com/sbc500/.

[58] Carol Pipes, "SBC Reports More Churches Serving Fewer People," June 10, 2015, *Lifeway Website* http://blog.lifeway.com/newsroom/2015/06/10/sbc-reports-more-churches-serving-fewer-people/.

50 – Freelance Minister

In 1996, the space shuttle Endeavour launched with six astronauts on board for a nine-day mission, Princess Diana and Prince Charles separated and were headed toward divorce, and the Internet, not yet a standard household tool, was nonetheless opening a vast new world of connectivity.

I was momentarily untethered, floating aimlessly. I had involuntarily disconnected from the organization that had been the center of my devotion, creativity, and tireless efforts for a decade.

After leaving Kingsland Baptist Church, I was certain of one thing—I never wanted to be a pastor again. If a small faction of disgruntled individuals could force me out of a community I loved—against the will of most of the members of the church—this was no longer a profession in which I wanted to serve.

Nothing about my commitment to live my life guided by Jesus had changed. My faith had been challenged, but it had not been shattered. I had experienced spiritual struggles and periods of questioning throughout my life, and while this was the most challenging, I still believed I had been called to ministry. Now, despite periodic moments of anger, shame, and sadness, I also felt free—suddenly—free to decide how I would practice my calling.

I was 48 years old. I had followed one career path and only that path since I was 16. Now, for the first time in my life, I was considering my options the way people normally do in their twenties. It felt exciting in its own way.

The 10 months of severance pay from Kingsland provided some breathing room—time to think about exactly what I wanted to do. And one of my goals was to develop multiple sources of income. Never again did I want to be dependent on a single source.

Since our days in New Jersey, Linda had offered tutoring services to students out of our home. She had continued for years until serving in her full-time position at Kingsland. After we left Kingsland, she began signing up tutoring students again. She also put her resume into circulation. She had developed a meaningful career path as a preschool and children's minister and wanted to find another church staff position.

Before the year was out, she was called as minister of preschool and children to a church demographically similar to Kingsland Baptist, in a Houston suburb 30 miles from our house in Katy. She quickly felt at home in her new job.

Within weeks of my resignation, I too was working, but in concert with my goal of multiple income sources, I took on a variety of roles—all ministry-related—from pastoral counselor to radio talk show host.

Starting new things was in my blood. With a trip to the county clerk's office, a few forms, and some help from a graphic artist, I set up a company called "Giant Steps." Armed with a new business card and all my organizational experience, I stepped into self-employment. My focus: helping people take Giant Steps toward self-awareness, recovery, and growth.

A little more than a month after leaving Kingsland, I was working as a pastoral counselor for the Union Baptist Association Center for Counseling. They relied on a team of 25 professional and pastoral counselors to provide services across the Houston metropolitan area.

My task—offering one-to-one counseling and leading *Making Peace with Your Past* support groups out of one of the center's offices. I realized it would take time to build a client base, but since I had other irons in the fire, that suited me fine. In a few short months, I was seeing a solid stream of clients in a high-rise office overlooking the city.

Since I had counseled church members in every pastorate, I thought this sort of counseling would feel entirely familiar. To a large extent, it did. But a surprising number of my clients seemed to be going through the motions, week after week sharing the same issues, and rather than changing behaviors, explaining why any course of action under consideration probably wouldn't work. Typically, this pattern would continue even after I had firmly but kindly confronted it. With these clients, I would eventually find myself staring out the window at passing traffic on the freeway six floors below. Then I would catch myself and feel guilty that I wasn't being patient enough, or that I wasn't somehow more engaged in hearing the client's recitation of problems one more time. In these cases, I wondered about my effectiveness. Sometimes I wound up recommending that a client stop our work together; without a different approach, no positive progress was likely to occur.

I had always loved playing even a small part in an individual's personal growth. In this new counseling setting, I found that the *Making Peace with Your Past Groups* could yield powerful results. Yet I couldn't help but notice that groups conducted outside of a congregational community were not as close-knit as those simultaneously connected to a dynamic church fellowship. The church provided a sense of belonging, a sense of family, and many other types of valuable support that created an oxygen-infused atmosphere for a Making Peace Group, an atmosphere not present in a sterile office in a commercial building.

Another reason that I was learning that counseling clients every day wasn't for me: Depression can be contagious. I have tremendous respect and empathy for counselors of all types who slog it out through complex and difficult—but negative—issues with their clients. I had been on the receiving end of counseling and remain grateful for the help I received, but I was finding that I couldn't be the counselor day in and day out. I needed an environment—and purpose—that felt more tangibly and consistently positive.

Public speaking was one of the things I most loved to do, and I took on several long-familiar types of engagements addressing topics like relationships and emotional healing as well as conducting workshops on support group leader training. In 1996 and 1997, I spoke in 19 cities in Florida, New Jersey, South Carolina, Tennessee, Texas, and Virginia.

For my out-of-town talks, I found myself in the entertaining position of being the semi-famous writer flown in from "somewhere else." This was something of a salve to the challenging mix of feelings I was dealing with in those days. I enjoyed these events. I might be asked to autograph a copy of one of my books, attendees were interested in what I had to say, and the always affirming attention was healing.

What took place in most of these meetings felt purposeful, significant, and even life-changing. After one of my training workshops for a large Florida church, I received a note signed by seven support group leaders in which every one of them said they had experienced personal healing while working through *Making Peace with Your Past*. They wrote: "Words can hardly express the gratitude and appreciation we feel towards you and your ministry. The training seminar and the information you shared are invaluable and are a real encouragement to us." Feedback like this reminded me that I still had something to contribute in some hybrid capacity as minister, public speaker, and counselor.

As a ministerial jack-of-all-trades, I also had the opportunity to be a stand-in preacher at Sunday services for vacationing pastors, which wasn't as fulfilling as I expected. I had loved giving sermons to my own congregations, but in Baptist churches, attendance is typically low when the regular pastor is away. Furthermore, in some churches, the second half of the Sunday morning worship service (the time for the sermon) was body-clocked as the ideal opportunity for a brief nap—undoubtedly the result of a steady diet of bad preaching, which had erased any positive anticipation of what might happen in the last half of the hour.

My communication skills had not waned, but in these situations, try as I might to give it everything I had, I was just the guy filling in for the pastor. I came to dread looking out at a disinterested audience.

I was about to learn the hard way that writing as a sideline is a different animal from making a living at it. I took on assignments for various Southern Baptist periodicals. During the first two years after leaving Kingsland, five of my articles were published for a national audience. Writing short articles for periodicals was fulfilling, but not financially significant. My paychecks for those five articles totaled $652.

Fortunately, the Galveston Gang was continuing to meet, and I enjoyed the support and lively discussions with my minister friends. The topics we discussed and my personal reflections on my own ministry generated an idea for a new book that would be titled, *Finding a Life of Your Own*. The book's intent: challenging ministers to live a balanced life that included self-care.

I drafted a book proposal that I submitted to LifeWay, the publisher of my previous books. I was flown in to Nashville to discuss the book at the LifeWay headquarters. I was shuffled from one office to another as I pitched my idea. Several people I talked to sounded interested. One commented that there was a better market for more traditional Christian books and encouraged me to write a book along those lines. It was *Congregation One* popping up in a Baptist publishing house.

Eventually, I talked to a LifeWay staff member who had himself written multiple books about the stresses and problems faced by ministers. As I sat in his office, I realized that he saw himself—accurately—as the Southern Baptist guru on the subject. He was cordial enough, but I think I was encroaching on his turf.

After returning home, I received a polite rejection of my book proposal.

Making Peace with Your Past was continuing to impact the lives of individuals across the country in significant, positive ways. I told myself that at least I had that; my book was making a difference.

I received the following letter from a woman in Florida.

> I am that adult child that you describe in the pages of your book. Although I usually highlight important sections of most books I read, I quickly gave up the highlighter because it seemed that almost every word and every scripture had significance to me. On the pages of your book, I saw myself so vividly... not being validated by my parents; at eight years old, being a "parent" to my two younger sisters; being a compulsive overachiever; entering a marriage that was doomed to fail; and I could go on and on. You were writing about me. This book was about my life! Once I could see that many of my traits are simply "reactions" to certain "actions" in my life, I felt this incredible freedom. If what I am experiencing is somehow so predictable that you could write a book about it, then what I was experiencing was somehow more a part of the human condition rather than a direct defect in me. As strange as it may seem, being part of that collective gave me a spark of hope.

It was rewarding and satisfying to know that words I had written 15 years earlier were still doing their job.

Specialized consulting jobs offered another avenue for my background and skills to be put to use, and I took on opportunities to help other pastors—regardless of denomination—take "giant steps" in their ministries.

A large United Methodist Church in Houston contracted me to consult with their young associate pastor who was preparing to launch a Saturday night worship service built around recovery and support groups. Their program was called Mercy Street. It's still going strong today.

I was marketing myself via another consulting service that I called "Visitor

Friendly." A church would pay me to visit on a Sunday morning without anyone knowing who I was. I would experience the church just like any first-time visitor—looking for a place to park, figuring out which door to enter, finding the right Bible Study class, and sitting through the worship service. I would then write a detailed report with recommendations for improvements.

I didn't do a large number of Visitor Friendly consultations, but each one was interesting, and I was able to offer helpful information to each church. I knew I was reaching my objective when one pastor wrote that my suggestions would help his church "to be more effective, friendlier, more attractive to people, and… to reach more people for the kingdom."

These efforts were ways for me to share what I had learned, make a little money, and help improve the work done by churches, even if only in a small way.

Talk Radio was widely popular in the late 1990s. A seminary friend was on the staff of an all-talk Christian radio station in Houston. My friend convinced the station manager that I would be an excellent talk show host. I signed an agreement for a one-hour talk show once a week. After I had four shows under my belt, I was given a new time slot. And, my program—aptly named *Giant Steps*—would be broadcast live not weekly, but every afternoon Monday through Friday.

The goal of my show was simple: "sharing biblically-oriented resources for emotional healing and wholeness." The summer edition of the station's newsletter introduced me to the listening audience describing my call-in show as one that "speaks to the rough edges in our lives, the many things that stand between us and a better, more rewarding relationship with God."

The broadcast studio was impressive—newly constructed, beautifully decorated, and its office spaces filled with light. In addition to all the latest technical equipment, one entire wall of the studio was glass—a huge, 11th-floor window with a panoramic view of Houston's business parks, freeways, and traffic.

Spending an hour a day doing talk radio wasn't hard duty. Radio is a personal, one-to-one medium, and the intimacy I felt with my listeners suited me. I loved sitting behind the microphone. I loved the conversations. I was having fun!

Most of my broadcasts began by interviewing a guest, usually a nationally recognized figure calling in from another city, though some of my guests were counselors and leaders from the Houston area. From time to time, I opened the program with my own short talk. After each interview or talk, I took calls from my listeners.

Since many of my guests were authors, I received promotional copies of their latest publications, skimming through multiple books every week and absorbing as much as I could to prepare as thoroughly as possible. Most of the authors on the show had written books on marriage, parenting, relationships, emotional wholeness, or some other self-improvement issue.

I had interesting conversations with the authors of books like *Help for the Perfectionist*, *Churches that Abuse*, and *High Maintenance Relationships*. I interviewed Dwight Carlson, the author of *Why Do Christians Shoot Their Wounded* and John Townsend, co-author of *Safe People*.

My friends and supporters sent encouraging letters, and the attorney who had represented me during my separation discussions with Kingsland had become one of my fans. He wrote:

> Congratulations. This is a valuable ministry and it calls for someone with a heart for people and for ministry such as you have. You are truly gifted and called to do this show. Your voice, your spirit, your tone, all manifest such calmness and inspire trust and friendship. And you speak with natural authority based on your extensive experience. I have always suspected that God decided to move you out of Kingsland because the job and the audience were too small.

Words of encouragement like these were priceless—and I loved doing a radio talk show.

Although I wasn't sending out my resume, occasionally someone I knew would recommend me to a church that was looking for a pastor. I wasn't interested. And I was growing accustomed to an exciting period in my life when I felt free to try anything as vocational work.

Whatever was coming next, I was glad for the breadth of experiences in my transitional pursuits. I hosted a daily radio program. I worked as a counselor and consultant. I applied myself to writing. I used my skills in ways that felt logical and familiar, and others that stretched my comfort zone.

I discovered that I did not want to be a pastoral counselor—full-time or part-time. And I also learned that there were efforts I enjoyed and was good at—including freelance writing and talk show hosting—but that didn't mean I could support my family doing them.

Figuring out what I wanted to do for a living and what would generate a livable income was going to take more time, but that was okay. And, I was about to experience a fantastic opportunity to expand my ministry.

51 – South Korea

In September of 1996, *Making Peace with Your Past* was translated and published in South Korea. Two months later, I went to South Korea on a speaking tour to help launch a nationwide Christian support group movement. During my 7-day visit, I experienced a part of the world that was completely new to me, made a dear friend, and learned that the healing concepts I had written about could cross cultural barriers.

The flight to Seoul was arduous—more than 16 hours—but soon after my arrival late in the afternoon, I met my host, the man who had translated my book. Dr. Andrew Chung was a widely respected professor of psychology at the Korean Baptist Seminary in Daejeon, South Korea—a distinguished 49-year-old man emanating boundless energy and extraordinary kindness.

As we drove out of Seoul that evening, I was reminded of Manhattan. The city was packed with people, traffic, and towering buildings. But the most distinguishing characteristic was unlike anything I had ever seen in any city—scores of red neon crosses mounted atop church buildings and steeples. In some locales, I could see five or six of these crosses perched high in the air, above any other lights, all within a few blocks of each other.

Waking early on Friday morning in the city of Incheon, I took in the harbor view from my hotel room window. I could see a half-dozen or more docked ships, and one vessel navigating out to sea. Farther still, on the distant horizon—a low range of purple-hazed mountains set against a grey-blue sky. This was my first daylight glimpse of South Korea.

After a morning to myself, Dr. Chung and I lunched at the hotel. He suggested Western food, so I ordered a hamburger. Dr. Chung asked me to call him Andrew, and while the burger wasn't great, the conversation was fascinating. He told me the heart-rending story of a childhood that felt painful, uncertain, and insecure. Listening carefully to his compelling account, I was struck by Andrew's apparent lack of emotion. And I wondered if, in South Korea, there were cultural barriers to the emotionally connected sharing of deeply personal childhood experiences that are so vital to a recovery ministry?

Then, as he shared a particularly painful part of his story, Andrew began to weep. For several minutes, he was unable to speak. In support groups, over and over, I had seen individuals reach this emotional tipping point where, suddenly, involuntarily, a backlog of pain spills into view.

In our groups, we had come to understand such moments of release were in response to an inner voice that was crying out, "You can't hold this inside anymore." Something about telling one's story in a safe environment has a way of triggering these releases and allowing decades of hurt to find a release.

It was only moments earlier that I was concerned about cultural obstacles to emotional sharing. Yet here we were, sitting in an upscale hotel bar with a

Michael Jackson music video playing in the background and businessmen passing in and out for lunch while Andrew was—with great emotion—pouring his heart out. What was happening at our table was completely out of sync with the surroundings, but for me, this sort of unguarded conversation was acceptable, familiar, and even normal.

I went into support group leader mode. "It's okay to feel the pain," I told Andrew. "Thank you for honoring me by showing your feelings."

Through tears, Andrew confided that because he read my book, he knew he could trust me and that I would understand. He was correct. He could indeed trust me, and I did understand.

Andrew's story was in fact, public. He had included it in a book that became a bestseller in South Korea. But I don't think he had yet experienced an opportunity quite like this—the opportunity to tell his story to someone who had walked a similar walk, and knew how to receive, support, and encourage his sharing.

At that moment, I knew with absolute certainty that this was where I was supposed to be—here, in South Korea. And I knew with equal certainty that the concepts I had come to share—the concepts in my newly-translated book—were significant, even in this faraway land.

One of the things that was apparent as I got better acquainted with Andrew, his work, and his influence: His goal of using my book and my visit to help launch a support group movement in South Korea's churches was not a fantasy. He was a nationally-known figure. He had translated 25 books from English into Korean. He was receiving 150 invitations a year to speak. He was widely respected and much loved.

If anyone could make support group ministries successful in this country, it was this man. An indicator of how Andrew's vision was unfolding: He told me that one of his colleagues was launching the first ever South Korean Christian counseling journal. That alone was a significant event in terms of bringing a more introspective and self-aware version of Christianity into play. And the first issue—just released—featured a piece outlining the lecture I would be presenting the next day.

We had been sitting and talking in the same spot for hours. As we continued getting to know one another, I learned that despite the embrace of Christianity in general and encouragement of home-based Bible study cell groups, just as there was pushback against support group and recovery ministries in the U.S., the same sort of opposition existed in South Korea.

We moved out into a seating area in the hotel lobby and continued our conversation. We had much in common and much to talk about. We were both dedicated ministers who fervently believed that psychology was a friend of faith, that support groups were a tool for building spiritual maturity, and that each of us had a part to play in helping other Christians understand what we knew to be true.

Andrew asked about Kingsland—specifically, my departure. It had been 10 months since my resignation. In fact, I was in the last month of my severance pay. I had prayed for guidance on how much to say on this subject while in South Korea. I wasn't sure what the response would be.

It was one thing to relate the details of my forced termination to someone I had known for decades, someone who knew my character, skills and ministry accomplishments, but quite another to talk about it with someone I had just met. But Andrew had taken the risk of being vulnerable with me. Now it was my turn to trust.

I walked Andrew through the events that led to my resignation, talked about the betrayal by leaders and staff, and described the emotional pain I experienced. I had shared all this many times by now, and could talk about it without much emotion, but talking about it with my new friend—a person whose intelligence and integrity I had come to respect in just one long afternoon conversation—did make me feel vulnerable. Andrew maintained eye contact, listened carefully, did not judge at any point, and responded with compassion, empathy, and support.

That day, without planning it, we had practiced the key principles that make groups work: an open attitude, honest talk, a willingness to be vulnerable, and non-judgmental support. These were the concepts I would be speaking about in my talks that week. Two men who were about to spend a week as cheerleaders for Christian recovery and support groups had just engaged in their own unscheduled support group meeting.

On Saturday morning, as we drove to the church where I would be speaking, I could see more of Incheon than the view from my hotel window allowed. Incheon was stacked, packed, and teeming—it reminded me of New York's Chinatown—no corridor or passageway was wasted. Even the alleys were paved and lined with storefronts instead of back entrances.

The conference that day was sponsored by the Incheon Family Culture Institute and was being held at a Methodist church. As we entered the church, we were welcomed by a string of greeters, each of whom bowed as we entered. Something about this gesture touched me deeply because it seemed so heartfelt—more than a formality. I was an honored guest, Andrew explained, and thus the recipient of a special welcome.

A registration table had been set up in the lobby of the church sanctuary. Copies of *Making Peace with Your Past* and a new book by Andrew, *How Can We Change Men*, were offered for sale. And, each participant was given a copy of the premier edition of the new Korean Christian counseling journal, the first Christian counseling journal in the country's history—the one containing the outline of my lecture for the day.

Entering the sanctuary made me feel like I was back home. It was a large, impressive space with a soaring, 50-foot ceiling. The pews were dark mahogany, the chancel was covered with red carpet, and positioned five feet higher than the main floor was a massive pulpit on the left and a smaller one on the right. The back wall was covered with an expanse of organ pipes.

It could have been an American church—with one exception. On the back of each pew was a surface that could be pulled in place like a small desk top—much like the seat-back tray table on a plane, except it extended outward from the top of the pew and was designed for setting one's Bible and taking notes. This is a common feature in South Korean churches, and notetaking is a usual practice.

Many of the 200 people in attendance were soon using these pew desks to take notes as a Korean pastor spoke, sharing his testimony, describing years of physical and verbal abuse he had dealt his wife, explaining how he had learned the ways his childhood had affected his behavior, and how he and his wife had experienced emotional and relational healing. Next, his wife spoke. Andrew sat beside me and interpreted. Both testimonies were moving and powerful.

When I began speaking, I wasn't nervous, but one thing did feel awkward—shoes are not allowed when standing on the chancel platform of a South Korean church. Each person who walks onto the platform removes his shoes and slips into a pair of open-toed house slippers. Koreans have a way of sliding their shoes off quickly and walking naturally in these flip-flops—as in one unobtrusive motion. Unfortunately, my slippers were an inch shorter than my size 12 feet, they flip-flopped noticeably when I walked, and my gait was conspicuous. I also felt strange lecturing in slippers and a business suit.

It helped that Andrew was at my side, interpreting as I was being introduced to the audience, and then as I spoke. In fact, the interpreting process went smoothly. My new friend was clearly adept at this task, and he displayed an excellent rapport with the audience—with each audience—throughout the course of the week.

In my morning talk, I shared some of my experiences as an adult child of an alcoholic, then described the characteristics of a dysfunctional family, and the nature of shame.

When it was time to stop for lunch, a group of us walked down a winding road to a local restaurant. We climbed a flight of steps to enter, took our shoes off at the threshold, and were escorted to a room with a large table about 18 inches high on which two small grills had been placed. We sat on a clean, heated, wooden floor. It was chilly outside and the warmth from the floor and the gas grills enhanced the cozy ambiance.

The order was placed for "fire beef," consisting of small pieces of grilled beef cooked at the table, dipped in a spicy sauce, then wrapped in lettuce and eaten like a sandwich. As we ate, Andrew and I were interviewed by a journalist from a South Korean Christian magazine who was anxious to learn about our message of emotional healing.

After lunch, in the second half of my lecture, I discussed compulsive behavior and described how support groups work. I hadn't made it all the way through my outline when the allotted time was almost up, so I asked Andrew what we should do. A man sitting about two rows back spoke out in Korean translated by Andrew, "Take until ten o'clock tonight if you need to." That was a good sign.

When I was finished speaking that afternoon, comments suggesting the possibility of my return to South Korea for a second visit were already circulating.

Sunday took us to Daejeon, a city in west-central South Korea where I spoke three times that day at the Daejeon Baptist Church—the largest and best-known Baptist Church in the city. Andrew introduced me to the congregation, and I began. I spoke on "Letting Go of a Painful Past" to a perfect audience— quiet, attentive, nodding in agreement as I spoke—with many taking notes using the writing boards mounted on the pews in front of them.

After speaking to two services in the morning and my sermon at the church's evening service, I had spoken to 2,500 people that day. The pastor said he hoped to invite me back for a three-day revival-type meeting to focus on emotional healing, and he was interested in starting a support group ministry in his church.

On Monday, I spoke to a weekly interdenominational pastors' meeting in Seoul. On Tuesday, I spoke to a group of students and ministers at the Korean Baptist Seminary located on the outskirts of Daejeon. After my lecture there, one South Korean minister told me in broken English, "Thank you so much for your message. This is really a problem in our culture. We need this." On Wednesday, I presented a 2-hour lecture to an undergraduate family life class at the seminary. When Andrew entered the room, the students cheered. He seemed to be the most popular professor on campus—another reminder that I was with a talented and highly respected man.

During the week, Andrew and I had lots of time for discussion. And the more we talked, the more in sync with him I felt in terms of our views on both theology and psychology. His insights into faith and unresolved emotional issues were brilliantly articulated.

We were so much on the same page in our views that as Andrew was interpreting my talks, it became common for me to speak a sentence or two, pause as usual, then Andrew would go on for a couple of minutes. He was so in agreement with the message I was sharing that now and then he added a culturally appropriate comment or a personal illustration. Though he later received some ribbing from his wife about embellishing my talk, the audience loved it.

As Andrew and I talked, I found myself telling him more about that the events that took place at Kingsland, specifically the week in October of 1994, when the three crises had occurred around the same time. As I spoke about these experiences, my new friend encouraged me to see that God would use what happened to broaden my ministry. Andrew's faith in God's plan for my future was affirming.

My final speaking event was in the heart of Seoul on Wednesday evening at the Sarong Presbyterian Church—a church with an average Sunday morning worship attendance of 15,000.

The exterior of the church looked as if it could have been a modern office building—with sloping, curved walls that seemed to be entirely of glass—but overlooking its courtyard was an impressive free-standing steeple of red brick topped by a copper dome supporting a large cross. In the courtyard, beneath our feet, were brick pavers interspersed with clear, transparent blocks emitting light from below, hinting that a large part of the facility was actually underground.

We were escorted down several flights of stairs. As we descended, we could hear magnificent singing—contemporary choruses, sung with a depth of emotion that was deeply moving.

Reaching the main floor of the massive underground sanctuary, 60 feet below street level, we found ourselves in a room with 2,300 people. The main floor and the first balcony were almost full. As I had witnessed at the Daejeon Baptist Church, everyone in this well-heeled congregation was joining in song wholeheartedly, and many were swaying side-to-side as they sang.

What followed was a period of prayer during which most people prayed aloud and some wept openly. After an introduction by Andrew, once again I spoke on "Letting Go of a Painful Past." The audience sat quietly and listened intently in a way that reflected the extra attention required when hearing something new for the first time—another significant opportunity to introduce the message of emotional healing to a new audience in a faraway land.

On Thursday, it was time to return home. That morning, Andrew and I made a visit to the publisher of the Korean version of my book, where I met the man in charge and several of his team members. We talked about additional writing projects we might pursue, and I was excited about each possibility.

I had spoken to more than 10,000 people in five days. Over lunch, Andrew said he felt the trip had been a success in every way—so much so that he wanted me to make a return visit in six months.

That week in South Korea, I felt that God hadn't forgotten me, was continuing to use me, and still had plans for my future. I may have been forced out of my pastorate in Texas but had just played a small part in launching an emphasis on Christian support groups for a nation of churches—and I was coming back.

In December, a few weeks after I returned home, an apologetic Andrew informed me that many in South Korea were experiencing financial difficulties. It would be necessary to postpone my next visit.

My first speaking tour in South Korea was my last.

52 – Still Struggling

In the first weeks and months after leaving Kingsland, I was fortunate to find multiple sources of support. Linda was my best and most constant source of encouragement, but she was hurting too.

The guys in the Galveston Gang, my minister's support group, were also tremendously encouraging. And I was continuing to work through the grief process with my therapist, who was an active member of a local Episcopal church. In her own way, she was now my spiritual mentor, unafraid to bring Christian principles into our therapeutic sessions.

One of the characteristics of grief is this: Just when you think it's over, it sweeps back in with renewed force like an unexpected slap in the face. The grief I felt at leaving Kingsland was no exception. Despite all the generous, meaningful support, 15 months after leaving Kingsland, my emotional pain could resurface unexpectedly and powerfully.

I journaled extensively. It was a primary mechanism for constructively processing a mix of sometimes confusing emotions.

Sunday, April 13, 1997

I had just returned home from leading a Saturday support group conference in the Dallas-Fort Worth area. I woke up at 4:00 a.m. on Sunday and began to journal: "These days I am working to survive financially. I have pushed to the end of our financial limits. I sometimes feel that I am drifting further and further from God. My sense of hurt, anger, and revulsion over what happened at Kingsland seems to be at its peak. If I died now, I think it would be from a broken heart."

The day before, as I led the support group leader training, I had, as I always did, asked for volunteers, and then conducted an actual group meeting so conference participants could see how it was done. In the meeting, a woman described living with a hypocritical father who was a minister. He had disappointed her deeply, and her disappointment spilled over to her relationship with God—to a point where the only thing she had to say to God was: "I don't have anything else to say to you."

As she shared her experience with strong emotion, I began to have trouble staying in the group leader role. I was identifying so strongly with her whole story, the root of which was disappointment with God and the church.

Reflecting on what she had shared, I journaled: "It seems that every time I do one of the groups, I hear a few more stories proving that the church is a heavy burden for many people. So many are hurting, and the church will not validate their pain."

After leading the Saturday training conference, I had visited two of my mother's sisters who lived in the area. First, I stopped to see Lena and her husband, Mike. Being in their home of 50 years, a place where I had fond memories of visiting as a boy, was always comforting. This time was no different. Though not religious themselves, they wanted to know what had happened at Kingsland and how my family was doing. Telling them what took place and how I felt about it was part of my healing process.

I then made a visit to my Aunt Blanche, who lived a short distance away. But unlike Lena and Mike, Blanche attended church every Sunday. I journaled about my time with her:

> Blanche was kind and glad to see me. She too wanted to know what happened at the church. She was sympathetic, but went on to list her pastor's foibles, and indicated the church might be asking him to leave that very week. One of the worst sins her pastor had committed was announcing that he was going to spend Christmas day (a Sunday) with his grandchildren. A few minutes of listening to Blanche strengthened my resolve never to be a pastor again.

Christian theology taught that I wouldn't be on the receiving end of warm, unconditional support from my irreligious aunt and uncle, and I would from my devout aunt. But the opposite was true. Blanche tried to be understanding, but the fact that she joined in critiquing her pastor as he was about to be ousted cancelled any positive words she had for me. This was one more *exception to the rule of faith*.

Wednesday, May 7, 1997

I continued struggling with my view of God, and I felt alone. I journaled:

> God, I don't know if I know who you are. I'm having trouble believing all the things I've been taught to believe about you.

> I am alone. I have skills and knowledge, but I don't know where to use them. I will not long be content with just earning a living. What will come of me?

Tuesday, May 20, 1997

After a meeting with my therapist, I described my struggle with what to believe about the church, about faith, and about God.

> I have given my life to a religious system called evangelical Christianity. I have tried to be a good student of its teachings. I have tried to live by its ethical standards. I have tried to excel in its ranks of leadership. I have tried to persuade others to join its ranks. Following this belief system as I have has led me to emptiness, loneliness, and a struggle to know what I can

continue to believe.

Having ended a 30-year ministry of preaching and pastoring in local churches, I am now in a time of questioning. I know that God exists. I agree with the Bible that only a fool says there is no God. But I need to find a sense of certainty about God's presence in my life. I have a great deal of respect for Jesus. I have always felt he was my friend and that he was with me. I am trying to understand better who he is.

Thursday, May 29, 1997

Nine days later, I journaled my questions about the nature of God, along with my conviction that some type of God does exist:

I know that the world is a wonderful and amazing place. I believe it was created by God. In this world, I see the reflection of a God of power, beauty, and great wisdom. I can tell from the world and the universe in which the world is placed that God the creator is wonderful and amazing.

But I cannot tell from looking at the world whether he is actively involved in the lives of individual people like me. Sometimes the world is a dangerous place. By looking at the world alone, I do not know for sure whether God will hurt me or take care of me.

Humans are too complex to be accidents. There is something pitiful and stupid about powerful humans who claim they do not need God.

Friday, June 6, 1997

I wrote about an incident with my therapist. She had asked me—repeatedly—"What do you think it is inside of you that keeps you going and gives you this energy for life?" I journaled: "It finally dawned on me that maybe this is the presence of God in me. This would be a different kind of God than the one who seems to produce so much anxiety and shame in me." I was wondering if I could see God in a new and broader way.

Monday, June 23, 1997

I described myself as a spiritually damaged person:

- A spiritually damaged person gets negative results from spiritual activities that once produced growth.
- A spiritually damaged person has the feeling that things will never be the same again.

- A spiritually damaged person feels frustrated, stuck, embarrassed.
- A spiritually damaged person is characterized by repeated, unsuccessful attempts at repair.

Grief takes time, but I was dealing with more than grief. I was wrestling with the loss of my lifelong vocation, and I was also struggling with faith—sometimes questioning it, sometimes redefining it, sometimes ready to throw it away. But I wasn't down for the count.

The strongest believers—including ministers—go through periods of doubt. In fact, doubt can sometimes fuel spiritual growth.

I was comforted by author Scott Peck's ideas on spiritual growth, seeing myself as having moved from what he described as stage two, in which one's spirituality is tied to an institution, to stage three, characterized by skepticism and searching. Step three could lead to step four, a state of peaceful enlightenment.[59] If Peck was correct, my questions could actually be a sign that I was growing spiritually.

My journal entries reflected my low points, but I wasn't giving up my Christian faith. I was still an active member of a Southern Baptist Church. And I was still available to preach a Sunday sermon or to speak about Christian recovery and support groups.

---

[59] Scott Peck, *Further Along the Road Less Traveled: The Unending Journey Toward Spiritual Growth* (New York: Simon and Schuster, 1993), 122-125.

53 – Prison Sentences

In 1997, a prison door was slammed shut and permanently locked behind me. I hadn't been incarcerated, but I had been working in a prison trying to help those who were locked inside.

Four years earlier, *Making Peace with Your Past* was having such a pronounced impact at the Julia Tutwiler Prison for Women in Wetumpka, Alabama, that the chairman of the Alabama State Board of Pardons and Paroles stated that every inmate should have an opportunity to participate in a Making Peace support group while in prison.[60]

One inmate described the Making Peace Group as "the hardest thing you'll ever do in your life," and said, "When I started the group, I was determined not to open up, and no one was going to make me do it." But as she began working through *Making Peace with Your Past*, she began to face things she had previously avoided, had many tear-filled phone conversations with her mother, and reconnected with her father after a separation of many years. Describing the change in her life, she said, "I'm not a violent person anymore and I don't solve everything with anger."

Frances, a 32-year-old inmate convicted of drug trafficking, talked about how she had changed as a result of participating in a Making Peace Group, "I was mean and low-down," she said. "For years, I hated me." She continued, "I feel a lot better about myself now. I used to jump on prison officers or anyone else, but after I made peace with myself, I see that I am somebody."[61]

It was strange to learn about the use of my book in a state correctional facility by reading a news article. But it felt good to know my words were making such an impact in a prison, where getting help could eventually lead to a meaningful life outside of prison walls.

* * *

In October of 1997, Texas Governor George W. Bush visited the Jester II Unit, a prison facility in Richmond, Texas, a suburb of Houston. Bush was there to help launch a new prison ministry, and his visit was reported by the *Houston Chronicle*. The article described how Bush had put his arm around a convicted murderer as he joined more than 50 prison inmates in singing *Amazing Grace*. Afterwards, Bush commented: "Standing up there, singing that song, reminded me that all of us need to think about our hearts, think about our lives. We're all human. We all make mistakes."

Also present that day was Chuck Colson, former special counsel to President Richard Nixon, who founded Prison Fellowship Ministries after serving a Watergate-related prison sentence. Colson joined Bush in touring the prison unit that was the new home for the InnerChange Freedom Initiative, a program designed to help inmates nearing release prepare for life outside of prison "through a change of heart, or spiritual and moral transformation." The program was a joint effort by Colson's Prison Fellowship organization, the Texas Department of Criminal Justice, and churches from the Houston area. The *Houston Chronicle* article reported: "The faith-based voluntary program has been called a Bible boot camp of sorts, with days and evenings filled with courses on subjects such as personal responsibility, parenting and financial management. The three-part program begins a year to a year and a half before an inmate is scheduled for release and continues outside prison with volunteer mentors from the community." Colson credited Bush for having the courage to be the first in the nation to try the program and said it was being watched "everywhere."[62]

About a month after George W. Bush visited the prison unit, I was hired to develop curriculum for the Jester II Unit InnerChange program. I was working through an intermediary firm under contract by Prison Fellowship—a New Hampshire-based consulting group called Dare Mighty Things. *Making Peace with Your Past* was already in use by the InnerChange program and was highly regarded. Thus, they called me about the new project.

The InnerChange program needed a family life course that dealt with some of the hard-core realities these male inmates were facing; every Christian family life book they had reviewed to date had too much of a rose-colored glasses approach—addressing issues faced by "more normal" families. What InnerChange needed instead: a family life study book written for inmates with relevant answers to questions specific to them.

I was not only interested but intrigued by the assignment. I signed a contract to write and test a 12-week family life course for the InnerChange program. I would be paid a flat fee, with one third of the amount paid up front. The payments for writing would be more than adequate income for the three months required for the project.

The plan was this. First, we would hold a Saturday and Sunday retreat at the correctional facility, and each inmate would be allowed to invite a family member. Next, we would meet weekly on Thursday nights for 12 weeks, holding support group meetings based on units from the study book that I would write.

Excited about this new challenge, I dove in enthusiastically. I developed a content outline for the whole course and wrote materials to be used at the weekend retreat, getting approval along the way from my contact person at Dare Mighty Things. I needed to write one unit each week, use it in an actual meeting, then fine-tune and finalize it for publishing. Once finished, the study book would be rolled out for use by support groups in prisons across the U.S.

During the retreat, I coached attendees on sharing and feedback, something that was understandably foreign to them, even more than it was to most congregants in a church. The retreat's format followed a pattern I had long used and found effective—giving a talk from the material I had prepared, then organizing into small groups of 6 to 8 for sharing, each group a mix of inmates and family members.

The room was about the size of a high school classroom, a little small for the 50 to 60 in attendance, so the group circles were closer to one another than I normally preferred. In fact, at church, we usually had one group per room, whereas here we had as many as 10 groups meeting in the same room. But it didn't matter. Everyone—the inmates and their family guests—were glad to be there. The feeling in the room was one of positive anticipation.

The content I shared in my talks connected, the small group format was effective, and encouraged unguarded exchanges. What was taking place was emotionally intense—you could see it and feel it in facial expressions and body language, and a change in the energy in the room. The process was working, and between sessions, both inmates and their visitors offered positive feedback.

The atmosphere felt so accepting of the work, it was easy to forget we were in a prison meeting room. I felt completely safe, and besides the fact that neither I nor any guest could leave without being escorted through multiple doors unlocked by a guard, the scene felt very comfortable and normal. And I was immensely pleased at the breakthroughs I saw taking place.

While it was always satisfying to help someone dig up unresolved pain from the past, wrestle with it, and move beyond it, this felt different. In a way, surreal. Here, the idea of helping an inmate return to a family he had hurt, embarrassed, and abandoned by committing a crime, perhaps a violent one— able to reconnect with a new level of calmness, self-awareness, and self-control—struck me as extremely important. I was honored to be part of something so significant.

God had opened this door for me. God was using me. God had not forgotten about calling me to minister.

As the retreat ended on Sunday, I felt a tremendous sense of satisfaction and hope. I told the men and their guests to read the materials each day, and that I would see them on Thursday night for our first weekly meeting.

On Monday, everything changed.

My contact person at Dare Mighty Things called. "Your writing project and weekly test groups have been cancelled."

At first, I wasn't sure I heard correctly. Hadn't the retreat met, no... exceeded expectations? Hadn't the on-site leader of the InnerChange ministry at Jester II Unit expressed approval and excitement? What on earth had happened?

The staff person calling was alternately dumbfounded, embarrassed, and empathetic. But her organization was the middleman, not the decision-maker. It was Prison Fellowship that issued the decision to end my involvement.

"Prison Fellowship has a new president," my contact person said. "His mentor is a man named Henry Brandt, and Brandt doesn't like your writing.

He thinks it's too psychological, not biblically based, and he's persuaded the new president of Prison Fellowship to cancel your project."

I asked, "Can I go back on Thursday and get closure with the inmates… just tell them goodbye and that I'm sorry I won't be able to come back?"

"No, Prison Fellowship does not want you to go back," she said.

It was an old, familiar tune. I couldn't believe I was dealing with this again—not being allowed to say goodbyes, and "too much psychology, not enough Bible."

Henry Brandt was the co-author of *The Heart of the Matter*, the book for which Henry Blackaby had written the forward. These were the God alone, psychology is dangerous, no social work, no introspection, "immediate healing" guys I had run into before.

I felt blindsided, hurt, humiliated, and in a way, blackballed. I was also upset at the lack of regard for the inmates. The retreat had elevated their hopes. They were looking forward to Thursday night. And now it wasn't going to happen.

For the third time in my life as a minister, I wouldn't be allowed to say goodbye to a group with whom I had formed a close connection. The inmates I engaged with were men who knew too much about broken promises. Now I was just one more authority figure who promised he would be there and wouldn't show up.

I called the InnerChange director at Jester II Unit and asked if I could simply have a short visit with the men to tell them goodbye. He said the higher-ups at Prison Fellowship would not allow it. What would it have hurt for me to spend 10 minutes with these men? What would it have hurt for me to tell them I was sorry it hadn't worked out? How could anyone who knew a typical inmate's family of origin story—filled with broken promises—do this to them?

How ironic. I wanted to get into prison, but I couldn't.

My project was done. There would be no more payments to cover my next two months of income. More importantly, I would not be writing a new book that would touch the lives of prison inmates across the U.S.

Making Peace with Your Past had a proven track record in prisons and jails across the country, but that didn't matter. This was a Christian turf war. I'd been there before, and I had my battle scars.

As I processed what happened, something inside me broke.

I was teaching emotional healing in a Christian world that should have embraced it, but that world was, itself, frequently emotionally unsafe. I was operating within a faith community where methods that could create meaningful positive change were, themselves, deemed a danger to those in need of that change. Kingsland Baptist taught me that I could never feel emotionally safe working for a church. And now, my prison experience was one more reminder that the larger Christian world in which I sought to make a difference shared the same characteristics.

---

[60] "Inmates Benefit from *Making Peace with Your Past*," *LifeTouch: Equipping Adults Through Discipleship and Family Development*, Volume 1, Number 4 (October 1993): 4.

[61] "Prison Ministry Setting Captives Free from Their Past" *Baptist Message*, March 24, 1994, 7.

[62] Patti Muck, "Bush Lends Voice to Prison Chorus," *Houston Chronicle*, (October 17, 1997): 1A, 19A. ©*Houston Chronicle*.

54 – High Tech

By the start of 1998, I had left my daily radio program—too much time and too little income. I had stopped working for the UBA Center for Counseling—it wasn't what I wanted to do. Opportunities for ministry-related consulting had faded. Plans to return to South Korea had been postponed indefinitely. Writing invitations from the denomination had ceased. The Prison Fellowship writing project had ended unexpectedly.

On a positive note, my books were still selling, and readers were offering praise. One *Making Peace with Your Past* reader wrote, "I have found nothing on dysfunctional families so insightful and penetrating. No matter what you have read before or how much counseling you may have had, you will gain tremendous insight from this study." My writing was helping people, and I was ready and willing to maintain my identity as a minister—with an emphasis on speaking about support groups and emotional healing—but my freelance ministry was losing momentum. As the number of speaking invitations declined, I needed other sources of income.

I had been interested in technology since I was a boy, tinkering with short wave radios and other electronic gadgets through my growing years. When the first personal computers went on sale in the early 1980s, I persuaded my Arizona church to buy one, just before I bought my own—a Compaq "portable" computer that weighed 35 pounds and looked like a small plastic suitcase.

I then taught myself to design database applications and developed the Smart Church software for use by my Arizona church. We put that same software to use at Kingsland as well, where we installed a network of multiple computers that were serviced by a Houston company called CNI. I got acquainted with the CNI tech who serviced our network and showed him the Smart Church software I had been working on for five years. He was impressed and mentioned my application to his boss.

When I resigned from Kingsland Baptist, CNI told me they needed someone to create database applications for their clients, and they wanted me to do contract work for them. They would bill the client their standard hourly rate and pay me roughly 70%.

I transitioned from working in a vocation for which I was educated at the doctoral level to working in a field where I had no training, credentials, or experience. But I was playing and replaying a mental tape of my dad's words: "You can do whatever you set your mind to." So, I approached this new work in the same way I was taught to sweep a floor—with energy, and persistence.

After three years of working with CNI, I went independent, started my own company, and purchased what soon became the largest custom software development ad in the *Houston Yellow Pages*.

My list of clients began to grow. I designed custom software applications for a major hospital in Houston, a senior adult care center, and a company that provided continuing education for Texas real estate agents. I worked with a wound-care nurse in developing software that helped medical personnel improve care for hard-to-heal wounds.

I learned that the most important phase of building a custom application begins with listening to the clients as they describe what they need. My counseling and people skills came into play as I sat in meetings, helping clients articulate their software requirements.

This was also a period when I was learning new things about myself. I had always thought that I drove myself so hard because I worked for God, but I was realizing that working hard was in my nature. I worked just as hard at designing software as I had in ministry.

But there was something different about me in my software designer role. One of my clients described me as easygoing. It made me laugh out loud because no one—and I mean no one—had ever described me as easygoing in the context of my work as a minister. In my new profession, I was more relaxed. Despite the financial uncertainty of whether I would have paying clients in a month or two, the stress level was a fraction of what it had been when I was a pastor.

And, not having a God-inspired message about what any software application was supposed to look like, I was less driven and more flexible. My clients told me what they needed, and I created it for them. The focus was on providing what was requested. And if the client wanted more of my time to talk about some aspect of a project—no problem. I was charging by the hour.

* * *

More than a decade earlier, my cousin Mike had lost all his businesses—a chain of restaurants and health clubs—because of his addictions. After multiple rounds in treatment centers and with several years of sobriety under his belt, he had started over and made half a million dollars in network marketing.

Network marketing works like this. You sign up with a company as a distributor to do two things: sell a product and recruit other people to sell the product under you—your downline. Some people think of network marketing companies as pyramid schemes, which is true in some cases, but there are network marketing companies that are completely legitimate and do help people make extra cash—sometimes a full-time income.

Mike—a natural born salesman—knew all the ins and outs of network marketing, and he knew many of the top leaders in the business. Over the years, we talked a lot about this type of business and how to succeed in it—starting with how to spot just the right opportunity. One of the most important principles I picked up from him was this: Get in on the ground floor.

In 1997, I found a company that met all the criteria Mike had taught me to seek. FlashNet was an early Internet Service Provider (ISP) that advertised heavily and sold its services directly to customers but had also created a separate arm to utilize a network marketing approach that would allow distributors to sell the Internet to friends and family. This subsidiary was called FlashNet Marketing.

FlashNet Marketing wasn't selling some unproven nutritional supplement or overpriced household product. It was just what it claimed to be—a way to connect to the Internet. And, it was one of the first companies to offer a one-year, flat-rate, unlimited-use Internet connection at a highly competitive price.

The CEO of FlashNet, Lee Thurburn, was a middle-aged man who hailed from Fort Worth. Before starting the company, his career was stalled, and by his own account, he was living with his mother. He and a friend with money to invest started a business to provide websites for real estate companies and decided to try selling the Internet services they were leasing for their real estate clients to everyone. Thus, FlashNet was born.

Lee Thurburn came to Houston in August of 1997 to recruit new distributors for FlashNet Marketing. When I heard him speak, I knew immediately that this company offered all the things I was looking for. Its network marketing division was brand new, which meant it provided an opportunity to get in on the ground floor. I signed up that night, paying $300 for the highest level of entry as a distributor. If I was going to do it, I would do it like I swept floors—wholeheartedly.

For the next two years, I continued my software development business, all the while working on developing my FlashNet business. I worked slowly but steadily to recruit other distributers, and to sell the company's Internet service plan.

A year or so later, the CEO hired Terri Maxwell to be the president of FlashNet Marketing. Not long after Terri took on this key position, she held a meeting in Fort Worth with the top 10 FlashNet distributors in the U.S. I was invited to the meeting and was surprised to learn I had built the fourth largest distributor organization in the company.

The top five distributors were given the title of "National Sales Director." Eventually, I was given the additional title of "National Director of Training" and helped Terri design and write some of the company's training materials for distributors. This was a brave new world for me—it was fun—and I loved it.

Not only was I part of a sea-change in terms of the use of the Internet just as it was exploding, but I was able to exercise many of the leadership skills I had refined as a pastor: leading weekly recruiting meetings in Houston, encouraging and training distributors in my organization, speaking at some of the company's national meetings, and building relationships with key leaders in my downline.

I became the number one distributor with 60% of FlashNet Marketing's Internet customers under me. A percentage of what each of these customers paid monthly was shared with me, and this would continue as long as they remained customers. This was the ground floor!

In October, November, and December of 1998, I traveled almost every week for FlashNet—Kansas City, Denver, St. Louis, and Oklahoma City. Everywhere I went on these trips, I would approach people, total strangers—in computer stores, in my hotel lobby, anywhere I could find— to sell them on signing up for our Internet service, or, more importantly, to enlist them as FlashNet distributors. I was a traveling evangelist for the Internet—proclaiming the good news about a high-tech opportunity to start a home-based business.

FlashNet was my first post-education experience of serving in an organization where my vocational identity was not related to ministry. As a pastor, I had regular interaction with people who didn't behave like themselves around me. They cleaned up their language. They were careful with their humor. They didn't drink alcohol around me. In my new role, people knew about my ministerial background, but pretty much ignored it. They saw me for who I was to them—a leader in an Internet sales company. This was a vastly different experience for me—and a good one. I found it refreshing when people didn't hide their real selves.

Things were going so well at FlashNet that in January of 1999, I walked into a Lexus car dealership in Fort Worth to see five new cars, each with a big red bow on top, and one of them was mine. I was one of five national sales directors to receive a Lexus sedan to drive as my own for two years.

The church had been my family—my life and calling—but it had forced me out. Now, I was part of a secular company that was providing generous rewards for my skills, abilities, and accomplishments—and they wanted me to make money. It felt good to be appreciated, and the accolades came with so little effort compared to the years I devoted to my role as a pastor. And I loved my new white Lexus sedan and its whisper-quiet ride.

FlashNet went public in March of 1999, and the CEO who had been living with his mother when the company started, owned stocks worth around $50 million. Nine months later, the company was bought by Prodigy, another Internet Service Provider, but continued to operate as a separate business entity.

In June of 2000, my monthly FlashNet check was close to what my monthly paycheck at Kingsland Baptist Church had been. With my FlashNet earnings, software development income, and Linda's salary from her new church position, we were making 50% more than we had in our last full year at Kingsland Baptist Church. Financially, this looked like a major win.

And FlashNet wasn't paying me a salary or hourly wage. My monthly earnings were residual income—a small share of what each customer in my downline organization paid the company for their service.

The number of distributors and customers under me was growing month by month. Piggybacking on the explosive growth of the Internet, I had a reasonable expectation that my checks would double, triple, and quadruple in the next few years. My financial future looked like it would be brighter than I had ever imagined.

I was delighted that I was making money, but also pleased to be doing something that was helping other people make money as well. It may sound hokey, but I found this to be true: Network marketing, when done properly, is about helping people believe in themselves, try things they are afraid to do, and inspiring them to live with a positive attitude.

My new role led to new friends across the country—in Illinois, Michigan, Oklahoma, Colorado, Arizona, California, and elsewhere. We all shared a dream of becoming financially independent, and believed we were on the path to achieving it.

Working with FlashNet was challenging and changing me, but I was having an impact on the company as well. I was still committed to my Christian faith, wasn't into judging others, and continued seeking to be a positive force for value-driven living. Within the organization, I became a voice for integrity.

In September of 2000, *Upline*, a network marketing magazine, published an article built around an interview with me titled "Integrity Is the Foundation."[63] The article shared my story of being forced out of my church, choosing FlashNet as a way to earn money, and described some of the things I had learned since first starting as a distributor for the company. The article further focused on the fact that network marketing was about relationships, personal growth, and teamwork. Then it turned to my emphasis on integrity, which I saw as foundational to running a successful business and a competitive advantage.

My leadership role with this secular company seemed too good to be true. I was making money, helping people grow, and still finding time for my software development business and occasional out-of-town, ministry-related, speaking engagements. In 2000, I spoke to church groups in North Carolina, South Carolina, Kentucky, Florida, New Mexico, and Texas.

FlashNet's explosive growth took place during the dial-up phase of the Internet. In those days, you clicked on an icon on your computer screen, then heard a dial tone, then waited as your land line connected to the Internet—at a speed no one would tolerate today.

As long as the Internet was dial-up only, the company had a tremendous advantage. We had an army of individuals across the country selling Internet accounts to family and friends—and our price was competitive. But as early forms of high-speed Internet connections became available, the value of a dial-up connection began to fade, and the new, faster connections were controlled by the nation's phone companies. One of those companies, SBC

Communications, bought FlashNet's parent company, Prodigy, in the fall of 2001.

Prodigy then closed the network marketing operation and bought out the FlashNet distributor contracts related to customer accounts. I received a sizable check, and that was that. My career with FlashNet was over.

I still had my software development business, royalty checks from my books, and a small amount of earnings from a few speaking engagements each year, but with the end of FlashNet, I lost 70% of my annual income and the dream of soon-to-be financial independence.

I felt discouraged, demoralized, and drained.

---

[63] "Integrity Is the Foundation," *Upline*, September 2000, 29-30.

55 – Longest Hour

Five years after Linda and I had been forced out of Kingsland Baptist, we were still living in the same house, just three minutes away from the church. Linda was starting her fifth year as the minister of preschool and children at a Baptist church in another part of Houston.

In those days, we didn't see each other as much as we had during our years at Kingsland, where Linda had been a staff member. On most days at Kingsland, Linda and I were minutes away from each other as we busily carried out our respective jobs in different parts of the same building. Now, Linda was making a 30-minute drive to work each morning. Her responsibilities frequently required evening meetings. Then she would make the 30-minute commute home.

In those same five years, I had worked in Houston as a radio talk show host and as a pastoral counselor, traveled across the country for FlashNet, and also traveled domestically and internationally as a Christian author. In addition, while all this was happening, I had built my own business as a developer of custom software applications.

With the demise of FlashNet, software development was now my primary source of income, and on most weekdays, I was alone in my office in our spacious two-story house—sitting in front of a computer, developing software for clients.

I still traveled occasionally to speak about *Making Peace with Your Past* or to lead related training seminars. And sometimes, I would fill in for a Houston-area pastor who was away on a Sunday. But on most Sunday mornings, I would be sitting beside my wife in the worship services of the church where she was serving on the staff.

I had known the pastor of our new church in seminary. As my first pastor in more than 20 years, he couldn't have been nicer to me, nor more supportive of Linda's work. And, he expressed a great deal of empathy for what had happened to us at Kingsland. More often than not, if he was away on a Sunday, he would ask me to preach for him.

This church, like Kingsland Baptist, had a well-educated congregation located in a growing suburb of Houston. But there was one big difference in the two churches. Our new church, though filled with bright, caring people and led by a bright, caring pastor, was a traditional Southern Baptist Church. No one was coming to observe or write about innovative ministries at this church.

Our pastor, a theological moderate, was also a leader in our state Baptist Convention. As much as he was universally loved in our congregation and by ministers around the state, I couldn't divorce myself from my reaction to his leadership style. It was the opposite of mine.

For example, from what I could tell, he never took a risky position, even if it made sense. When the church, originally named for the street where it was located, moved to a busy freeway and its name became a source of confusion, he stuck with the original name. Apparently, several key members were sentimentally attached to it. Since he was a masterful reader of the tea leaves when it came to church politics, he waited to initiate renaming the church until the opposition had died down.

No one ever forced him out.

More importantly, in my view, the pastor's sermons were tedious. Despite his contagious geniality, cheerfulness, and love of people that expressed itself so freely one-to-one, my gut told me that he had grown weary of ministry, or at least with some aspects of it, and that his heart wasn't fully present in his sermons. Nevertheless, I was supportive. He was my pastor. I never said anything negative about him or the church. I didn't believe in taking potshots; I knew what it was to be on the receiving end.

Although I didn't want to be a pastor again, it was hard to be good at something and watch someone else do it with a lack of passion. Sitting in the congregation on Sunday mornings became the longest hour of the week.

On the other hand, Linda's ministry was a bright spot in the church, and I wanted to be supportive of her work. Our roles had reversed; for years, she was by my side to support my ministry. Now it was my turn.

After leaving the profession in which I had invested so much time, study, and emotional intensity, I was pleased that I had found a way to make a living as a self-taught software developer. I was also glad that I still did a sufficient amount of speaking to feel a connection with my call to ministry. Sometimes this felt like enough, a good balance—working for myself and speaking occasionally. But at other times, loneliness and isolation were a painful reality.

Over the years, my work in ministry, and later, Linda's emerging role in ministry, had defined certain aspects of our marriage. Once it was clear that I was not going to be a pastor again, Linda said, "I'm going to have to get used to my husband not being the one up at the front of the room."

The changing circumstances of our evolving job situations, the challenges of parenting, and the stresses we endured as we left Kingsland were leaving us relationally weakened. We both had a sense that we were no longer as connected as we used to be. Our marriage ended in 2002.

And more than a decade later, the pastor of the last church we attended together—in a state of deep depression—took his own life.

Ultimately, I became one of the estimated one in ten ministers who leave the ministry after a forced termination. And for me, the exit process eventually included leaving religion and faith and beginning to think in a new way about my life purpose.

56 – New Purpose

In 2002, I stopped doing any kind of ministry-related activity. My vocational focus shifted entirely to what had been a part-time venture, my software development business. Instead of sermons and religious articles, for the last 16 years, I have written tens of thousands of lines of software code.

I was fortunate to excel in my new venture. I learned by doing. I taught myself new skills, not just in the first year or two, but every year, time and time again. And that is one aspect of the work that I always enjoyed.

Today, businesses run on software I built for them. I created software applications for departments of the federal government. I designed and built a medical application used by orthopedic surgeons in the U.S. and Europe. One of my business apps creates legal documents for financial institutions across the U.S. each business day. A global technology company uses an application I built to track career development for its top 100 executives around the world. I was happy that I could build a new career doing something that I enjoyed, paid me well, and challenged me intellectually. I am proof that you can leave the ministry, start over, make a good living, and like what you do.

In late 2016, I decided to rethink my vocational focus as I looked toward the last decades of my life. Thinking about values and goals had been a regular discipline for many years. But now it was time for more than a cursory review of my direction and values. And I decided to enlist the help of a personal coach.

The person I selected to work with me was Terri Maxwell, an old friend, the former President of FlashNet Marketing. The name of her company, "Succeed on Purpose," describes what Terri helps people do: Find your purpose, then align your work with it.

Terri helped me start from scratch in working to describe my current life purpose in one sentence. Here's the result: *My purpose is providing inspiration and insights that lead to personal growth.*

Terri's help was tremendously significant in multiple ways. With her guidance, I wrote a vision statement to go with my purpose statement.

> The inspiration and insights I provide for growth will flow from me in one-to-one personal relationships and in spoken and written products that I create and skillfully deliver. A wonderful aspect of my vision is that I can never get too old to do it. I will view the pursuit of this purpose as an adventure and will be open to course corrections as the journey unfolds.

As part of my vision work, I listed five core values:

- Love gives life meaning. I will excel at giving and receiving love.
- I will follow the truth wherever it leads, and I will tell the truth with

sensitivity.
- I will be strong enough to be kind to everyone.
- I will be courageous.
- I will express gratitude every day.

And, I listed some expectations:

- I expect to enjoy the new version of me.
- I will stick to pursing my new vision. I will not give up.
- I expect a feeling of lightness and flow as I experience the unfolding of my new sense of purpose.
- My inspiration and insights will have the power of attraction and will not need to be forced on anyone.
- Providing inspiration and insights to others will be one more reason to get up in the morning, and to stay healthy, energetic, and vital for years to come.

Today, I choose to live a value-driven life, to embrace life's ups and downs, to seek purpose and significance, and to find meaning and joy in the process. This is the new me, yet also the me that has always been here. I am excited about creating new avenues for personal growth in the lives of others. I want to help make the world a better place, at least in some small way, and it feels good to have this renewed sense of direction.

One place where I share insights and inspiration is on my website, www.MovingTruths.com. I hope you will visit me there, and if you would like, there is a link on the site where you can contact me.

My book, *Goodbye Jesus: An Evangelical Preacher's Journey Beyond Faith*, shares a longer version of my story. In addition to the material included in this book, you will find more information about the last 20 years of my journey and more details about the early stages of my life trek.

57 – Self-Care

Ten Self-Care Principles for Ministers

1. I will be honest with myself about what is going on in my life, my family, and my ministry.

2. I will learn to identify what I am feeling and to give outward signals which match what is really happening inside of me.

3. Since ministry is not about medicating my emotional pain, I will find ways outside my work to find nurture and healing.

4. I will resist the impulse to try to control everything that happens.

5. I will learn to build emotional intimacy with the key people in my life, starting with my family and friends.

6. I will not assume that I am responsible for all the problems of the people to whom I minister.

7. Understanding that my family will be around when my church isn't, I will take care of my family better than I take care of my church.

8. I will find safe places in my life where I can be vulnerable, but when I am with sharks, I will not bleed.

9. I will participate in a support group outside my church, maintaining accountability for my personal life.

10. I will maintain my commitment to a balanced life even if no one else supports me.

www.ingramcontent.com/pod-product-compliance
Lightning Source LLC
LaVergne TN
LVHW011220080426
835509LV00005B/232